D0810793

Jimi Hendrix
Made in England

by Brian Southall

This edition © Ovolo Books Ltd 2012
Text © Brian Southall 2012

Print edition: ISBN: 978 1 905959 4 19

Printed in Italy

Front Cover photograph by kind permission of Gered Mankowitz

www.clarksdalebooks.co.uk

CLARKSDALE

CONTENTS

THE JIMI HENDRIX WHO'S WHO

Lou Adler
American record producer who launched Ode Records and helped organize the pop music festival in Monterey, California, at which Hendrix appeared in 1967.

Daevid Allen
Australian singer and guitarist who was an original member of Soft Machine. Formed Gong in France after being refused admission to Britain.

John Allen
Guitarist with The Nashville Teens who bought his first fuzz box from Roger Mayer.

Keith Altham
A journalist for the NME who became the band's publicist. Suggested Jimi should set his guitar on fire at a gig for first time. Continued in PR with many high-profile clients including The Rolling Stones, The Who, Jeff Beck, The Beach Boys, Police, Slade, Status Quo and ELP before retiring in 1993.

Ian 'Tich' Amey
Guitarist with Dave Dee, Dozy, Beaky, Mick & Tich.

David Arden
The son of Don Arden and brother of Sharon Osbourne, David Arden was brought up in the entertainment and music business and even as a teenager he was at his father's side as he oversaw the careers of The Small Faces, The Nashville Teens, Amen Corner and The Move from his office in Carnaby Street, in the heart of Soho. By 1967, David, a long-time associate of Chas Chandler's, had taken over booking the dates for The Move

Ginger Baker
Drummer with Cream alongside Eric Clapton and Jack Bruce.

Syd Barrett

Singer and founder member of Pink Floyd, who died in 2006. The Nice's David O'List deputised on occasions in the 1967 Experience package tour when the erratic Barrett was ill or absent.

Jeff Beck

Like Eric Clapton, Beck was a former Yardbird who went on to find further fame, in his case with the Jeff Beck Group. Has specialized in instrumental jazz-rock for the last four decades and is still at the top. Adopted Jimi and Kathy Etchingham's dog.

Andrew Black

He joined Polydor Records in early 1967 as an ambitious artist and repertoire (A&R) man and moved on to EMI before leaving the music industry.

Jean-Michel Boris

Former stage manager-cum-director of L'Olympia Theatre in Paris.

Joe Boyd

The respected producer of early Pink Floyd records and founder of the UFO club in Tottenham Court Road, the American was the instigator of the UFO club, which shared a basement in Tottenham Court Road with an Irish dance hall called the Blarney. He signed and produced early recordings by The Incredible String Band and would later produce both R.E.M. and Billy Bragg.

Tony Bramwell

The man who ran London's Saville Theatre worked for The Beatles and manager Brian Epstein's NEMS organization. He played the major role in booking the Experience for their theatre debut.

Vic Briggs

Bass player of The Animals who joined the band in early 1967 as replacement for Chas Chandler.

Chris Britton

Guitarist of the Troggs, original hitmakers with 'Wild Thing'.

Mickey Brookes

The Californians guitarist toured Britain with Hendrix on the infamous Walker Brothers 1967 package tour.

Jack Bruce
Bass player with Cream, the first ever supergroup, featuring Eric Clapton and Ginger Baker, was a veteran of Graham Bond's Organisation and Alexis Korner's band. Allegedly wrote 'Sunshine of Your Love' when inspired by Hendrix. Still performs today.

Eric Burdon
Lead singer with 'House Of The Rising Sun' hitmakers the Animals, whose ranks included Chas Chandler. Hendrix was on stage jamming with him and his funk band War two nights before he died. Still performs today.

Tito Burns
Impresario and promoter of the 1967 gig at London's Finsbury Park Astoria where Jimi set his guitar on fire for reputedly the first time.

Trevor Burton
Birmingham-born guitarist who found fame alongside Roy Wood in The Move. Who had scored two Top 5 hits – 'Night Of Fear' and 'I Can Hear The Grass Grow' – by May 1967. He worked with fellow Brummies Steve Gibbons and Denny Laine in a band called Balls and admits to being "absolutely" influenced by Hendrix's playing, both then and today.

Ed Chalpin
Ran the PPX Productions company. His deals with Hendrix led to problems for Track Records that would rumble on in the courts, and led to him receiving the proceeds of the Band Of Gypsys album.

Chas Chandler
Born Bryan Chandler, the former bass player with The Animals signed and brought the 20-year-old Jim Hendrix to Britain. He acted as manager, producer and confidant to Hendrix, though their business relationship split acrimoniously in late 1968. Chandler. He died in his home town of Newcastle Upon Tyne in 1996. He was 58 years old and had played a solo gig just a few days earlier.

Eric Clapton
The "King of Britain's blues guitarists" saw Hendrix as the major contender for his crown. He followed stints with the Yardbirds and John Mayall's Bliuesbreakers by

forming supergroup Cream with Jack Bruce and Ginger Baker. Plays on as a solo bandleader after spells with Blind Faith and Derek & The Dominos; briefly re-formed Cream in 2005.

Dick Clark
Monkees tour promoter and host from 1956 onwards of American's earliest pop TV show American Bandstand. Died in 2012.

Petula Clark
A former child star and hitmaker with the likes of 'Downtown' who made her negative feelings about Hendrix known to Melody Maker in 1968.

Stan Cornyn
A man who was closely involved in all aspects of Reprise (Hendrix's US label) and Warner Bros.' creative imagery, being charged with much of the writing to emerge from both labels in the mid Sixties. Won Grammy awards in 1966 and 1967 for his sleevenotes for two Frank Sinatra albums and went on to become Executive Vice President of Warner Bros. Records.

Billy Cox
Bass player of Hendrix's post-Experience Band of Gypsys and a former US Army colleague.

Robbie Dale
A regular host of TV's Ready Steady Go! and a Radio Caroline DJ, who now owns a holiday complex in the Canary Islands.

Monika Dannemann
A friend of Hendrix's who discovered his lifeless body in the Samarkand Hotel in Bayswater on September 18, 1970.

Dave Davies
The Kinks' guitarist whose work on 'You Really Got Me' in 1964 helped create the foundations of heavy rock.

Barry Dickins
A young booking agent who worked at the important Harold Davidson Agency under the direction of Dick Katz, the former agent for The Animals. Dickins is still

booking artists such as Bob Dylan, Fleetwood Mac and Aerosmith through his ITB Agency.

Micky Dolenz

The Monkees drummer, later a TV director.

Donovan

British folk singer, born Donovan Leitch, who hung out with the Beatles and had hit singles like 'Sunshine Superman' and 'Mellow Yellow'.

Pete Drummond

BBC Radio 1 disc jockey who learnt to be a DJ in America and been on air on the pirate radio station Radio London until August 1967. He spent his early years training to be an actor before turning to radio. He moved on to a career in voiceovers after leaving the BBC.

Keith Emerson

The keyboard-playing founder member of The Nice – including Brian Davison, Lee Jackson and David O'List who moved on to form Emerson, Lake & Palmer in August 1970 with Greg Lake and Carl Palmer. Now resident in the United States.

Brian Epstein

Beatles manager who was also the owner of the Saville Theatre in London's West End. Died in August 1967.

Kathy Etchingham

Hendrix's girlfriend in his first years in London was a hairdresser. In the first week of December 1966, the pair moved into the flat in Montagu Square owned by Beatles drummer Ringo Starr and occupied by Chandler and his Swedish wife Lotta. Now resident in Australia.

Andy Fairweather Low

Singer with Amen Corner, Experience package-tour members in late 1967. Scored solo hits in the Seventies like 'Wide Eyed And Legless'. Went on to be a stellar session guitarist, and was a long-time musical director for Eric Clapton and Roger Waters.

Bruce Fleming

A former press snapper with Melody Maker who eventually became a personal photographer to the likes of Lulu, The Hollies, The Dave Clark Five and The Animals.

THE JIMI HENDRIX WHO'S WHO

Bill Graham
US West Coast promoter who booked the Experience in for six nights at the
Fillmore West in San Francisco in 67 and paid The Hendrix Experience $500 a night.
Died in a helicopter crash in October 1991.

Richard J. Green
Track Records' first press officer.

Germaine Greer
Australian feminist writer who wrote for the underground magazine Oz, launched in
the UK earlier in 1967 and acquitted of obscenity charges in 1971 before closing two
years later.

Jeff Griffin
A BBC producer who saw and worked with the finest musicians of the day, Griffin
went on to produce radio shows with John Peel and was the BBC's radio co-
ordinator for Live Aid in 1985.

Keith Guster
Drummer with London pop band Les Fleur De Lys and allegedly Jimi's one-time
flatmate. Runs the band's website.

Johnny Hallyday
France's very own Elvis who spotted Hendrix in London in 1966 and asked him to
come to play at the Paris L'Olympia with him.

Gordon Haskell
Les Fleur De Lys member and former Hendrix flatmate who was later to find fame
with King Crimson before hitting Number 2 in the UK singles chart in 2001 with
'How Wonderful You Are'. Lives on a Greek island.

Bryn Haworth
Les Fleur De Lys guitarist and later Island Records solo act. Now records religious
music.

David Hughes
Reporter for the Kent Messenger who later went on to write for Disc and also work
for Polydor and EMI Records.

David Jacobs
Top radio DJ and host of TV's Juke Box Jury panel show.

Mick Jagger
Then, as now, Rolling Stones frontman.

Bert Jansch
A leading folk player and a veteran of Britain's folk music scene for over 40 years.

Mike Jeffery
Deliberately mysterious co-manager of Jimi Hendrix with Chas Chandler. Their partnership was dissolved in December 1968 when Jeffrey bought out his former business partner for $300,000. He died in 1973 in a plane crash, the circumstances of which remain unclear.

Peter Jenner
The former London School of Economics lecturer turned rock manager whose Blackhill Enterprises company would assume the management of Pink Floyd. He later managed artists such as Syd Barrett, Roy Harper and Billy Bragg,

Brian Jones
Rolling Stones guitarist and early Hendrix mentor who died in 1969, two years after introducing Jimi on stage at Monterey.

Peter Jones
Wrote for Record Mirror, and reported on Hendrix's Bag O'Nails showcase on November 25, 1966. He went on to write for the US music magazine Billboard before retiring.

François Jouffa
Legendary French music broadcaster and writer who witnessed Hendrix's shows at L'Olympia Theatre in Paris and broadcast excerpts on radio.

Linda Keith
Keith Richards' sometime girlfriend who persuaded Chas Chandler to see Hendrix.

Curtis Knight
Hendrix's pre-Experience bandleader in the Squires. Recordings with him were issued in late 1967 by producer Ed Chalpin as Get That Feeling, causing much ill-will. Knight

THE JIMI HENDRIX WHO'S WHO

wrote a book about Hendrix, Jimi, in 1974 and died in 1999.

Kit Lambert
Co-manager of the Who and Hendrix with Chris Stamp, Lambert was fired by the Who in 1971. The son of composer Constant Lambert, he died of a cerebral haemorrhage after falling down the stairs of his mother's house in 1981.

Peter Lee
The Californians bass player (real name Peter Abberley) toured Britain with Hendrix on the infamous Walker Brothers 1967 package.

Gary Leeds, see Gary Walker

Lemmy
Born Ian Kilmister, the bass-player and singer, formerly of the Rockin' Vickers, served time (and earned £10 a week) as Hendrix's roadie before his days with Hawkwind and, for the last three and a half decades, fronting Motörhead

Deke Leonard
His band Lucifur and the Corncrackers met Hendrix on their first Speakeasy appearance. Later a mainstay of progressive rockers Man, he has written three books, two autobiographical.

Little Richard
Richard Penniman first hit the charts in America with 'Tutti Frutti' in 1956, and employed Hendrix as a sideman before his move to the UK.

Paul McCartney
Beatles bass-player McCartney was a big fan of the The Jimi Hendrix Experience, rating them one of the most important UK acts.

Henry McCullough
Up-and-coming Irish musician from the band Eire Apparent, signed to the same ANIM management company as Hendrix. He would miss out on a later trip to America with his band because of a drugs conviction and was on the bill with Hendrix at Woodstock as a member of Joe Cocker's Greaseband.

Gered Mankowitz
The son of celebrated writer Wolf Mankowitz, he toured America in 1965 as The

Rolling Stones' official lensman before photographing the Experience and striking up a friendship with Hendrix.

John Mansfield
The owner/promoter of the Ricky Tick clubs in Hounslow and Windsor.

Greil Marcus
Rolling Stone writer who eloquently reviewed Hendrix's show at Woodstock.

Jim Marshall
The founder of Marshall Amplification died in 2012, having set the industry standard in rock guitar amp technology. He called Hendrix, an early and avid customer, his company's 'greatest ambassador'.

Dave Mason
Ex-Deep Feeling guitarist, later a member of Traffic with Steve Winwood, Chris Wood and Jim Capaldi. Appeared on later Hendrix recordings, notably 'All Along The Watchtower'.

Nick Mason
The Pink Floyd drummer.

Brian May
The future Queen guitarist grew up in the Twickenham and Richmond areas, May spent his youth at the Crawdaddy and Eel Pie Island clubs, where he witnessed the likes of Eric Clapton and The Yardbirds. He was a member of the entertainments committee that paid £1,000 for the Experience to play Imperial College, London, in 1967.

Roger Mayer
The man who helped create Hendrix's unique guitar sound was a young electrical engineer employed by the Royal Navy Scientific Service in sound analysis. Worked alongside the former right-hand man to Barnes Wallis (the inventor of the famous 'bouncing bomb' which was used in World War II. Today runs a thriving business creating guitar effects.

Buddy Miles
Drummer of Hendrix's post-Experience Band of Gypsys.

THE JIMI HENDRIX WHO'S WHO

Mitch Mitchell
Having just left Georgie Fame's Blue Flames, John 'Mitch' Mitchell competed with
Aynsley Dunbar for a place in the Experience line-up in 1966 and last played with
him in 1970. In December 1968, Mitchell played in The Dirty Mac, an all-star band
assembled for The Rolling Stones' Rock And Roll Circus. He was found dead in his
hotel room in Portland, Oregon, in 2008, just days after finishing a string of dates on
the 2008 Experience Hendrix Tour.

Zoot Money
Legendary leader of the Big Roll Band (born George Bruno Money) and all-round
good guy whose house was Hendrix's first port of call in London. Still performing at
the time of publication.

Chris Morrison
Young manager of Felder's Orioles who went on to look after Thin Lizzy, Ultravox,
Blur and Damon Albarn. In 1985 he was a co-organizer of Live Aid with Bob Geldof
and Harvey Goldsmith.

Mike Nesmith
Guitarist of the Monkees and future solo star/video director.

Jimmy Page
Former Yardbird and session guitarist who would found Led Zeppelin in 1968. An
early customer of Roger Mayer.

John Phillips
Founder of The Mamas & The Papas and co-organizer the pop music festival Hendrix
played in Monterey, California in 1967. The writer and singer died in 2001 aged 65.

Alan Price
Keyboardist and Chas Chandler's former bandmate in The Animals, whose solo hits
included 'Simon Smith And His Amazing Dancing Bear'.

Noel Redding
Kent-based guitarist who had worked with The Loving Kind arrived in London
search of a gig with Eric Burdon's New Animals but ended up playing bass with the
Experience. Formed Fat Mattress to milk his Hendrix fame, but failed to sustain any
long-term success. Redding died at his home in Ireland in 2003, aged 57.

Terry Reid
Critically acclaimed singer who was first choice for the Led Zeppelin gig.

Roland Rennie
The man chosen by Polydor to head up their British operation after a career at EMI which involved a period in New York setting up deals for the company's UK acts that their US operation Capitol passed on. The man who funded (rather than founded) Track Records.

Keith Richards
Then, as now, Rolling Stones guitarist.

Mike Ross-Taylor
Engineer on CBS Studios sessions for Are You Experienced. He went on to make recordings with the likes of John Barry, John Williams, Ennio Morricone and Lesley Garrett. Was awarded a Gold Badge from the British Association of Songwriters, Composers & Authors (BASCA) in 2011 for "a special contribution to Britain's entertainment industry".

Jimmy Savile
Top disc jockey and legendary presenter of TV's Top Of The Pops who died in 2011.

Arthur Sharp
Nashville Teens co-vocalist. His band aimed for chart action in late 1968 with a cover of Dylan's 'All Along The Watchtower', which Hendrix would also record about a month later. While Hendrix reached the UK Top 5 with his effort, The Teens' record sank without trace.

Chris Stamp
The co-founder of Track Records in partnership with Kit Lambert, and the co-manager of The Who. Brother of film star Terence Stamp.

Gerry Stickells
A friend of Redding who earned extra money by driving dance bands around Kent before linking up with Redding's early bands and becoming the Experience's roadie. Was also Queen's road manager at the height of their fame.

Stephen Stills
A member of Buffalo Springfield in July 1967. Hendrix would play on his first

solo album, while in 2008 he claimed to have unearthed a whole album of their collaborations.

Andy Summers
Sometimes known as Somers, the guitarist with Zoot Money's Big Roll Band found Seventies fame as a member of The Police.

Phil Swern
Back in 1967 he worked for Strike Records as a 17-year-old runner for the label which was set up and run by Pete Richards. Now a highly respected radio producer (and avid record collector) who currently oversees Brian Matthew's Sounds Of The Sixties show and Pick Of The Pops for BBC Radio 2.

Peter Tork
Member of the Monkees who made a point of going to see Hendrix play "because he was a world-class musician".

Pete Townshend
Guitarist and songwriter of Experience labelmates The Who. While initially unimpressed, he became a convert of the man also managed by Lambert and Stamp.

Hilton Valentine
Ex-Animals guitarist who, like Chas Chandler, wanted to move on from performer to producer.

Gary Walker
Born Gary Leeds, he was The Walker Brothers' drummer and a regular on the London club scene who lobbied to get Jimi Hendrix onto the bill of their 1967 UK tour.

John Walker
The Walker Brother born John Maus enjoyed seven UK Top 20 hits with his 'brothers' by March 1967 after linking up with Scott Engel and Gary Leeds in Los Angeles in 1964. New Yorker died of cancer aged 67 in May 2011.

Geno Washington
Born in Indiana and stationed in Britain with the US Air Force before he joined forces with The Ram Jam Band, Washington was among the country's biggest crowd-pullers.

Their non-stop, high energy shows made them a sell-out top of the bill act. The genial soul singer also trained as a hypnotist.

Roger Waters

Art student turned Pink Floyd bass player.

Jann Wenner

Renowned American journalist who wrote for Melody Maker and would launch Rolling Stone magazine in November 1967

Jerry Wexler

Atlantic Records co-founder and a personal friend of Hendrix.

Dave Wilkinson

Veteran guitar salesman in the Selmer shop on London's Charing Cross Road.

Tom Wilkinson

Worked in Selmer music store and still runs his own drum workshop in London's Soho district.

Ronnie Wood

Birds, Creation guitarist; Jeff Beck Group bassist, later Faces and Rolling Stones guitarist.

James 'Tappy' Wright

Former Hendrix road manager.

Robert Wyatt

Drummer, vocalist and founder of Soft Machine, who were also managed and produced by Chas Chandler. Pursued a music career even after breaking his back in a fall and being confined to a wheelchair.

Bill Wyman

The Rolling Stones bassist until 1992.

BIBLIOGRAPHY

Tony Bacon – London Live (Balafon, 1999)

Ginger Baker – Hellraiser (John Blake Publishing, 2010)

The Beatles – Anthology (Cassell & Co, 2000)

Johnny Black – Eyewitness Hendrix (Carlton, 2004)

Joe Boyd – White Bicycles: Making Music In The 1960s (Serpent's Tail, 2006)

Tony Brown – Jimi Hendrix: Concert Files (Omnibus, 2009)

Tony Brown – Jimi Hendrix "Talking": Jimi Hendrix In His Own Words (Omnibus, 2003)

Eric Clapton – The Autobiography (Century, 2007)

Ray Coleman – Brian Epstein: The Man Who Made The Beatles (Viking, 1989)

Stan Cornyn with Paul Scanlon – Exploding: The Highs, Hits, Hype, Heroes, And Hustlers Of The Warner Music Group (Harper Collins, 2002)

Charles R Cross – Room Full Of Mirrors: A Biography Of Jimi Hendrix (Hodder & Stoughton, 2005)

Donovan – The Hurdy Gurdy Man (Arrow Books, 2006)

Sean Egan – Not Necessarily Stoned, But Beautiful (Unanimous, 2002)

Kathy Etchingham – My Life, The 60s, And Jimi Hendrix: Through Gypsy Eyes (Orion, 1999)

Colin Harper – Dazzling Stranger: Bert Jansch And The British Folk And Blues Revival (Bloomsbury, 2000)

Michael Heatley – Jimi Hendrix Gear (Voyageur Press, 2009)

Boris Johnson – Johnson's Life Of London: The People Who Made The City That Made The World (Harper Press, 2011)

Sharon Lawrence – Jimi Hendrix: The Man, The Magic, The Truth (Sidgwick & Jackson, 2005)

Deke Leonard – The Twang Dynasty (Northdown Publishing, 2012)

Shawn Levy – Ready, Steady, Go! (Fourth Estate, 2002)

John McDermott with Eddie Kramer and Billy Cox – Ultimate Hendrix (Backbeat Books, 2009)

Barry Miles – Paul McCartney: Many Years From Now (Secker & Warburg, 1997)

Mitch Mitchell with John Platt – Jimi Hendrix: Inside The Experience (Hamlyn, 1998)

Julian Palacios – Syd Barrett And Pink Floyd (Boxtree, 1998)

Joe Smith – Off The Record: An Oral History Of Popular Music (Sidgwick & Jackson, 1989)

Richie Unterberger – The Rough Guide To Jimi Hendrix (Rough Guides, 2009)

Chris Welch – Hendrix: A Biography (Omnibus, 1982)

Mark Wilkerson – Who Are You: The Life Of Pete Townshend (Omnibus, 2008)

James 'Tappy' Wright and Rod Weinberg – Rock Roadie: Backstage And Confidential (JR Books, 2009)

Bill Wyman with Ray Coleman – Stone Alone: The Story Of A Rock'n'roll Band (Viking, 1990)

Plus… back issues of Billboard, Melody Maker, Mojo, New Musical Express, Q, Record Mirror, Rolling Stone and assorted local newspapers.

ACKNOWLEDGEMENTS

Acknowledgements: In addition to thanking all those people who took time out to talk to me and pass on their 'Hendrix moments' – it would not have been the same book without you – I owe a debt of thanks to publisher Mark Neeter for his support and enthusiasm for this project and also to the people in the Clarksdale team, including David Roberts and Matthew White, for all their help in getting my words into some sort of readable format.

Thanks also to photographer Gered Mankowitz, whose cover photograph shows exactly why his work is so treasured. Finally, behind every man, great or otherwise (and believe me I am otherwise), there is a great woman and my wife Pat is one of them and once again she has lent her considerable skills as a reader and corrector to this book.

My thanks also go to the British Library and their Newspaper Library.

INTRODUCTION

"Unquestionably one of music's most influential figures ... brought an unparalleled vision to the art of playing electric guitar" – The Encyclopedia of Popular Music

"Guitar ace and hugely influential 20th century icon" – Guinness Book of British Hit Singles & Albums

"Legendary psychedelic-blues guitarist" – Billboard Book of Albums

"A truly revolutionary musician – perhaps the only one in the end to come out of the whole mid-Sixties psychedelic explosion" – Rolling Stone magazine

"Over the top, overwhelming, over here ... it took Jimi Hendrix less than a year to cement his place in music history" – Guitar & Bass magazine

"Guitar genius ... his gymnastic style remains the benchmark by which rock guitarists are measured" – The Guinness Rockopedia

"Psychedelic super-spade according to hip writers. He was unquestionably the sexiest rock performer of the Sixties" – Swinging Sixties

A million or more fans, a host of distinguished commentators plus hundreds of esteemed musicians have made their feelings known about Jimi Hendrix. This young man from Seattle travelled to London in the autumn of 1966 and, by the winter of the following year, had become arguably the most famous rock star on the planet.

Within three months of his arrival – while he still waited to be discovered by the rest of the country – Hendrix had not just won over the great and the good of London's celebrated swingin' Sixties scene but also had them reviewing his ability in the most glowing terms.

The top-selling acts from the most creative and successful decade of British pop were in raptures about the man who arrived as an almost complete unknown. But manager Chas Chandler's plan to plunge his protégé in at the deepest of deep ends paid off in a way even he could not have imagined, as one celebrated musician after another told the world about the newest kid on the block.

For Eric Clapton, seeing Hendrix was a "wow" experience which "opened my mind to listening to a lot of other things and playing a lot of other things", while Jeff Beck's reaction to what he heard was simply "I couldn't believe it."

The most famous fan of all turned out to be Paul McCartney, who recalled, "He was fantastic … when he picked up that guitar he was a monster". Singer-songwriter Donovan revealed, "Before that moment I had no sense of the revolution this young shamen would conjure", while The Kinks' Dave Davies considered him "a fabulous rock'n'roll character and a great and unique guitarist."

Guitarists in particular didn't hesitate to lay praise at the feet of a 'rival'. Trevor Burton from The Move told me that "it was an extraordinary experience – and nobody had done anything like it before", while John Walker of The Walker Brothers agreed that "he developed a lot of guitar techniques and chord structures that we really hadn't seen before."

John McLaughlin, who founded the renowned Mahavishnu Orchestra, once worked as a guitar technician in the London music shop where Hendrix bought his guitars. "Jimi played such great guitar I think he could have played great while standing on his head – he was truly unique." Established guitar gods like Pete Townshend from The Who and the Rolling Stones' Brian Jones were excited and amazed in equal measure.

Aspiring 19-year-old Brian May fancied he might have a career in pop music … until he saw Jimi Hendrix. Four years before he helped form Queen, he made a pilgrimage to see and hear Hendrix and it left him in a quandary. "When I first heard him, it was a close thing between wanting to give up and wanting to try a lot harder. It was truly wonderful when Jimi played – like the heavens opening."

Hendrix's road to stardom beckoned as first the music industry and then the record-buying public caught on to a new phenomenon. Gradually he began to play to sell-out crowds in clubs around the country as not just his powerful music but his 'sexy' stage show became the must-see event.

However, Fairport Convention founder member Richard Thompson was one of those who missed out on a 'live' Hendrix moment and, together with Tubular Bells creator Mike Oldfield, once listed "seeing Hendrix perform live" as the event he most wished he had seen.

During the 15 months between September 1966 and December 1967, as Hendrix went from sideman to frontman, he played close to 200 UK dates – many of them involving two shows a night – and released three Top 10 hit singles and two Top 5 albums. At the same time, thanks to his outrageous talent, extraordinary appearance and rock'n'roll lifestyle, he became the stuff of headlines and rumours.

This book – courtesy of the memories and reminiscences of people who were there – will chart, analyze and assess this most definitive period in the life of Jimi Hendrix, who was born in the USA but made in England. The late Derek Taylor, long time confidant and friend of The Beatles, once observed that it was in Britain in 1966 and 1967 that "Jimi Hendrix became a pop star, irresistible to women – the feeling was mutual – and a hero to men."

And according to Kathy Etchingham, Hendrix's girlfriend throughout this most extraordinary and never-to-be-forgotten period in his short life, it was a special time. "He was at his peak in 1967, at his most creative. In the early days he had a lot of fun …" She added that it was, most importantly, the year "when he found success and [there were] no hard drugs in the early days".

American record producer Joe Boyd, who co-produced and co-directed the 1973 documentary Jimi Hendrix, also reflects on how the time was right for Hendrix to burst into people's lives. "His transition from an American living in Harlem to England – that cultural collision – was unique to him and is a great story of that period. That was the time for it to happen."

In short, when a once-in-a-lifetime talent hit the fertile ground of swingin' London, alchemy was inevitable.

A LITTLE DREAM OF MINE

1

HENDRIX LEARNS TO PLAY GUITAR – JOINS AND LEAVES US
ARMY – SIGNS RECORDING DEAL IN NEW YORK – IS PICKED UP BY
CHAS CHANDLER – BROUGHT TO LONDON BY CHANDLER AND
ANIMALS MANAGER MIKE JEFFERY

The story of James Marshall Hendrix began in Seattle on America's west coast on November 27, 1942. Had he lived, he would be celebrating his 70th birthday in the year of this book's publication.

The youngster bought a guitar for $5 and, being left-handed, turned it upside down and taught himself how to play. The musicians who influenced him most in those early days were, not surprisingly, elder statesmen of blues such as Elmore James, B.B. King and Muddy Waters, while emerging rock guitarists such as Chuck Berry and Eddie Cochran also made an impression. And though the young Hendrix readily admitted that "school wasn't for me", he did have one other interest alongside music. "I used to like to paint … I'd do abstract stuff like Martian sunsets."

But music was his abiding passion and, in his late teens, Hendrix was to be found gigging regularly around Washington State with The Rocking Kings, earning the princely sum of 35 cents a night for his efforts.

Signing up for three years in the US Army in May 1961, Hendrix found himself assigned to the 101st Airborne Division stationed in Kentucky, where he not only qualified as a parachutist but was also able to indulge his love of the blues. He teamed up with fellow soldier and bass player Billy Cox to form The Kasuals, who played bases in the South.

By 1962 Hendrix had had enough of Army life and managed to obtain a discharge, although the circumstances of his exit from Uncle Sam's armed forces are still not clear. Originally Hendrix claimed ankle and back injuries sustained during his 26th parachute jump were the reasons for his departure, but later stories suggest he was discharged for pretending to be a homosexual. Others argue that he was just a bad soldier who

1

preferred music to life in the Army.

By his own admission, Hendrix was no more enamoured with his time in the forces than the authorities were. "I got tired of that [the Army] and it was very boring" was his assessment, while his military records reported, "He has no interest whatsoever in the Army." Either way, by the middle of 1962 Hendrix had become, according to British journalist Charles Shaar Murray, "a sideman for hire" and was back on the music circuit touring with the likes of Sam Cooke, Jackie Wilson, B.B. King and The Isley Brothers. But this was sometimes no easier than submitting to military discipline.

"I had to conform when I was playing with groups like that," he once explained. "The so-called grooming bit, with mohair suits. If our shoelaces were two different types we'd get fined five dollars." And when he wound up in New York in 1965 working with Little Richard (born Richard Penniman), another issue reared its head … upstaging the self-styled King of Rock and Rhythm.

"Me and another guy got fancy shirts 'cos we were tired of wearing the uniform," recalls Hendrix, who then recounted Mr Penniman's reaction. "He said 'I am Little Richard, I am Little Richard. I am the only one allowed to be pretty. Take off those shirts.' It was all like that. Bad pay, lousy living and getting burned."

Speaking in 1970, Little Richard listed some of the people he claimed he had helped along the way and, alongside The Beatles, The Stones and James Brown, he included the guitar player from Seattle. "I put Jimi Hendrix in the business – he played in my band for two years before he made a record," said the man who first hit the charts in America with 'Tutti Frutti' in 1956, before adding, "You know, all these people, I put them in it and they never mention what you've done – not that you want credit."

While in New York, a naïve but ambitious Hendrix signed a three-year recording contract with producer Ed Chalpin and his PPX Productions which saw the young guitarist receive $1 and a one per cent royalty on the records he was making with US soul singer and band leader Curtis Knight. (The agreement was the subject of a long-running legal dispute between Chalpin and Hendrix plus his management and record companies which was only partially settled in 1970.)

Even though Knight wrote the prophetic 'The Ballad Of Jimi' in 1965 – which predicted Hendrix's own death in five years' time – being one of Knight's Squires was not the job for Hendrix, who had served enough time on the infamous 'chitlin circuit' – a collection of clubs and theatres where African-American acts could perform during America's years of racial segregation.

A LITTLE DREAM OF MINE

In January Jimi sits in with sax-player King Curtis in New York's Smalls Club when his guitarist is indisposed, and is so impressive he is added to the band. On May 13 Hendrix uses a fuzz box for the first documented time when playing a two-week residency with Curtis Knight and the Squires at the Club Cheetah on Broadway. He would play his last gig with Knight a week later.

He now had a hankering for being out front and centre stage, and began playing around the clubs of New York under the name Jimmy James with a band called The Blue Flames. It wasn't long before he started making an impression on any critic who happened to be in the audience. New York Post journalist Al Aronowitz was one such writer and in June 1966 he was moved to say "I'd never seen anything like him. There was a point where I could not take my eyes off him."

Suitably encouraged, Hendrix became a regular around New York and the Greenwich Village area in particular, where the locals hung out and played chess, read poetry, listened to music and generally put to the world to rights. He even made a bee-line for the famous club where one of his heroes had started out a few years earlier. "One of the first places I set foot in was Café Wha? Dylan had played there so of course I hoped they'd let me play there too," Hendrix once explained. "It was a little dream of mine."

It was during these early shows that Hendrix began putting together his own set of songs and two of his earliest choices were 'Hey Joe', written by Billy Roberts, and Chip Taylor's 'Wild Thing'. He was beginning to make an impression and, in June 1966, an Englishwoman named Linda Keith was among the first to sing his praises. She was Rolling Stone Keith Richards' girlfriend and she persuaded the band and their manager Andrew Loog Oldham to see Hendrix in action.

Oldham was seemingly unimpressed, but The Stones in general were very much taken by the young pretender, lead guitarist Brian Jones being completely captivated by his new 'rival'. He took on the role of mentor to the emerging Hendrix, who was just about the only African-American playing around the Village in those days and certainly the only one playing Bob Dylan songs.

Reminiscing years later, Keith Richards recounted his own version of events involving his then-girlfriend who was, it seems, determined to promote the young guitarist. "In her enthusiasm for him, during a long evening with him, as she tells it, she gave him a Fender Stratocaster of mine that was in my hotel room." He then goes on to add, "And then, so Linda says, she also picked up a copy of a demo I had of Tim Rose singing 'Hey Joe' … she took it round to where Jimi was and played it to him. This is rock'n'roll

1

history. So he got the song from me apparently."

While Hendrix was busy making a bit of a name for himself around the clubs of New York, The Animals had embarked on their final Stateside tour alongside fellow Brits Herman's Hermits, starting in Honolulu on July 1.

Some reports have suggested that it was during the first week of this tour – on July 5 in fact – that the band's bass player Bryan 'Chas' Chandler first saw Hendrix play in the Café Wha? But as The Animals' tour schedule shows them recording in Los Angeles on July 4 and playing in Denver on July 6, it seems unlikely that Chandler would have taken a round trip of over 4,000 miles to see somebody he had never heard of.

It seems more likely that it was in the first week of August 1966 when the founding member of the band who hit the US chart with the likes of 'The House Of The Rising Sun', 'I'm Crying', 'Don't Let Me Be Misunderstood', 'Bring It On Home To Me' and 'We've Gotta Get Out Of This Place' became aware of Hendrix.

Already disenchanted with life on the road, 27-year-old Chandler had his eyes set on a career as a producer, and an unlikely opportunity came his way when he flew to New York after the band's show at the Cape Cod A-Go-Go in West Hyannis on August 2. At a club called Ondine's he met Linda Keith, who had not given up on the young guitarist she had first come across a couple of months earlier.

She told Chandler all about the man she had found playing in the Village and, following his own band's show in New York's Central Park on August 3, he found himself sitting alongside her in Café Wha? watching Hendrix do his stuff.

A giant of a man who stood well over six feet tall, Newcastle-born Chandler was aware of his own limitations as both a bass player and a pop star. He also knew he wasn't making a fortune despite hit records and sell-out tours. Spurred on by these circumstances, alongside in-fighting within The Animals, he immediately saw the young Hendrix as the answer to his prayer.

Like The Rolling Stones, he saw enormous potential in the young man's talent as both a guitarist and singer – particularly when he performed 'Hey Joe', a song Chandler was already familiar with. He later recalled that an old girlfriend had played him US singer Tim Rose's version a few weeks earlier and he'd vowed to find an artist to record it as soon as he was off the road.

Little wonder, then, that he was astounded to hear that the opening number of Hendrix's set was 'Hey Joe'. "It was the first song he played and I just thought 'that's it, don't look any more'. Then we sat and talked for about two hours and I told him that

HELLO ENGLAND, GLAD TO SEE YOU

2

ARRIVES IN UK 1966 – ADOPTS THE NAME JIMI – FIRST LONDON
APPEARANCES – MEETS GIRLFRIEND KATHY ETCHINGHAM –
FORMS BAND – PLAYS WITH JOHNNY HALLYDAY IN FRANCE –
RECORDS 'HEY JOE'

In 1966, the England which was about to embrace Jimi Hendrix was still celebrating the success of its World Cup-winning football team. Home-grown cultural icons included Twiggy, the newest and tiniest fashion model, and Michael Caine, the womanizing 'hero' of swingin' London in his role of Alfie. Musically, The Beatles had made their final UK stage appearance on May 1 at the New Musical Express Awards.

You could buy "genuine red and blue military jackets" for 35 shillings and pre-World War 1 Infantry tunics for just 52 shillings and six pence from Lord Kitchener's Valet in the Portobello Road market, a magnet that attracted those in search of second-hand fashionable bric-a-brac. For those with deeper pockets and more sophisticated tastes, Britain's first Playboy Club opened in the capital's plushest area of Mayfair.

London was the place to be, the city that swung like no other. American magazine Time told the world in April 1966, "In this century every decade has its city ... and for the Sixties that city is London." And 45 years on, in October 2011, mayor Boris Johnson reflected in his book Johnson's Life Of London: The People Who Made The City That Made The World, that, "It is one of the greatest triumphs of British culture that rock/pop had its most beautiful and psychedelic flowering in London in the Sixties."

This, then, was the London about to greet Hendrix and Chandler as they left New York's John F. Kennedy Airport on September 23, 1966 on a Pan Am flight bound for Heathrow. They flew first class, thanks to Mike Jeffery, although the young American had with him less than $50 in cash plus a small bag containing a few clothes, a set of plastic hair curlers and medicine for his acne.

He also had with him a white Fender Stratocaster which, in order to avoid arousing

JIMI HENDRIX MADE IN ENGLAND

2

the suspicions of customs officials as to whether the 'alien' from the US was on a working or social visit, was carried into the country on Saturday September 24 by Animals road manager Terry McVay.

The ambitious young musician used the flight to determine that James Hendrix and Jimmy James were names of the past and that Jimi Hendrix was the way forward. "Chas always liked to believe he thought of it," Hendrix once told author Sharon Lawrence, adding, "the spelling had crossed my mind before that."

Hendrix's first port of call on arriving in swingin' London at around 9am on a Saturday morning was the Fulham home of effervescent bandleader Zoot Money. The household was home to the whole of Money's band plus a young girl named Kathy Etchingham, a hairdresser and friend of musicians such as Brian Jones and Keith Moon.

The guitarist with Money's Big Roll Band was Andy Summers. As he was out, Money raided his basement flat and retrieved a Telecaster guitar which he lent to the new arrival, who straightaway turned his unannounced visit into a jam session.

"Jimi jammed for two or three hours ... the house was full of musicians and it made him feel he could settle in London" is Chandler's memory, while Money recalls, "It was obvious that all forms of blues, or black music had gone through him. He was able to play all forms of blues, gospel – whatever you want to call it."

Although Hendrix visited the west London house she called home, 20-year-old Etchingham didn't actually meet him on that first morning, despite Zoot's wife Roni Money's urging. "She came running up to my flat," recounts Etchingham, and said, 'You gotta come down, Chas has brought this guy back from America and he looks like the Wild Man of Borneo.' But I wasn't keen to get out of bed."

However, the girl from Derby got her chance to meet the man from Seattle later the same day when Chandler, Hendrix, Mr. and Mrs. Money and their friends descended on the fashionable Scotch of St James club in Mason's Yard, just south of Piccadilly. The favourite watering-hole of The Beatles, The Who and a host of other pop stars seeking a quiet drink and was about to become even more famous as the place where Hendrix made his UK debut.

Tony Bramwell, who worked for The Beatles and manager Brian Epstein's NEMS organization, recalls Hendrix's first British performance. "He got up on stage and played a couple of numbers, just blues stuff. He was just like sat on a stool. It wasn't explosive stuff or anything like that." Chas Chandler tried to get him off the stage, protesting that "he's only got a seven-day visa and he's not supposed to be working, paid or unpaid", while The Who's Pete Townshend, watching from the raised platform reserved for the celebrities of the day, was unimpressed. "He looked scruffy, jet-lagged and pock-marked. I thought 'light'."

Bramwell took the opportunity to speak with Chandler, "who was telling me about this guy he had found in New York and he never doubted that he was going to be a huge star."

One man who would play a major role in making Hendrix the huge star Chandler predicted was also in the Scotch that night. Chris Stamp, brother of film star Terence, was in partnership with Kit Lambert as co-manager of The Who. He was a familiar man-about-town with a host of influential connections and, on the night Hendrix first played in London, he and his partner liked what they saw. "He (Hendrix) had a special look about him. I loved his face and his hair. It was just the dynamic that got you."

It got to Stamp to such an extent that, after unsuccessfully attempting to persuade Chandler to let them manage or produce the young Hendrix, they were left with one final roll of the dice. "We said we were thinking of starting a record label and Chas said, 'Well I'd love to talk to you about that.' Chas was looking for money but our label at that moment didn't even exist."

From the moment she walked into the club and first saw Hendrix, Kathy Etchingham was taken with the young American musician. "I was instantly attracted. I had never seen such an exotic man before," she recalled. Dressed in flared beige trousers and a white satin shirt with a large collar and wide sleeves, she saw Hendrix as "dangerous and exciting" with a voice that was "very seductive" and manners that were "quiet and polite".

During the evening Hendrix had spent most of his time sitting next to Linda Keith, his old friend from New York, but when she left to go to the ladies room he called over the young trainee hairdresser to sit by his side. After that he leant over, kissed her on the ear and whispered "I think you're beautiful."

With the evening over – and Hendrix and Etchingham ensconced in London's swanky Hyde Park Towers Hotel, presumably courtesy once again of Chandler's Animals earnings – the process of settling Hendrix into London became a priority for the bass player-turned-manager.

Some of The Animals had lived in the basement flat at 24 Cranley Gardens in South Kensington. While they were away on their final tour of America in July, it became home to two members of Les Fleur De Lys, a band that gigged regularly on the London club circuit.

JIMI HENDRIX MADE IN ENGLAND

2

Apparently their manager had some connection with The Animals and had swung it so that two of his band could move in during the summer of 1966. "Nicky Wright (the band's manager) clearly had the keys to the flat but what's not so clear is whether we had permission to move in or not," recounts bass player Gordon Haskell.

Drummer Keith Guster explains the benefits of the arrangement. "It was an amazing ground floor set of rooms and we moved in rent free. Our manager said The Animals wouldn't mind and that they'd be pleased we were looking after the place for them." Guster and Haskell shared a large bedroom looking out on to the garden area with a kitchen and bathroom at the end of the hallway. He also recalls two rooms neither of them ever entered. "There was one door on the right-hand side that was locked and another that was also locked … I think that was Hilton Valentine's room, although we never saw him."

With The Animals' tour of America coming to an end, Haskell and Guster were preparing themselves for their inevitable departure when Chandler turned up and explained that he had just returned from the US with a new mate in tow. "He told us we were all right to stay for a bit longer," said Guster before adding, "then he said, 'I'm going to bring a guy round and he's going to stay in the other room.' We asked what his name was and Chas just said 'Oh it's Jimi.'"

When Jimi arrived the next day, he quickly disappeared into the room at the front of the house. "We hardly ever saw him really. On odd occasions he'd sit on the floor in his room drawing pictures and picking on an acoustic guitar – that's about all we ever saw him do." Haskell has few more memories of their life together in a South Kensington flat in late 1966. "We did a few domestic things together in the kitchen but Jimi seemed to be completely on his own most of the time. I do remember him playing acoustic guitar in the flat, but never electric."

Guster also explains that, as three working musicians, they were rarely in the house at the same time. "We didn't cook or eat together and there were never any fights over the bathroom, but we were out most of the time trying to get more work while Jimi was presumably out with Chas working on getting their band together."

Kathy Etchingham remembers the flat in Cranley Gardens as "where Hilton Valentine and Eric Burdon lived and I visited it on occasions before Jimi ever arrived in the UK." She is adamant that "Jimi never lived there because he was in the Hyde Park Towers Hotel with me from the first night he arrived. Chas had already booked him there." Hilton Valentine still has no knowledge of the guy who moved in down the corridor. "I didn't know that … or I don't remember" is all he can add.

2

Etchingham does concede that Hendrix might have been a visitor to the flat. "He may have gone round there with Chas at some time and met these guys and he might even have fallen asleep on the sofa, but they are all mistaken about Jimi living there. It couldn't have happened because Chas would not have let Jimi out of his sight when he first arrived because he had too much money invested in him." Etchingham also disputes that Hendrix was seen doing some drawing at the flat. "He wasn't painting or drawing at that time, to my knowledge, as he didn't have any painting material when he arrived and wouldn't have been able to afford any."

During one of Chandler's visits to the flat, he told Guster that "he was planning to put together a three-piece – Jimi with a drummer and a bass player. Gordon and I looked at each other and thought one of us plays bass and the other plays drums and we haven't got much work at the moment.

"I think we sort of mentioned it to Chas and he said, 'Well thanks boys but we'll see'," Guster recalls, while Haskell suggests, "I never thought that Chas should have hired us to be with Jimi. We were very loyal to Les Fleurs, and while we would have done a very good job behind Jimi – been very tight – we probably wouldn't have got into the showmanship stuff."

Chandler set about organizing auditions for the two musicians he was looking for at the Birdland Club in Mayfair's Jermyn Street. First on board in late September was guitarist Noel Redding, who arrived in search of a gig with Eric Burdon's New Animals but ended up borrowing Chandler's Gibson bass and running through a handful of numbers.

According to Chandler, Redding, who had worked with The Loving Kind and played on sessions for Gerry Dorsey before he became Engelbert Humperdinck, was badly in need of a gig. "He told me he was skint and would try anything so I lent him my bass." And the plan worked as, according to Redding, the main man was impressed – and not just with what he heard. Redding's wild, untamed hair also appealed to Hendrix, whose own locks were naturally unruly.

"I saw this ad in Melody Maker that Eric Burdon was forming the New Animals," Redding explained in 2000. "He'd sung with my band from Folkestone called the Loving Kind about six months before. We'd played in a club in London and he'd come up and sung a couple of tunes, and said 'You lot are good.' Basically in September '66 I thought I'd go for an audition playing guitar for Eric Burdon in case he might remember me. Did he? No, and that was my bit of good luck!

2

"At this point I played a couple of tunes on guitar and that was when Chas Chandler wandered over to me. He was like a star to me, I was only 20 years old. He said 'Can you play bass?', and I said 'No, but I'll try it.' I was handed a bass and played three songs with this American gentleman, a drummer, myself and a keyboard player. Three songs with no vocal at all. Then the American gentleman said 'Can I have a word with you?'

"There was a nice little pub next door to the place and he discovered he liked best bitter. He talked about music, I asked him about the American scene, had he ever seen Sam Cooke, that sort of stuff, Booker T and he was asking me about the English scene which at that point was the Small Faces, the Move, the Kinks. Then he said to me 'Do you want to join my band?' And that was Mr. James Hendrix."

Despite still being without the work permit that would allow him to perform legally in the UK, Hendrix continued to jam wherever and whenever he could. Late September found him playing as part of Brian Auger's set-up in the basement of the Imperial Hotel in Queen's Gate, Knightsbridge, which housed the Blaises club.

In the audience on September 29 was Andy Summers, the man whose guitar he had been loaned by Money a few days earlier. "At the time it was amazing. He had a white Strat and, as I walked in, he had it in his mouth and he had on a sort of buckskin jacket with fringes. It was intense and it turned all the other guitarists in London upside-down."

Also there that night was Tony Bramwell, who had been in the audience three nights earlier when Hendrix first played. "I was with Graham Nash (from The Hollies) and Gary Leeds (from The Walker Brothers) when Brian Auger was playing. And Jimi just got up and played. He just sat on a stool and just played. He didn't do the whole show." And according to Bramwell there were some other interested people in the room that night. "Johnny Hallyday was there with his brother and Otis Redding and they started chatting about Jimi being amazing. Hallyday's brother wanted him [Hendrix] to go to France to join Johnny's band or something ... it all sounded very weird."

While a number of people seem to seriously doubt that Hallyday's brother was actually there, and others have even suggested that Redding was not present either (although he was touring the UK around that time and you could catch his show at a Mecca Ballroom for 10 shillings), there is no doubt that France's very own Elvis was among the crowd. "I was with Otis Redding when I heard this totally unknown guitar player, this fantastic black guy who even played very good guitar with his teeth. I asked him to become part of my next show."

Hendrix also recalled the meeting as an early opportunity for his new group. "Johnny Hallyday asked whether we would like to come to play at the Paris Olympia with him. We did, after being together only about four days and having about four hours of practice."

The chance to play with Hallyday in France gave Chandler the opportunity to solve two problems in one go. Firstly he could get Hendrix out of London where, as word of his performances spread, there was a growing chance of him being caught and possibly deported for playing without a work permit. Secondly it was a chance to rehearse the band and create an act in a country where he didn't need a permit and was a complete unknown.

However, before the trip to France, an opening presented itself for Chandler to keep a promise he had made to Hendrix during their meetings in New York. The young guitarist was keen to know if his British musician friend-turned-manager knew Eric Clapton and if he could arrange a meeting or even a jam session.

Within a week of their arrival in London, opportunity reared its head when Cream, rock's first ever supergroup featuring Clapton, Jack Bruce and Ginger Baker, were booked to play at the London Polytechnic in Regent Street on October 1. A moment like this could only come the way of the aspiring young American thanks to his manager's standing. "When he arrived in London he was, thanks to Chas Chandler, right at the centre of the rock scene," according to journalist and author Charles Shaar Murray. "He was a local hero within weeks of arriving."

Tony Bramwell turned up at the London Poly on October 1 in his role as a scout for potential acts for a series of Sunday-evening rock shows being planned by Epstein for his Saville Theatre and met the band's bassist before the show. "I was with Jack Bruce in a pub somewhere off Regent Street, and Jimi was there too."

According to Bruce, a veteran of Graham Bond's Organisation and Alexis Korner's band, "Jimi just asked to sit in and I said 'OK'. Ginger wasn't too keen but we walked over to the gig and he sat in and played incredibly." Frontman Clapton, who had a reputation as the number one guitarist in town at the time, didn't raise any objection when he met Hendrix backstage. "I thought he looked cool and that he probably knew what he was doing. We got talking about music and he liked the same people I liked, so I was all for it."

So, a month after they had released their debut single 'Wrapping Paper', Cream were joined on stage by Hendrix to play Howling Wolf's blues number 'Killing Floor'. "Jimi just went for it," recalls Clapton. "He played the guitar with his teeth, behind his head, laying on the floor, doing the splits, the whole business. It was amazing." While his official

JIMI HENDRIX MADE IN ENGLAND

2

reaction was, "It scared me because he was clearly going to be a huge star and just as we were finding our own speed, here was the real thing", according to those who were there on the night Clapton came off stage and uttered the immortal words, "You didn't tell me he was that fucking good, did you?"

Looking back, Baker admits that he was less than enthusiastic about letting the young unknown on stage. "Finally, and with great reluctance on my part, it was agreed that we would let him sit in," says the drummer before adding, "I was not impressed. Yeah, he could play a bit … but what really got up my nose was Jimi's onstage cavorting. Jimi was getting down on his knees and simulating oral sex with his axe. I was not into it."

Standing at the back of the hall that night was Pete Jenner of Blackhill Enterprises. "My recollection is of it being extraordinary – Hendrix was quite stunning even though he only did a couple of numbers," says the man who was there to see his friend Eric Clapton. Kathy Etchingham was also at the show and she still rates it as one of the best gigs she saw him play. "He was very good that night, but he only did one number and then they wanted to get him off," she recalls.

Also in the hall that night in Upper Regent Street, close to the BBC's Broadcasting House headquarters, was Roger Waters, 22, who was already making an impression on the emerging London 'underground' scene with fellow Poly student Nick Mason in a new group called Pink Floyd. "I remember seeing them [Jimi Hendrix and Cream] as a callow youth. They both played the Regent Street Poly as part of our end-of-term hop," recalls the bass player. "It was outstanding to see and hear their long improvisations."

Although he was there to see if Cream were right for a show at his theatre, Bramwell remembers the night for another reason. "It was one of the first times the general public got to see Hendrix because his appearances, up to then, had been in clubs in front of a load of drunks from the business … this was a proper audience."

A couple of weeks after gigging with Clapton and a few days after officially hiring Redding as the band's bass player, Hendrix began auditioning drummers. The final two were Aynsley Dunbar and Mitch Mitchell, who had just left Georgie Fame's Blue Flames. After auditioning in Les Cousins, an old folk and skiffle hang-out in Soho's Greek Street, it's rumoured the choice was made on the toss of a coin.

Either way, Mitchell recalls walking into a very dingy club one afternoon and seeing "this guy with pretty wild hair and like a Humphrey Bogart-type raincoat – very quiet and very unassuming", before being told by Hendrix, "OK I'll see you around."

With just two weeks' work in France on the books, Mitchell formally joined the

HELLO ENGLAND, GLAD TO SEE YOU

newly created Jimi Hendrix Experience just as the NME dated October 7, 1966 carried the first-ever UK mention of the new frontman in its Alley Cat gossip column: "Blues singer Jimi Hendrix managed by Chas Chandler, former member of The Animals."

With Mitchell and Redding on board, two other musicians were left to think about what might have been. Haskell reckons that he and fellow band member Guster "were better than what he ended up with", while Guster adds, "I don't think they [Redding and Mitchell] were the right guys to be in Jimi's group – I thought it was all very makeshift." He admits that "if Gordon and I had been invited to rehearse with Jimi we would not have had the same impact."

One thing the two members of Les Fleurs were able to help Hendrix with was shopping. "One day he said he wanted to get a guitar and asked if we'd go with him because he didn't know his way around London," says Guster. "We traipsed around Denmark Street and Charing Cross Road but I can't remember if he bought anything."

A man who remembers a lot more about Jimi's guitar-shopping trips is Dave Wilkinson, who worked at Selmer at 114 Charing Cross Road. In the autumn of 1966, he welcomed Chandler and Hendrix into the shop.

"Chas came in with this guy who he introduced to our manager. After that day, Jimi came back on his own and just sat in the shop and picked up guitars and asked if he could play them. He took hold of a right-handed Stratocaster – just took it down off the wall – and played it upside-down and the stuff he came out with was absolutely mind-blowing."

The instructions for Dave and his brother Tom Wilkinson, who started out in the Selmer store in 1964, were to sell 13 guitars a day and as many Selmer amps as possible. "Hendrix did try a 4 x 12 cabinet one but didn't like it," says Tom, who still runs a drum workshop in Denmark Street. "But he just walked in, picked up a guitar, turned it up the other way and played it ... you thought, 'Shit, what's going on?'"

One particular visit by Hendrix remains a vivid memory for Dave. "One of the guys who worked in the basement was John McLaughlin, and I'm sure he came running up the stairs one day when Hendrix was playing and shouted, 'Who the fuck is that?' I just said, 'It's Jimi Hendrix.'" Interestingly, 45 years on, McLaughlin, who worked in the downstairs workshop, has no recollection of the incident.

While Chandler was well known to the staff at Selmer as one of the throng of musicians who visited the store to buy equipment, the young man he brought in with him caused something of a stir. "Hendrix looked very different with his big fuzzy hair,

2

but he was a very quiet man and always very polite and he shook hands with everyone he met," explains Dave, who also noticed a particular Americanism. "He always called you 'sir', which was something that Presley seemed to do as well when you heard him talk. Once I got to know him he called me by my name, but it was 'sir' for a while."

Hendrix's enduring politeness and use of the word 'sir' when talking to people has been a constant feature of recollections. Fellow ex-US serviceman and musician Geno Washington can provide an explanation. "We were both ex-GIs and his politeness came from the services and his parents. In the services it was 'Yes sir, yes ma'am' all day, and that was something we continued after we left … it stays with you."

Selmer became a regular hang-out for Hendrix according to Dave Wilkinson. "He came in quite a few times when he was at a loose end. He would just come in and play on his own – not to buy anything but just to sit and play. He lived for the guitar."

Dave recalls a customer who came in to buy a guitar but wanted to hear how it sounded. "Jimi was in the shop, and there was no way I was going to play the guitar in front of him," says the guitarist-turned-salesman. "I just said I would ask someone else if they would mind playing it for him, then turned to Jimi and said, 'Can I ask a favour? Would you mind demonstrating this guitar for this customer?'"

Hendrix picked up the guitar, turned it upside-down and played. "It was mind-blowing," says Dave. "The customer didn't seem to know who Jimi was, but he was absolutely gob-smacked and bought the guitar. I took Jimi's commission for him selling that guitar."

Later, when Hendrix visited the Marshall Amplification factory in October 1966 with Mitchell and Redding, he was greeted by sceptical owner Jim Marshall, who immediately saw the young American guitarist as another musician wanting something for nothing. "But his [Hendrix's] first words were, 'I don't want you to give them to me. I will pay full price. I just want to know that wherever I am in the world, I won't be let down,'" said Marshall, before adding, "without doubt Jimi became our greatest ambassador."

While the band may not have bought any amps from Selmer, Mitch Mitchell did buy his kits from Dave Wilkinson's shop. Newly recruited bass player Redding was also a customer. "I knew Noel from before Hendrix and was pleased that he got the job," says the veteran salesman. "He didn't really want to play bass, but it was that or nothing. It was a job with regular money so he knuckled down, but there was a certain amount of jealousy on Noel's part about Jimi being the frontman and the guitarist."

Ahead of the new band's visit to France, Chandler and Jeffery began to talk about signing the trio to their own ANIM management company ahead of any record-company contracts that might come along. Jeffery led the negotiations with Hendrix, Mitchell and Redding, and these initial contract proposals would turn out to be the cause of much discussion and resentment on the part of the two British sidemen, who regularly claimed that they received only a straight weekly wage rather than any percentage or even a royalty on future record sales.

As success and sales increased, Redding and Mitchell were dismayed at an arrangement which saw Hendrix take a major cut and all the artist royalties. It was something Redding talked about to a number of people, including Dave Wilkinson: "He was a bit cheesed off about not getting anything more than a straight wage." Geno Washington also understood the situation Mitchell and Redding found themselves in with Jeffery, who was co-owner of the Flamingo club where his Ram Jam Band were regulars. "That Mike Jeffery, he was a slippery monkey. If you worked with him it was always 20 per cent for you and 80 per cent for him."

Joe Boyd, producer of early Pink Floyd and founder of the UFO club in Tottenham Court Road, believes "Jeffery never understood Hendrix the musician. There was a fascination with black music in Britain at that time, and even though you hate to give Jeffery the credit, the idea of the black guy with the two white guys did help as an image thing."

Tony Bramwell was another who was also wary of Jeffery and his partnership with the ever-popular and outgoing Chandler. "I don't think Chas had much nous about the details or the money part. He was always broke – nobody seemed to make any money out of The Animals – but he was a good man to have around," he says. "Mike Jeffery was like one of those criminal comedy characters from [TV crime show] Taggart and he reckoned that he was due a share of anything Chas did after he left The Animals."

Chandler himself went on record to air his concerns about his partner, whose name has also appeared as Jeffrey, Jeffries and Jeffreys. "If I regret one thing it was getting Mike Jeffery involved. I didn't really have a choice – Jeffery was the one with the money and the contacts." Trixie Sullivan, Jeffery's personal assistant, held a different view. "He was really something special. He was shy and always stood back but he was one tough guy and bloody clever."

Kathy Etchingham has both a soft spot and a good word for Jeffery who, she believes, was brought in by Chandler because he didn't have any cash. "Both Jimi and I liked him," she says. "He was different to all the other people … older, better educated, slicker and more businesslike. To Jimi and me he seemed like someone we could look to for guidance, someone we could trust."

JIMI HENDRIX MADE IN ENGLAND

2

However, just two days before leaving for France in October 1966, all three members of the Jimi Hendrix Experience gathered in ANIM's offices in Gerrard Street – in the heart of London's 'Chinatown' – and signed amended production deals with Chandler and Jeffery. These contracts apparently paid Chandler and Jeffery 20 per cent of all income earned by the group, while the band would share a royalty of 2.5 per cent on record sales. Each member of the band was also put on a weekly salary, starting at £15 a week, which was an advance against future earnings.

While it wasn't a generous deal, it was not an unduly unfair agreement at that time in the UK music business. Between 1963 and 1966, The Beatles received from EMI a royalty of two old pence (0.82 new pence) per single and, after that, were paid 6.5 per cent on the first 100,000 singles and first 30,000 albums. However, they were by this time the biggest act in the world with global album sales of over 180 million records, while The Experience had been together for less than a month and hadn't released a record.

In addition, Hendrix agreed a publishing deal with Chandler that saw the manager take a 50 per cent share of Hendrix's songwriting for six years. This too, compared to The Beatles' deal with their publishing company, was not particularly unfair as John Lennon and Paul McCartney shared their publishing royalties 50/50 with Northern Songs – who also took a 10 per cent administration charge, leaving 40 per cent to be shared equally between the two Beatles and their manager Brian Epstein.

According to David Arden, son of larger-than-life pop impresario Don Arden, ANIM was not in the top bracket when it came to pop management companies. "Nobody attached much importance to it at the time and apparently very few people who were signed there ever actually saw Jeffery in the office," he says. "For Chas in the early days of Hendrix, it was a case of better the devil you know than the devil you don't, and they had been together for many years with The Animals so there was some sort of relationship."

After three warm-up shows supporting Hallyday and local French acts The Blackbirds and Long Chris, Hendrix and his two cohorts arrived in Paris for their show at the legendary L'Olympia Theatre on October 18, with Brian Auger a late addition to the bill.

The Paris L'Olympia was opened as a music hall in 1889 and is now preserved as an historic building. It has played host to acts as diverse as Edith Piaf, Jacques Brel, Marlene Dietrich, The Beatles, The Shadows and the Grateful Dead. French rock star Hallyday was no stranger to L'Olympia and its 1,700 seats would have been sold out for his October 1966 date.

2

But, according to former stage manager-cum-director of the theatre, Jean-Michel Boris, "People knew who Hendrix was even though no record had come out and they knew Johnny Hallyday wanted him on the show. And the public went crazy about the sound … I remember the sound and his dress – he was wearing a big hat and a red Army jacket."

While Boris, who served at L'Olympia for 46 years, never met Hendrix – "He stayed in his dressing room, which was packed with many girls" – reports from his staff were of a modest man who was easy to speak to.

Also at the show was legendary French music broadcaster and writer François Jouffa, who claims he knows where Hendrix got his stage gear. "He went with a friend of mine to a flea market in Paris and that is where he bought his military jacket." He shares the view that Hendrix was polite and not very exuberant – "You know, when you are a stranger in a country you are a little bit shy and reserved" – but has little recollection of the show itself.

"Many people in France do not care about the first act so not so many people saw this first Hendrix show at L'Olympia. I did see him but don't remember anything about it … I was with other people talking and did not really notice him, although we did say 'hello' briefly when I was backstage."

Boris, however, has a better memory of that night's events. "Hendrix and Julie Driscoll (the singer with Brian Auger) were both in the first part and had about 20 to 30 minutes each," he says, and also recalls that the French star and the American debutant got together that night. "I think he played with Johnny Hallyday – I am sure he went on stage with him." Indeed Hendrix, complete with his white Stratocaster, joined in with Hallyday and the rest of the performers during the finale.

These shows in France were an eye-opener for new drummer Mitchell, who saw three new Marshall cabinets being loaded on to the plane. "There were no flight cases, they were just wrapped in corrugated cardboard sheeting." He had come to know the band's frontman as amiable and quiet, but the first show changed all that. "We saw a whole other person, completely different from anything I had ever seen before. It was like 'whoosh'. The showmanship – playing behind his head, with his teeth, was amazing – but it was obviously not just flashiness, he really did have the musicianship to go with it."

Mitchell also heard that one of their sets from France was broadcast on a radio station called Europe 1, although he reckons it was probably just a by-product of Hallyday's show being recorded. Jouffa, who had a show on Europe 1, confirms the

2

rumour. "The L'Olympia show was recorded for my radio show and there is a pirate CD which has me speaking over the music, which I did deliberately because I did not want the show pirated even back then."

If Chandler had viewed the shows in France as a means to get Hendrix out of the way of prying UK immigration officials and as an opportunity to get his new band, together, he returned overjoyed with the outcome. "Really the Hendrix Experience act – the entire basis of the act – was established on that Johnny Hallyday tour, no question about it."

But things went surprisingly quiet for the trio when they returned from France. Work was hard to come by on the over-crowded London club scene, although Bramwell recalls Hendrix, who was still without a work permit, joining in around town for some solo sessions. "The Pretty Things had a club called Knuckles just off Soho Square and Jimi turned up there and played with Dave Mason and Jim Capaldi [soon to be members of Traffic] and he played with the VIPs [who became Art, and later still Spooky Tooth] a few times."

Plans were put in place for the Experience to record for the first time, and on October 23 the trio assembled in De Lane Lea Studios to record 'Hey Joe' with Chandler at the production desk. The studio was where The Animals had done most of their recording, but had only enough cash to make one track. Mitchell noted that "Studio time was expensive and I'm sure that not a lot of time was spent on 'Hey Joe'."

Chandler was never going to be wasteful when it came to the studio. After all, he had been there when producer Mickie Most booked The Animals in for a three-hour session – at £8 an hour – to record their US and UK chart-topping single 'The House Of The Rising Sun', only to find the track was done in under 20 minutes. "We found ourselves with over two-and-a-half hours to spare, so we made an album," Most recounted years later. "It cost £24 and stayed in the British and American charts for over 30 weeks, so it was a good deal."

This was the model for Chandler's production style, which Mitchell described as "No need to piss around wasting time and money in the studio." Bandmate Redding recalled that they got 'Hey Joe' recorded despite Hendrix's reluctance as a vocalist. "He hated singing – he used to turn the lights off in the studio. But then Chas threw in three girls' voices which actually made the song – it was when it started sounding good."

Kathy Etchingham was present at the session and remembered the backing singers. "Keep an eye out for The Breakaways, they're doing the backing vocals," she recalls

HELLO ENGLAND, GLAD TO SEE YOU

Chandler telling her. When she asked what they would look like, the manager-turned-producer told her, "You'll think they're the cleaning ladies, they don't dress up for recording sessions."

Sure enough, they arrived looking very unglamorous and wearing headscarves – and also unrehearsed because that would have cost Chandler more money. "He wrote the words on pieces of paper and held them up behind the glass for the girls to read as they sang," says Etchingham, who was "impressed with their professionalism."

Hendrix's girlfriend has another memory of the first ever recording session for The Experience. "I went to the loo during the first session for 'Hey Joe' and when I came back I had no idea what a red light outside a studio door meant, so I just walked in," she says. "They were doing it all in one take, playing it together, and I ruined the first take by opening the door. I got into real trouble, not from Jimi but from Chas. It was Chas's money, of course, that was paying for the session and he was always careful with money."

Chandler accepted that Hendrix was not only a great musician but also "incredibly particular about the sound." And Jimi's ambitions were already extending beyond his first single. "We're trying to get our own particular sound, like a freakish blues only with a little more feeling," he said. "'Hey Joe' is a phase, one very small part of us."

Exactly what else the Experience had to offer would soon become apparent, not only to London but the rest of the United Kingdom, in the months ahead.

2

BRITAIN IS REALLY GROOVY

3

GIGS IN GERMANY – SMASHES FIRST GUITAR – SIGNS TO
TRACK – DEVELOPS EX-MILITARY LOOK – APPEARS ON
READY STEADY GO! – FIRST SINGLE RELEASED – GETS
EXTENSION TO WORK PERMIT – APPEARS ON TOP OF THE
POPS – CRITICAL ACCLAIM

In the space of one whirlwind month after arriving in Britain, Hendrix had jammed with some of the country's finest musicians, rehearsed and recruited two new players for his band, played a series of gigs in France and recorded his debut track as The Jimi Hendrix Experience.

The next step, on October 25, 1966, was for the band to play a showcase gig for the music industry and media. This was at the Scotch of St James club, where Jimi had played on the night he arrived in London just 32 days earlier.

Word of the young guitarist had spread around the city as the musicians who jammed with him or saw him play spoke in glowing terms about his prowess and stage presence. Dave Mason was so "blown away" after his first experience that he considered a complete change of career. "I remember thinking I might as well take up another instrument." Lemmy (aka Ian Kilmister), who served time and earned £10 a week as Hendrix's roadie before his days with Hawkwind and Motörhead, recalls, "When he performed he was magic. You would watch him and time and space would stop … on stage he was a howling demon."

Robert Wyatt, the founder of Soft Machine who were also managed and produced by Chandler, compared Hendrix's arrival with a major change in the movie business. "Films were in black and white, but then along came Technicolor and that was like hearing Hendrix play – like Technicolor had just been invented in a black and white world."

With such references and recommendations ringing in their ears, a cross-section of

JIMI HENDRIX MADE IN ENGLAND

3

agents, managers, musicians, journalists, disc jockeys, broadcasters and record company executives descended on the Scotch for the Tuesday showcase.

One of the guests was Dick Katz, who had booked dates for The Animals and was a man Chandler knew well. Sharing a table with the pair was Paul McCartney who, according to Chandler, leant over to ask Katz if he had signed Hendrix as he "would be a giant".

Also on duty that day was Gerry Stickells, a friend of Redding who had been recruited as the band's roadie. A trained mechanic, he had earned extra money by driving dance bands around Kent before linking up with Redding's early bands. "He got a job with Jimi Hendrix by switching to bass and I got a job too," explained Stickells.

He was the man who, in his own words, "did pretty much everything – drove the band, settled the show, took care of the gear" – and that night was in charge of the sound. "The owner kept trying to get me to turn down Hendrix's amp. I kept saying I would at the end of the next song, but then I ran to the bathroom to hide."

Before the month of October was out, Hendrix had made it into the columns of the British music press when Richard Green wrote in the October 29 issue of Record Mirror that "Chas Chandler has signed and brought to this country a 20-year-old Negro called Jim Hendrix who – among other things – plays the guitar with his teeth and is being hailed in some quarters as the main contender for the title of 'the next big thing'."

The quarter-page article shared page six with a feature on singer Lee Dorsey defining soul music (with help from his manager Marshall Sehorn), an advert for new Decca singles from the likes of Unit Four Plus Two, The Mockingbirds and The Righteous Brothers and an in-depth probe into the life and times of Walker Brother Gary Leeds. Journalist Green focused on life after The Animals for Chandler and Valentine.

While confirming that Chandler had first heard 'John' – the paper managed to give him that name as well – playing in Greenwich Village, Record Mirror went on to report the ex-musician-turned-manager's comments on his new discovery. "He looks like Dylan, he's got all that hair sticking out all over the place. He's coloured but he doesn't think like a coloured person. He's got a very good idea of what he wants to do," adding, just for good measure, "He's better than Eric Clapton." So now, whether he was Jim, John or Jimi, at least Hendrix had his name in the papers!

By November 2, Chandler had got enough money together for another studio session – but, as he "couldn't afford to have the band learn the song in the studio", they rehearsed elsewhere before going into De Lane Lea. 'Stone Free' was a song Hendrix had written after his manager explained the financial advantages of recording self-penned songs rather than cover versions.

After their initial sojourn to France, the Experience went off to Germany between November 8 and 11 for a series of gigs at the Big Apple Club in Munich, where they played two shows a night.

According to Chandler it was during one of these that Hendrix, having been pulled off stage by fans, threw his guitar back up on to the stage. "When he picked it up he saw that it was cracked and several strings were broken. Then he just went barmy and smashed everything in sight. The Germans loved it and we decided to keep it as part of the act."

While the band was away, it was the turn of Chandler and Jeffery to try to negotiate a major record for their young charges. It's likely that EMI would have shied away from dealing with Jeffery, who had begun to compare himself with Beatles manager Brian Epstein, while Decca apparently doubted the band's "long-term potential".

Finally, their attention turned to Chris Stamp and Kit Lambert, who had told Chandler in September of their plans to start a label. This was mainly as an outlet for their best-selling act The Who, who had moved from Decca (and its Brunswick label) to a new independent called Reaction in March 1966.

Reaction, like its sister indie label Creation, was formed by Australian entrepreneur Robert Stigwood in partnership with Germany's Polydor Records, which had launched a UK operation in 1965. Having seen The Who and Stigwood's own act Cream ride up the charts on two small labels – bringing some profile and profit to Polydor – Stamp and Lambert saw the opportunity to launch Track Records with the backing and support of Polydor.

The two young managers were inspired by the likes of Island Records, founded in 1962 by Chris Blackwell, and Andrew Loog Oldham's Immediate label, created in 1965. In an industry that was still controlled by three UK majors – EMI, Decca and Pye – plus the Dutch company Philips, they took the view that independent labels were needed to break the stranglehold the 'big boys' held over artist signing and retail opportunities.

"We wanted to make money," said Stamp, "but it wasn't the be-all and end-all. Track was not conceived as a company that was gonna put out a gimmick record because it was gonna to be a hit." They nailed their 'indie' colours firmly to the mast in 1968 with the release of John Lennon's Two Virgins album, which had a cover featuring a photograph of Lennon and Yoko Ono in all their naked glory. When EMI refused to distribute the album, Track stepped in and put it into the shops – albeit in a brown paper bag.

Stamp admits that one thing alone clinched the deal with Chandler and Jeffery for Hendrix – money. "They insisted, 'You have to give us some sort of money', and because we didn't want to lose Hendrix we eventually came up with £1,000 and we promised that we would get Hendrix on Ready Steady Go!"

According to Etchingham, the deal to sign Hendrix to Track Records might well have been clinched during one of the long nights spent in the Scotch of St James. "I can remember Chris Stamp and Kit Lambert sitting with Chas and Mike one night in the early days and Chas saying, 'We've got a deal.'"

Ready Steady Go! was commercial television's all-important Friday evening pop show which went out with the tag 'The weekend starts here' and had been running since August 1963. The two men who managed The Who believed they would be able to influence the show's producers to feature their new unknown signing when the time was right.

Hendrix's wild and exciting guitar style drew immediate comparisons with the established master of destruction, Pete Townshend from The Who. Stamp and Lambert knew all about dealing with controversy and both on-stage and off-stage antics, and in Hendrix's amplified blues and rock trio they had the perfect stablemates to their group of deafening pop and R&B pioneers.

In addition to the money, and the promise of a TV show, the two partners also convinced Chandler and Jeffery that they had something else in their locker. "We said to them, and they already knew this, 'Look, we are the best sort of concept promotion going at the moment.'"

Roland Rennie was the man chosen by Polydor to head their British operation as managing director. One of Rennie's first contacts was Robert Stigwood, and it was through Stigwood that Rennie met up with Lambert and Stamp and ultimately signed a £50,000 deal to bring The Who to Polydor via Reaction. "Everybody wanted a label in those days and Kit and Chris wanted to start a label called Track. So we said 'OK'. We paid for everything and we owned it all."

The idea was to create Track with Polydor's funding, but even now Rennie remembers Stamp's attitude to the deal. "He said they didn't want to go with a major and that going with Polydor was the best of a bad lot." Joe Boyd believes the inspiration behind Polydor's transition into a major label was A&R chief Horst Schmolzi. "He was the guy who invented it all, the deals with independents like Giorgio Gomelsky, Robert Stigwood and the guys at Track. He liked the idea of empowering people like Chris Stamp and Kit Lambert who had new ideas. He welcomed independents and doled out the German money, which nobody had ever done before, and Polydor went from zero to around 12 per cent of the pop market in a year."

Chas was hopeful the Polydor A&R head would be more receptive on his first hearing of Are You Experienced. The German listened impassively to both sides, saying nothing, and Chandler, who hadn't yet played the acetate to an 'outsider', admitted he was waiting for 'the men in white coats to take me away'. At the end of side two came the German bigwig's verdict: 'This is brilliant, the greatest thing I ever heard.'

With the promised funding for their new label, Stamp and Lambert set about signing The Jimi Hendrix Experience as Track's first act. With Hendrix signed to Track for the world outside the US, even though the label didn't officially exist in November 1966, Rennie was forced to deal with the team of the inexperienced Chandler ("Chas was never born to be a manager") and Jeffery, plus the unique pairing of Stamp and Lambert.

"Kit was a headcase" is Rennie's simple summing-up of the Oxford graduate son of the composer Constant Lambert. "He came into my office one day while I was dealing with a load of bills. I asked him to wait a minute, but he just picked up the whole tray of papers and threw them out of the window."

While Stamp, the son of a tugboat captain from London's East End, was less of a handful, he still posed problems for the head of Polydor. "Neither of them were really business people and it was an odd partnership because Chris was straight and Kit was gay, but we agreed we would leave it to them to deliver what they thought was right."

Joe Boyd believes the pairing of Stamp and Lambert at Track came along at the right time. "They were great and both very creative. I think Kit had that theatrical side and Chris was a clever guy who perhaps knew more about the nuts and bolts of the business.

Track gave Chas the money and also gave him the independence to make records and deliver them to Track, who were good at marketing, and Chas made good records for Jimi."

Kathy Etchingham sees the fact that Track dealt direct with Chas as the best way for things to be handled back then. "Jimi didn't really have a lot to do with Track – he just signed whatever he was told to and it was Chas's job to handle things with Track and deal with the record releases." That said, she admits "We really didn't discuss the business side of things and I can't really say what was in his mind about records, sleeves or tours."

JIMI HENDRIX MADE IN ENGLAND

3

Teenager David Arden saw Stamp and Lambert around the London scene and, even then, understood their appeal to acts. "They were great characters and they seemed to be a bit cavalier and a bit different, although Lambert was a bit airy-fairy about business and a bit oily."

He also understood what Polydor was trying to do with Track Records. "They were one of the first companies to invest in talented executives like Stigwood and then Stamp and Lambert who wanted to start up their own operations. For some reason they [Polydor] didn't seem to have confidence in their own people to find talent, so they invested in these smaller independent labels."

The late Tony Stratton-Smith, who launched Charisma Records in 1969, rated his inspirations for pursuing a career in the music business as Brian Epstein, Andrew Loog Oldham and Kit Lambert. "Of the three I would say that Kit was the model in those days," said the man known throughout the industry as 'Strat'. "Before he started running off to Paris and drinking too much and drugging too much, before all these things ruined Kit's life, he had a fine mind. If he could have controlled himself he could have become the best manager in the world."

Although he could play legally overseas, Jimi Hendrix was still unable to perform professionally in Britain until he could obtain a UK work permit. With a few pounds in his pocket from the band's first professional gigs, he spent his spare time strolling around London. He took in bookshops, searching for his favourite sci-fi titles, and the plethora of fancy clothes stores that filled Soho's Carnaby Street and the King's Road in Chelsea.

He was fast developing a fashion style that was both unique and highly distinctive and it was something leading photographer Gered Mankowitz, who had toured America in 1965 with The Rolling Stones, spotted. "As the London scene and the music business embraced him, he developed his own individual and flamboyant sense of style as he took to the look of the day – velvets, silk, satins, lace and chiffon."

Mankowitz regarded Hendrix, with his slim, almost hipless body, broad shoulders and larger than average head, as "the perfect rock'n'roll figure" even before he had photographed him. Hendrix, who had been considered quite eccentric in New York, quickly developed an affection for the London fashion scene of the swingin' Sixties. "He particularly loved the military jackets you could buy from Lord Kitchener's Valet around that time," says Mankowitz.

Hendrix found genuine antique houses sitting next to junk shops on west London's trendy Portobello Road. One of the coolest was the previously mentioned Lord Kitchener's Valet, quaintly named after the personal assistant to the leader of Britain's army in the Boer War and in India at the start of the twentieth century. Hendrix would browse through the colourful army tunics of Britain's imperial past. He was in good company, as Manfred Mann, Eric Clapton and members of The Stones were regular customers. This was not just the usual ex-army merchandise and owner Paul Robinson refused to reveal the source of his exotic military outfits.

Apart from The Beatles, who adopted faux military band uniforms for the Sgt Pepper shoot, it was Hendrix who embraced the military fashion most successfully. Like many Royal Guardsman, his height enabled him to carry off the look.

Ram Jam Band frontman Geno Washington tells how Hendrix got one of his jackets in particularly sneaky fashion after the pair went to a shop just off Carnaby Street, London's hip fashion thoroughfare, and spotted a black and gold Hungarian Hussars jacket. "I was a uniform freak and was looking for something for my image and I fell in love with this jacket. The guy wanted £75 for it but I only had 50 quid on me which I gave him as a deposit to keep the jacket," says Washington.

In need of another £25, and in the days long before ATM cash machines, Washington and band went off in search of a bank. "He gave us 25 minutes to get the cash and get back, otherwise he would sell the jacket to anyone else who wanted it. We got back in around 10 minutes, I gave him the money and said 'Bring out my jacket.'"

The shop owner gave Washington his £50 back and explained that he had sold the jacket to Hendrix, who had given him £150. "I could not believe it and you're damn right I mentioned it to Jimi when I saw him next. In fact I mentioned it to him many, many times and then he used to tease me and say, 'Do you want to touch my jacket?' We were about the same size back in those days – skinny and just under six foot tall except for his hair sticking up in the air, which gave him another few inches."

The next step in manager Chandler's plan was for a full-scale reception to present his artist to the press. With cash in short supply, he was forced to sell the only things he had left from his days with The Animals – his bass guitars – to fund the Tuesday lunchtime show in the cellar that was known as the Bag O'Nails.

If the show at the Scotch a month earlier had been a success, then the reception at the Bag on November 25 would have an even greater impact on Hendrix's rise to fame and fortune. Etchingham considers the Bag O'Nails one of her favourite Hendrix gigs, "because it was his own night". Members of The Beatles, The Stones,

JIMI HENDRIX MADE IN ENGLAND

3

The Who and The Hollies, witnessed The Experience putting on a show that inspired Pete Townshend, memorably unmoved by Hendrix's debut performance two months earlier, to comment, "It was a shock to see somebody like Hendrix. We were witnessing something quite remarkable."

"There were guitar players weeping … everybody was completely in shock," according to singer Terry Reid, while among the visitors to Hendrix's dressing room was John Lennon, who, according to Noel Redding, wandered into the room after the show and simply said, "Fucking grand, lads".

Folk singer Donovan saw that something else was in the air and observed, "Watch out you white boys. He [Hendrix] is going to reverse the process and take centre-stage as the Afro-guitar wizard." For Tony Bramwell, the show at the Bag was "like a guitarist's convention", while Polydor boss Rennie thought his new signing was "terrific", but acknowledged that he was "35 and dealing with 20-year-olds who weren't interested in what I thought".

Both men found the newly emerging American star's down-to-earth nature refreshing. "He was a lovely guy, absolutely charming, although he always mumbled and was hard to understand," says Rennie, and Bramwell's abiding memory is much the same. "He was always polite but never said much to anybody, although as he spent time in London he gradually gained more of a personality."

The Bag was located in Kingly Street, a side street between Carnaby Street and Regent Street. Revived by agent and manager John Gunnell with club owner Lawrie Leslie, the Bag was a favourite with most of the major pop acts of the time. On the day Hendrix and his band appeared, admittance was free and the drinks were paid for by Chandler, who had invited Gered Mankowitz along with an eye to hiring him to capture his new star on film. "Chas said he had this 'fantastic guy' he'd like me to photograph, and when I arrived people were clambering on the stage and the noise was absolutely extraordinary."

While he is the first to admit that the music – which included Hendrix's take on Dylan's 'Like A Rolling Stone', 'Everybody Needs Somebody To Love' (a hit for Solomon Burke) and Chuck Berry's 'Johnny B Goode' – "went way over my head", Mankowitz was still excited by what he saw on stage. "What was most enthralling was his charisma, his extraordinary skill, and most of all the total mystery of how he was doing it … it was like a three-card trick."

Impressed by the frontman's flamboyant appearance and charismatic stage presence,

Mankowitz was taken to meet the man he might have to photograph. "He was surrounded by people but Chas ushered me over. He stood up, called me 'sir' and we shook hands and I said I looked forward to seeing him in the studio in the coming weeks. It was ridiculous after what I'd seen on stage that there was this quietly spoken, ridiculously polite, very American young man."

The Bag was the venue for Geno Washington's next meeting with Chas Chandler, who was keen to get the soul singer to return a favour. "His group The Animals had helped me get started, so he laid it on me as to whether I could help him out with Jimi, who was just doing small clubs and things."

Washington's Ram Jam Band were a top-of-the-bill act and Chandler saw an opportunity for his new group to play bigger venues. "He asked me if I could get him to support me on my gigs – we had lots of gigs back then and thousands of people were coming to see us." An agreement was reached between the rookie manager and the popular singer for The Jimi Hendrix Experience to support The Ram Jam Band, starting with a show just before Christmas 1966.

In 1966, 19-year-old Barry Dickins worked at the Harold Davidson Agency under the direction of Dick Katz, the former agent for The Animals who had been at the Scotch of St James showcase in October. "Dick summoned me to his office one day when Chas was there. He showed me some pictures of this guy with hair like Bob Dylan had put his finger in a socket and wearing an old military jacket."

Even then, it was obvious to the young agent that his boss didn't really understand what was going on with Hendrix and Chandler. When it came to the music, "It was like nothing else I had ever heard. I thought it was interesting, so Dick said I should do the bookings for Jimi Hendrix."

Dickins and Chandler decided that the best move was to book the new Jimi Hendrix Experience on the regular club circuit, which covered the Ricky Tick, Uppercut, Ram Jam, 7½, Speakeasy and Marquee clubs in and around London. "When we started out, the aim was to try and book him out for seven nights a week," says Dickins.

"Chas would be saying, 'He's got a night off, what's wrong?', and I would just be negotiating for as much as I could get. There was no standard rate and promoters wanted an opening act to play for nothing, but once they had seen Hendrix in their club they came back asking for more – then I was turning down offers." According to Etchingham, Chandler's ploy was to tell club owners that his new act "weren't too loud" and, as they were just a trio, they were "cheap as well".

JIMI HENDRIX MADE IN ENGLAND

3

The first date Dickins booked for his new act was at the Ricky Tick club in Hounslow as support to Eric Burdon and The New Animals. "I got £25 for Jimi to open the show which wasn't very much, but it was worth at least £100 in today's money." The Ricky Tick was located in a room above Burton's High Street tailors shop that held no more than 500 people, and was run by promoter John Mansfield.

"Ricky Tick meant syncopated music in America in the Twenties and Thirties," Mansfield later explained, "and from 1963 onwards we used it with the logo of a big, screaming Negro face." On the night of November 26, he recalls that the manager of his club got a call about the evening's support act. "He said to Chas Chandler, 'Where's the support?', and was told, 'They're over there.' Once they started playing he turned to Chas and said, 'That guy with the fuzzy hair's playing the guitar back to front, what's wrong with him?', and Chas just said, 'That's Jimi.'"

Recounting that he first paid The Rolling Stones £12 for their services and then upped it to £20 for the likes of The Animals and The Yardbirds, Mansfield remembers Hendrix as "very humble, there was nothing showbiz at all about him."

For Dickins, the show was his introduction to the live experience that was The Experience. "They came on stage and it was Jimi and all these guys with crazy hair and suddenly 'Wham!' … there was the most amazing thing you had ever seen."

As a dedicated follower of Bob Dylan, Dickins was interested in the band's set list that night. "He did 'Like A Rolling Stone' but nothing like Dylan did it, and 'Hey Joe', which I was aware of because it was a song Tim Rose sang. But this was Hendrix's version and you thought this guy has got something. It was like goosebumps down your back."

For drummer Mitchell, for whom playing the Ricky Tick was not a new experience as he had been there with Georgie Fame, "The Hounslow club was tiny with a low ceiling. We were set up in the corner and had very little room to move. The audience weren't exactly hostile but they didn't know what to make of us."

Like so many others, Dickins found Hendrix to be quiet and polite – until he went to work. "Then suddenly you saw this maniac on stage, where he also had Mitch the mad drummer and Noel Redding, who was sort of just there. Nobody played guitar like Hendrix and nobody was a showman like him."

Many had noticed the young American's reserved, almost laid-back, attitude to life and it was apparent to most of them what his secret was. "He was stoned most of the times I saw him," says Dickins, while Lemmy simply states, "He had a legendary capacity to take more drugs than anybody else. He was totally stoned most of the time and it helped him with some of the experimenting he did with the guitar."

Peter Jones, who wrote for Record Mirror, reported on the Bag O'Nails showcase on November 25. "He also remembers seeing him play "in the afternoon once at Charlie Chester's club in Archer Street, which was an old gambling club. It was something that Chas put together early on. The show was shambolic. Nobody made any introductions or anything, but he just electrified the people who were there. Him playing the guitar with his teeth is embedded in my memory forever … Chas was right in thinking that Hendrix had a great future." Sadly, there is no record of Hendrix ever setting foot in the club owned by one the UK's most successful and colourful post-war comedians.

Record Mirror, the smallest of the UK's weekly pop newspapers in the Sixties behind New Musical Express and Melody Maker, ploughed an unique editorial path. "We did write about unknowns while nobody else would," Jones says, explaining how he came to interview Hendrix in November 1966. "It was a favour for Chas, whom I got on with very well."

The meeting was set to take place in De Hems, an Anglo-Dutch pub just a stone's throw from Record Mirror's office and a popular watering hole for media and musicians alike. Hendrix arrived at De Hems to meet Jones, accompanied by Chandler and, over a drink, turned out to be a reluctant talker – even about himself. "It wasn't really an interview," recalls Jones. "He was really very quiet and you almost had to drag him into the conversation. I got some background stuff and he praised Chas a lot."

Despite the American's reluctance, Jones managed to put together a feature which appeared on page 2 of the December 10 issue of Record Mirror, alongside readers' letters. Under the headline "MR. PHENOMENON!", and alongside a photograph captioned "a moody pic of Jimi Hendrix", Jones advised fans who believed there was nothing new happening in pop music that here was "a new artist, a new star in the making who we predict is going to whirl round the business like a tornado."

Jones went on to recount in print going to the Bag O'Nails with Bill Harry, the founding editor of Mersey Beat magazine. "Jimi was in full flight, whirling like a demon, swirling his guitar every which-way; this 20-year-old [in fact he was just two days away from celebrating his 24th birthday!] was quite amazing."

If Jones managed to get few words out of Hendrix during their encounter in the London pub, he seemingly got some quotes after his showcase performance. "Sweatily exhausted Jimi said afterwards, 'I've only been in London three months, but Britain is really groovy. Just been working in Paris and Munich.'" He then went on to explain the type of music his new three-piece line-up played. "We don't want to be classed in any

JIMI HENDRIX MADE IN ENGLAND

3

category. If it must have a tag, I'd like it to be called Free Feeling. It's a mixture of rock, freak-out, blues and rave music."

Explaining that the group had been playing on the Continent while awaiting Hendrix's official work permit, Chandler also confirmed that the three-piece line-up was permanent. "Noel and Mitch can follow his every mood – if we get even one more [person] in it could spoil the understanding." Looking to end on a lighter note, Jones asked about the effect of playing the guitar with your teeth and Hendrix apparently told him, "I do have to brush my teeth three times a day."

While he remained a friend of Chandler's for many years, Jones never saw Hendrix play again, nor did he interview him a second time. "Once he became really famous he was out of Record Mirror's range." He did, however, see him around London. "He used to come into De Hems and I saw him in there a few times. I would be standing at the bar and suddenly I'd be aware that somebody was sitting very quietly and waiting patiently to be served, and it was Jimi Hendrix. He did recognize me and we talked briefly. He was living nearby by then, so maybe it became one of his locals."

Jones caught sight of Hendrix walking around Soho and Mayfair more than once during those heady mid-Sixties days. "The amazing thing was that nobody took very much notice at all. He was never dressed outrageously, usually in very sombre black things, but he did still have the very wild hair, which was very shocking."

Being so readily accepted in London and settled within the UK music business was important to Hendrix after what he had experienced in areas of America where black people were banned from restaurants, stores, buses and hotels and made to use separate bathrooms and entrances.

Looking back on those days in the swingin' London of the Sixties, photographer Mankowitz also sensed that Hendrix liked his newly adopted country. "He found London comfortable and certainly experienced less racial problems than in America," says the man who first visited the US in 1965. "I was completely shocked by the segregation that I saw in the South. I was fascinated by it and Hendrix was just about the first American black artist I worked with after that."

Throughout their photo session, Hendrix chatted openly about his own experiences on the chitlin' circuit and told Mankowitz what he found "so wonderful" about the UK. "He said he didn't feel any of that prejudice here. He could be seen with white girls without many problems and he recognized that the whole music scene took to him – they loved black music and loved him as a black man playing music."

BRITAIN IS REALLY GROOVY

Hearing comments like that made Mankowitz proud. "That made us all feel great, that we should be part of a society that just accepted him." Tony Bramwell, too, shares the view that Hendrix had found a new home. "I think he really loved England in those days."

Dave Wilkinson also recalls how Hendrix slowly but surely took to his new life in Britain. "He did become more English as time went by, although he was probably already more polite than many of our customers. On more than one occasion, I used to send out for tea for him while he was sitting in the shop and just playing. He did adopt us … in a sense."

In the first week of December 1966, Hendrix and Kathy Etchingham, his girlfriend from day one in the UK, moved into the flat in Montagu Square owned by Beatles drummer Ringo Starr and occupied by Chandler and his Swedish wife Lotta. Located between Baker Street and the Edgware Road, the apartment was spread over two floors, which meant that Hendrix and his manager could live on separate levels. Hendrix, Etchingham and the Chandlers lived here until the neighbours complained about the noise being made by the 'rock star' tenants.

When Chandler told Hendrix and Etchingham they all had to move out, she recalls Chandler claimed there was a clause in the lease which barred 'blacks' from living in the flat and that Ringo had received some complaints. The next place the four of them called home was a fourth-floor flat in nearby Upper Berkeley Street and once again the manager and his wife took the best room. Eventually, in 1968, Hendrix and Etchingham would move to 25 Brook Street, in the heart of London's prestigious Mayfair, where composer George Frideric Handel had lived from 1723 until his death in 1759.

After they moved out, the Montagu Square flat was taken over by John Lennon and Yoko Ono and the Beatle, concerned about Hendrix's reputation for drug use, is reported to have had the place meticulously scoured and vacuumed in order to remove any remnants of the previous occupants. It obviously wasn't enough; despite Lennon and Ono's insistence that they were 'clean', a seven-strong police force discovered a small piece of hash in a clothes trunk during a drugs raid.

Despite alleging that the dope had been planted and he had been framed, Lennon ultimately pleaded guilty to possessing 219 grains of cannabis and was fined £150. The conviction for the offence committed in Hendrix's old flat would become a major issue in his quest for US citizenship. George Harrison was later moved to comment, "Jimi Hendrix rented it as well. It has a history, that flat."

The two members of Les Fleur De Lys had still not seen their former 'flatmate' play

3

live. While Hendrix and his band were making a noise in London, Gordon Haskell, Keith Guster and their group were themselves busy gigging in the capital and around the Home Counties but, oddly, their paths seemingly never crossed. According to Haskell, the man they claim was in the front flat was still "the bloke in the next room".

With an all-important extension to his work permit which would see him through until mid-January 1967, Hendrix took to the stage at Brixton's Ram Jam Club on December 10 to support John Mayall and chose a set that would appeal to the man who was the UK's leading blues exponent. How it went down with the predominantly West Indian crowd who filled out the south London reggae club we may never know. But, having run through 'Catfish Blues' and 'Dust My Blues', Hendrix thrust his guitar through the ceiling and then carried on playing slide guitar, using bits of the roof as the bottleneck.

The next day the man who fired Hendrix for being too audacious and up-front hit London. Jimi visited Little Richard in his London hotel and, according to legend, borrowed $50 from him. Recalling the meeting as the last time he ever saw Hendrix, Little Richard confirmed that he lent him some money and heard about his new record. "He said he'd got this new record coming out which was gonna be a hit. Sure enough, when it comes out, it was a mighty hit."

Part of the attraction for Chandler when he chose Track Records as the home for his act was the promise of an appearance on Ready Steady Go!, and on December 13 Stamp and Lambert came up with goods. For the standard fee of £91 eight shillings and five pence, The Jimi Hendrix Experience shared the bill with The Troggs, The Merseybeats and Marc Bolan and, in front of an assembled audience of interested youngsters, belted out a live version of 'Hey Joe'. According to Bolan, this was "really loud ... all the machines [in the control room] were shaking".

The Troggs' Chris Britton recalls that although The Experience were miming, there was still something magical about the performance. "Both the music and the act were stunning."

For Stamp and Lambert, RSG! offered them the perfect opportunity to plug Hendrix's debut single, released on Friday December 16 – the same day as the one-hour show was broadcast. While no one doubted that Hendrix would be able to deal with what was his first television performance as frontman, bass player Redding was a little less confident. "I'd never done television before ... I was terrified."

"We knew that the audience of RSG! were musically a little bit hip," recounts Stamp. "They weren't as broad as the Top Of The Pops audience but we knew they would get off on Jimi."

Show over, the group moved on to CBS Studios where they installed four Marshall cabinets, planted Hendrix's microphone just eight feet away and laid down 'Foxy Lady','Red House','Can You See Me' and 'Third Stone From The Sun' under Chandler's watchful eye.

Engineer on those sessions was 21-year-old Mike Ross-Taylor who, in exchange for his weekly wage of £10, worked on "whoever and whatever came into the studio". Located in Whitfield Street in central London, CBS had begun business as Levy's Sound Studios and had a relaxed attitude to booking. "We weren't as strict as other studios – people could hire the studio for as long as they wanted," says Ross-Taylor. "They booked by the hour basically or could book up to eight hours. Sessions did go on into the evening, starting at four and going through to close to midnight."

Recalling that The Experience were booked in for three days, starting at 4pm on December 13, 1966, Ross-Taylor explains, "It came in as a regular booking and I had no idea who Hendrix was. Chas booked it and I knew who he was – it was quite exciting that he was coming in."

The start of the two days of recording – "the last day was just mixing" – was when Ross-Taylor first caught sight of Hendrix. "Chas turned up with this guy who was very tall and had a lot of hair and wore a strange military-style jacket. He was a lovely guy, very quiet, very shy, and he never said much. He just seemed to be locked in this little world of guitars. He seemed like a bit of a loner who lived just for guitars."

Ross-Taylor worked on three tracks – 'Foxy Lady','Red House' and 'Third Stone From The Sun' – that would eventually appear on the first Experience album. From the outset he realized who was calling the shots. "There was a definite feeling that Chas was in charge, he was the boss. He had got Noel and Mitch into the band and I got the feeling that they were expected to feel lucky that he had employed them," he explains. "But it was still all very relaxed and not the least hurried by Chas, who was hands-on and definitely in control."

As the main man in the trio, Hendrix focused his attention on his own work, spending his time in the studio away from the other two members of his group. This was one of the first things Ross-Taylor noticed when they started to prepare for their session. "He kind of rehearsed for a while, plugged everything in and just played around on his own and I could not believe the sound coming out of his amp."

Hendrix's amps were all the engineer and the guitarist ever spoke to each other about. "The only conversation I had with Jimi was about recording his amp, which was

3

just so loud," says Ross-Taylor, who was more used to the small amps brought in by session players. "He came in with four Marshall stacks and started to play and it was just unbelievably loud – everything in the room was shaking.

"He knew it was loud and he wanted it loud, and I remember thinking that if I put a microphone on his amp it was going to shatter so I said to Jimi, 'How do they normally record your amp?', He just said, 'If you put the microphone over there and sort of point it'," explains Ross-Taylor, remembering that Hendrix and his Experience had only been recorded once before when they made 'Hey Joe'. "He just suggested that I didn't put the mike too near the guitar."

Drummer Mitchell was even more involved in how his drum kit was miked for the sessions, as Ross-Taylor recollects. "He turned up and said that he had been at Lansdowne Road studios and they had put a microphone on every drum – about eight mikes in all as opposed to the normal of a mike on the bass drum and a mike on the top. I remember feeling a bit put out by this and thinking that if they could do it then so could I. It was the first time I had ever multi-miked a drum kit and I think Mitch told me the story in order to get me to do it."

Ross-Taylor also recalls that Hendrix didn't spend all his time in the studio. "He was in the control room for all the playbacks, but that wasn't unusual for a solo musician and I saw Jimi as a solo musician," he says. "But he had no idea what was going on in the control room. He turned up and listened and did what Chas said. He didn't seem to have many ideas of his own and I got the feeling that it was very much a case of 'OK Chas, you paid for all this. What do you want?'"

As Hendrix moved between studio and control room – "I got the impression that he was very pleased to be there and pleased to be making a record," suggests Ross-Taylor – Redding was intent on burning the midnight oil and running up the bills. "I remember Chas saying late one night that we should wrap and go home and Noel saying that he wanted to play all night. Chas looked at him and said, 'You don't want to go home because you live in a pit', and I do recall that Noel looked as if he was on his uppers."

The fact that, according to Ross-Taylor, the sessions were not rushed was a bit of a surprise as it soon became apparent to the engineer that Chas had financial issues. "It was obvious money was tight. Chas hired the studio, and in those days you were expected to pay your bills before you left with the tapes, but Chas didn't have any money at the end of the day," he says.

This situation resulted in a row with the studio manager, who wanted to be paid for the work that had been done. "He wanted payment for the three days before he would let Chas book any more time, but Chas was arguing, 'This is not the way I normally do business. I come in and I finish my recordings and then at the end of it all I pay my bill'," recalls Ross-Taylor.

"About a week later I got a call to say that Chas was coming in to settle the bill, so I could give him the tapes we had done. He was really upset because he said he was really happy with the work we had done but he said to me, 'Your studio manager is unworkable. I can't work under these conditions.'" With studio costs at CBS, according to Ross-Taylor, running at around £42 an hour in 1966, Chandler's first three days must have cost close to £700 and it seems the Experience's early departure left at least two people disappointed.

"Chas actually loved the studio and he thanked me for all my work," says Ross-Taylor. "And I was upset because if he had been able to pay the bill I would have recorded the whole of the first Hendrix album. I enjoyed what we were doing – it kinda blew me away because I had never heard anything like it before. It was amazing."

Although he firmly believes that Are You Experienced is "one of the greatest albums of all time", Ross-Taylor finds it hard to analyze his own contribution. "As the years pass you don't hear it as your work, you hear it as someone else's work – you don't feel connected any more."

While the group's television debut on RSG! was the focal point of the promotion for 'Hey Joe', Stamp and Lambert were also busy priming the press about their new act, and portraying Hendrix as savage, wild and even primeval was an acceptable part of the PR game they were playing. It paid off in part as at least one writer did use the phrase 'Wild Man of Borneo' when describing Hendrix, a six-foot black man with an extraordinary, unruly hair style who was very much the opposite of the suited-and-booted black musicians who had toured the UK in soul and R&B bands.

Agent Dickins was one man who was certainly taken aback, firstly by Hendrix's musical ability and then by the appearance of the frontman and his two cohorts. "He just exploded like nothing else you had ever seen at the time," he explains. "First of all he was black, and black for everybody back then was Otis Redding; black meant a soul singer. And then he had hair like no other person you had ever seen." As if that were not enough, Dickins recounts, "he had these two white guys. Mitch was the closest thing you could get to Keith Moon in manic drumming and Noel, with his round glasses, looked like a schoolteacher with a wig on."

JIMI HENDRIX MADE IN ENGLAND

Then there was Hendrix's extraordinary stage presence which, in contrast to his reticent, retiring, off-stage persona, shone out the moment the spotlight was turned on. "You walked in and just looked at him and thought this guy has to be a star," says Dickins. "You had Clapton who was the God and then there was Jeff Beck but Hendrix was so totally different. There was this guy who looked like he'd come to clean your windows who became the biggest thing since sliced bread."

Reports of the arrival of a new guitar hero were picking up speed, and being seen by millions of youngsters on Ready Steady Go! only added to the tidal wave of interest. In his role as general manager of the Saville Theatre, Tony Bramwell was constantly on the lookout for new acts and he was particularly drawn to those who offered something different in their performance. "Suddenly we were seeing somebody playing rock properly and loud and being entertaining without being stupid."

Comparing Hendrix with the two biggest bands in the land, he says, "You were either mop-tops like The Beatles, or The Stones with Jagger doing his little dance thing. With them you didn't have a whirlwind in front of you shaking a guitar in the air." At that time, other than the odd ceiling incident and neck-breaking moment, there wasn't, according to Dickins, too much deliberate on-stage vandalism. "He certainly didn't set fire to his guitar when I was getting him 25 quid a night. You can only afford to do that sort of thing when you're earning good money."

Even though he was a whirling dervish on the guitar, it seems Hendrix didn't spend a lot of time discussing the merits of different makes and styles. Ex-Animal Hilton Valentine spent quite a bit of time with Hendrix but doesn't recall too many guitar seminars – "Some players love to talk technical about their gear but not Jimi" – while former Move man Trevor Burton adds, "All the times I met him I never actually sat and had him teach me anything, but I would watch him as he played and that was enough."

Valentine was a regular visitor to the flat where Chandler and Hendrix lived with their partners, but probably spent more time in the Hendrix wing. "We'd hang together at Chas's place and take drugs there. Then our minds would just wander and we'd talk philosophically about anything from the state of the world to inane things like the pattern on the wallpaper … like stoned people do!"

Burton, too, saw Hendrix on occasion, this time through sharing a house with Redding which Hendrix would often visit. "He used to come round now and again and I met Chas a few times. He was a nice bloke but I don't think he ever really understood all the drug culture surrounding Jimi, and he didn't like it at all."

BRITAIN IS REALLY GROOVY

Following the broadcast of RSG!, and on the day their first single was officially released, Hendrix and The Experience took off for Kent to play at the Chislehurst Caves. Here a sell-out crowd assembled for the show organized by pirate radio station Radio Caroline, which initially broadcast off the coast of Suffolk until it fell foul of British Government legislation in 1967 and was forced to operate under Dutch regulations.

The rock gigs held in a section of the 22 miles of tunnels formed from man-made mines dating back to 1250 were, according to regular host and Caroline DJ Robbie Dale, "the wildest shows on Earth". He remembers the venue as "a sweaty hole in the ground filled with throbbing new music … and young, horny bodies." He also recalls the impact The Experience had on the audience. "They stood open-mouthed and wide-eyed. Nobody had ever seen a guitar player eat electricity quite like Jimi. You could hear and see him develop his skill playing with feedback."

'Hey Joe' by The Jimi Hendrix Experience was officially released just ten days before Christmas 1966 on the Polydor label with the number 56139 – despite the best efforts of Stamp and Lambert to make it Track's debut release. "Track wasn't ready by the time Hendrix made his first record," explains Rennie. "I hadn't signed off on their label because I still wasn't really sure why they wanted one and we did have a bit of a ding-dong about it before it was officially launched. We had to keep an eye on all the Track accounts and business dealings from day one."

The singles chart into which 'Hey Joe' was writing Hendrix's name for the first time was very much dominated by middle-of the road names. Tom Jones, the Seekers, Cliff Richard and Val Doonican were all in the Top 10, while the Monkees' made-for-kids TV 'I'm A Believer' was about to hit Number 1. Only Cream ('I Feel Free') and The Who ('Happy Jack') were really flying the flag for rock alongside the newcomer.

Hilton Valentine, meanwhile, was busy wearing a new hat as a producer, and the first people he turned to were Haskell, Guster and the rest of Les Fleur De Lys. "He came back to the flat while we were still living there, but after Jimi had gone he said he wanted to do some songs with us," says Guster. While nobody can remember which studio they used, the band played three songs – 'You've Got To Earn It', 'Ring Of Fire' and an old Impressions song called 'Amen' – with Valentine at the desk. "I have got 'You've Got To Earn It' and did have 'Ring Of Fire'," says Guster, who temptingly adds, "There was a rumour that Jimi Hendrix was going to turn up and overdub guitar on the tracks, but I can't honestly remember whether he did or not."

His bandmate Haskell is more certain. "I'm sure Jimi came in and put some guitar

3

on one of the tracks, which may well have been 'Amen', but we have never heard it." When prompted, Valentine too recalls an involvement with the band. "You've got to understand that we were all doing a lot of drugs back then so a lot of stuff is very hazy, but I've got a vague recollection of doing a session with Les Fleurs. But the only thing I really remember is the track 'Amen' and that Jimi was there, but I can't remember in what capacity."

Two tracks have survived as acetates, the song that might have featured Hendrix seems to have disappeared. Guster suggests, "If Jimi was on it maybe Chas took it" before ruefully adding, "If Jimi had put anything on any of the tracks they would be worth a fortune." Haskell had half a theory that keyboardist Pete Sears, who left soon after for America, might have taken it with him.

In 2003, Sears recalled the session to journalist Michael Heatley. "Chas Chandler and Mike Jeffery were recording us [playing] a demo of the Impressions song called 'Amen'. I was there at Eric Burdon's house with the band in his living room and they brought Jimi Hendrix over … we had no idea who he was, he just seemed like a nice guy. Then he overdubbed some guitar on 'Amen', but it was never released."

Guster and Haskell were invited by Chandler to see his protégé at his next London club date. "Chas came round and said he wanted us to go to Blaises," Guster says. "We walked up there from the flat and it was filling up with everybody who was anybody – there was Clapton, Townshend, Jack Bruce and Jeff Beck. The rock aristocracy was in and we felt like nobodies."

Opened as an upmarket club, Blaises was located in the basement of the Imperial Hotel, which was eventually demolished in 1992. When Hendrix, Mitchell and Redding came on stage, Guster saw the man they spent time with in their flat perform for the first time. "I had never seen or heard anything like it in my life. It was amazing, just phenomenal. Nobody had seen anyone play guitar like that … with his teeth, behind his back, and he banged it on the floor."

For Haskell too, Hendrix represented a special talent. "He was unique. I put Hendrix at the peak, but only just ahead of Jeff Beck. We were in awe of these God-like musicians and it was the greatest time for anyone to be around … and that was what we were – we were just around."

Also in the audience at Blaises was Gary Leeds of The Walker Brothers, who shared a table that night with Paul McCartney. "After Hendrix played the place went wild," he says. Sharing another table were BBC producers Jeff Griffin and Bernie Andrews. "I was doing a World Service programme with Alexis Korner," says Griffin, "and the first person who brought anything in – I think it was a reel of tape or maybe an acetate of 'Hey Joe' – was Dick Katz." Having explained to Griffin that "It's not really my cup of tea", the agent went on to say that he felt it might be the sort of thing they would like.

"He said that if we did like it and wanted to go and see him [Hendrix] then we should give him a call," explains Griffin. "Both Bernie and I thought it was good and we went along to see him. I think it was at Blaises and I remember just standing there open-mouthed and thinking, 'Bloody hell – this is something really special.'"

Thanks to his string of dates in and around the capital, musicians, broadcasters, record executives and punters had all been brought on board the Hendrix express, and after RSG! a new television audience had also bought tickets. Over at Selmer in the Charing Cross Road, Dave Wilkinson was also hearing all about the new guitar hero. "There was lots of talk about him when other musicians came into the shop. He made an enormous impression on all the other bands that were around."

Now it was the turn of the press to play their part in the story. Soon after the show at Blaises, Melody Maker's Chris Welch told his readers, "Jimi Hendrix, a fantastic American guitarist, blew the minds of the star-packed crowd who went to see him at Blaises club. Jimi has great stage presence and an exceptional guitar technique which involved him playing with his teeth on occasions and no hands at all on others!"

Pete Townshend, who was also at Blaises, laid bare his thoughts years later. "Seeing Jimi absolutely completely destroyed me. It was horrifying because he took back black music. He came and stole R&B back."

Down in Kent, David Hughes was busy reviewing the first Experience single for the December 23 issue of the Kent Messenger. He told his readers all about 'Hey Joe'. "Standout single this week comes from Jimi Hendrix, a coloured refugee from New York's Greenwich Village brought to our shores by ex-Animal Chas Chandler. 'Hey Joe' has the feeling of the urban bluesman and brings a new sound to the rather stagnant scene. The flip 'Stone Free' reminds me of The Stones as they were in their Crawdaddy days, up-tempo and containing much of Jimi's 'free feeling' sound. Strongly recommended."

Looking back over 45 years later, Hughes reflects on the fact they could use the word coloured in those days and is impressed that he also reviewed the B-side. "Maybe things were a bit tedious at that time and I remember that 'Hey Joe' stood out from the rest," he says. "In those days you got no information about the record or the act.

3

You were just grateful to get singles on a local paper so you played everything, including the B-side." 'Stone Free', Hendrix's writing debut, certainly made an impression on the young writer. "I'd never heard anything like it before. It wasn't even like Cream – this bloke's guitar was completely different."

The following day, Melody Maker printed a news story announcing that Jimi Hendrix – "the young American artist who came to Britain with ex-Animal Chas Chandler" – was the first signing to Polydor's new Track label. Explaining that 'Hey Joe' would appear on Polydor and not Track – the label that would be "fully operational in 1967" – they carried a quote from label executive Lambert which said, "We think Jimi's record is so good we didn't want to hold it back until Track officially came into being."

The press was now in full cry about The Jimi Hendrix Experience and their first record, with the NME's Christmas Eve edition announcing, "Here's a young man who could make a profound impression in the future. This is a raw, uninhibited treatment of a traditional number. It's guttural, earthy, convincing and authentic." Meanwhile Record Mirror's Peter Jones added, "Should justice prevail, this'll be a first-time hit. The genuinely most soulful record ever made in Britain. The best record Polydor has issued."

As Christmas approached, so finally did the opportunity for Geno Washington to repay his debt to Chandler. The Ram Jam Band were headlining two shows (8pm and midnight, entrance fee eight shillings) at the Guildhall in Southampton. "Jimi opened the show and came out with this little crappy PA [public address system]," recalls Washington. "He wanted to use our PA and he'd say, 'Come on man, we're brothers from America, you can let a brother use your PA.' So I let him use it and he loved it and it was good playing together and seeing him reach a wider audience."

Even though they were light-years apart in musical styles, Washington appreciated Hendrix and his group. "He was doing his thing and I admired his image – flower [power] was not big then and soul still ruled the house. I could see what he was doing, although I didn't know much about it. I knew he was changing the way things were presented and liked his image." However, the singer still had reservations about mixing their musical styles. "Him supporting me never really worked. We were pumping out dance music with a band rocking the house and my audience – mainly mods – was definitely not into flower power. We had different audiences."

Before the year ended, Hendrix, Mitchell and Redding had another show to do at a club in Forest Gate, to the east of London. Co-owned by businessman George Walker and his boxing champion brother Billy, the Upper Cut was a former ice-skating rink which was cavernous in comparison to most of its competitors and could hold up to 1,500 people. It featured big bands on Fridays for the over-18s, new groups on Sundays with dancers, and DJs playing records and hosting competitions on other nights – and all for an entrance fee of around six shillings.

In fact, the club had only been open five days when Hendrix was booked to appear on the afternoon of Monday December 26, posters advertising his show as "Boxing Day Fun For All The Family". The Who had opened the club on December 21 – the entrance fee was 17 shillings and six pence for 'gentlemen' and 15 shillings for 'ladies' – while both men and women paid £1 to see Eric Burdon and The New Animals on Christmas Eve. For the unknown and hitless Hendrix Experience, you could get in at 2.30 in the afternoon for just five shillings.

The show had been booked by Dickins, who recalls that, despite the lowly entrance fee, Hendrix was already a big draw. "He had exploded by then. It was unbelievable. No one had heard of him three months earlier." The band's reputation, which was being built up by word-of-mouth, radio play and media reports, allowed Dickins to start upping Hendrix's fee from the paltry £25 he started with in Croydon to anywhere between £100 and £500 nightly.

"A hundred quid was decent money for bookings for an unknown act in 1966," says Dickins, "and when he exploded on the back of 'Hey Joe' I remember trying to get him out of earlier dates. I used to phone up everybody and say, 'You know that date you got for £60 quid on Jimi Hendrix? We'll pay you £100 quid to let us out of it.' I knew I could get more for him somewhere else."

One thing Dickins was never sure about was how the money he negotiated for The Experience for their live shows was split between Hendrix and his fellow band members, let alone the details of their deal with Chandler, Jeffery and Track Records. "As far as I know, and I'm not absolutely sure about it, I think Jimi got paid it all and the other two just got paid a salary and I'm not even sure they got any royalties on record sales either."

He does, however, know that the Upper Cut was one of the clubs that would not let Hendrix out of his deal. "Some did let us out, but the Upper Cut wouldn't budge and we had to honour the date for the original money – which was a pity, as there were about 3,000 people there and they really made a fortune."

With no regard for heath and safety regulations, the Upper Cut seemingly broke all the rules that night as kids poured into the Woodgrange Road venue to see the latest phenomenon perform live – and all for just five bob!

JIMI HENDRIX MADE IN ENGLAND

3

While he was hanging around in his dressing room waiting for the 4pm show, Hendrix took up his pen and began to write the song that would eventually become his second biggest hit single.

"It was just a straight dream I had linked upon a story I read in a science fiction magazine about a purple death ray" is how Jimi remembers 'Purple Haze'. Manager Chandler, who was with Hendrix that afternoon, recollects, "It was written in the dressing room that afternoon. The gig was at 4pm … he just started playing the riff and I said, 'Write the rest of it, that's the next single' – so he did."

Dickins, who wasn't backstage, has a different memory of Hendrix's appearance at the Upper Cut club. "They never even gave him a bottle of Scotch in his dressing room and I remember Chas saying, 'I don't care if they offer me £10,000, I will never play this place again.'"

On the back of the group's TV debut on RSG! and the release of 'Hey Joe', The Experience found themselves booked for their debut appearance on the BBC's top music show Top Of The Pops. The edition filmed on December 29 was hosted by disc jockey Jimmy Savile, who recalled that there was often a four or five-hour wait to do the show, which in those days was usually produced in Manchester.

"You'd be stuck in the studio with nothing much to do. We got quite a rapport going but it was very much casual chat – the weather, where we'd been working, who was around and so on," said the legendary presenter. "But sitting having a cup of tea or coffee was something he [Hendrix] really enjoyed."

The day after brought Hendrix into contact with fellow psychedelic act Pink Floyd for possibly the first time during his three months in Britain. The band, named after American bluesmen Pink Anderson and Floyd Council, had become the hippest band in town as they began experimenting with feedback and electronic sound plus film and light shows.

Hendrix was in the crowd at the UFO club on December 30, 1966 to see jazz-rock group Soft Machine open the show, and midway through the set leapt on to the stage to jam with the band. After that he stayed for the Floyd's set, although he seemingly decided against joining in with the quartet.

Soft Machine's Daevid Allen had fond memories of the guitarist when interviewed in 2000. "We had the same management originally when he first arrived from America; he arrived right in the room where I was sitting. He started playing the guitar left-handed and filling the room with amazing sound. I got to know him immediately; it was easy to talk to him, he was one of those sunshine personalities. "We used to play chess. And yeah, we were both guitar players.

"When I had my guitar stolen, he once travelled across London in a taxi to bring me his. It was the wrong way round, of course, 'cos he was left-handed, I smashed it on the ground in frustration, but he didn't give a shit. It [our friendship] was fairly brief … but it was a really lovely connection."

Hendrix's first year in the UK ended with a New Year's Eve concert, which was hastily put together by their bass player in his home town of Folkestone when it became apparent the band had no show that night. It was set for the Hillside Social Club, and after the gig the trio retired to Redding's family home for a party to see in the New Year. It was there that, according to the bass player's mother, Hendrix got the inspiration for another song. "It was very cold that night," recounts Margaret Redding, "and Jimi asked me if it would be alright to stand next to the fire. That's how he got the idea for the song 'Fire'."

While it seems the family's German Shepherd dog was reluctant to share his warm retreat – hence the line, "Oh move over Rover and let Jimi take over" – there would be many established rock acts looking nervously over their shoulder in the coming year of 1967.

3

SOME PEOPLE THINK I'M GOOD

4

'HEY JOE' ENTERS UK CHART IN JANUARY 1967 – STARTS TO PERFORM IN PROVINCES – RECORDS 'PURPLE HAZE' – BUYS OCTAVIA FUZZ BOX – CLASSIC MANKOWITZ PHOTO SHOOT

L ess than four months after arriving in the UK as a complete unknown with no band and no record deal, Jimi Hendrix and his Experience began the New Year of 1967 with their first ever appearance in any record chart anywhere in the world.

Both major music papers Melody Maker and Record Mirror ran charts with 'Hey Joe' debuting in the MM at Number 48 on January 7 and entering the RM chart seven places higher at 41. Over the next four weeks, the record slowly gained ground in both and, by February 4, Melody Maker listed the record at Number 4 while Record Mirror placed it two slots lower.

In all, the record – which Hendrix had earlier told Little Richard would be a hit – stayed on the British chart for a total of 11 weeks and firmly established the Anglo-American Jimi Hendrix Experience at the heart of Britain's pop empire. 'Hey Joe's chart success had come at just the right time for Chandler, who was rapidly running short of money. "It was all done by the skin of my teeth," he recalled. "The DJs hadn't been playing it on the radio but the word had spread through the ballrooms and it started to sell. I think we had about 30 shillings left between us."

Two people who were turned on to Hendrix by his debut single were producer Joe Boyd and musician Keith Emerson, the keyboard-playing founder member of The Nice. "'Hey Joe' was my first introduction to him [Hendrix]," says Boyd. "Somebody said, 'Wow, listen to this', and when I heard it I remember thinking 'This is really good' and then going out and buying it. The minute I heard 'Hey Joe' it was clear that this guy was a superstar. I never had a nanosecond of doubt about his talent." Emerson was surprised to hear the song on the radio. "It wasn't usual to hear a lyric like 'Hey Joe, where you going with that gun in your hand?' played on the BBC."

4

'Foxy Lady' was not only one of the first songs recorded by the Experience, it was also for many music fans around the country their first chance, outside of the 'Hey Joe' single, to hear the Experience when it was recorded at a BBC Radio Saturday Club session in February 1967. For some aficionados, these rougher-edged, live in the BBC studio versions were more exciting than the polished album recordings, and Hendrix's six sessions recorded that year would form the basis of a later album..

For agent Barry Dickins, 1967 meant spreading the net wider so The Jimi Hendrix Experience would be seen and heard around the country. While they had travelled to France, Luxembourg and Germany, they had rarely stepped outside a comfort zone of London and its suburbs, plus odd shows in Kent and Southampton. Now it was time for the band to spread their wings, and in January Dickins booked them to appear in Manchester, Sheffield, Nottingham, Middlesbrough, Oldham and Norwich. "He did go up and down the country a few times – you were looking for the maximum exposure in the shortest amount of time, which sometimes involved a bit of travelling."

These new venues alternated between clubs and small theatres but, according to girlfriend Kathy Etchingham, they represented something new and good for her man. "That's when I remember him at his very best … and at his happiest." She recalls it being a time when Hendrix was "desperate to make a name for himself while also playing for himself", and these new out-of-town venues provided a perfect opportunity. "In the working men's clubs, they just wanted to hear some music to enjoy while they drank their beer. In the small theatres people had come to hear him."

She is also convinced it helped him produce something special. "That was his best music ever – played for its own sake. None of these crazy expectations – no one hanging on." However, if the fans had no expectations, the local promoters and media were not afraid to milk the situation as the UK's latest chart act came their way … and probably at a bargain price.

In Manchester, it was claimed that "300,000 people had voted them a hit on TV", while the folk in Sheffield were invited along to see "The New Weirdo Trio". Despite these excesses and near insults, Dickins knew exactly what the promoters and the fans were getting for their money. "This crazy, big-haired guy played with his teeth. James Brown was the only other exciting, outrageous black act in those days and some of that rubbed off on Jimi."

Hendrix's on-stage/off-stage persona still fascinated Dickins. "On stage he was this extraordinary showman and then he could come off and just be really quiet, although he was stoned nearly all of the time. But he was a professional musician who played with some great musicians and learnt a lot from them."

While 'Hey Joe' was making its way up the chart, Chandler found the time (and money) to book The Experience into De Lane Lea studios to record 'Purple Haze', 'The Wind Cries Mary' and '51st Anniversary'. That was on January 11, 1967, the day Hendrix formally signed to Track Records. The next three years would see him expected to deliver four singles and two albums annually in exchange for an advance of £1,000.

It seems that Hendrix was the only one of the trio to be named in the contract, which left Mitch Mitchell and Noel Redding as wage-earning sidemen. "Had Mitch and I known that Jimi was the only one being signed to contracts, The Experience would have ended" was how Redding later summed up the situation, although the confusion over who got paid and for what in the early days has never been clarified.

The official formation of Track allowed Chris Stamp and Kit Lambert to exert a degree of influence over their new signing. "All the imagery was basically done at Track," says Stamp. The cream of London's rock photographers were brought in to shoot pictures, which included shots of Hendrix posing bare-chested. "Track was doing a semi-management job but that was because Kit and I were managers who operated a record label," added one half of the team which had, by that time, already steered The Who to eight hit singles and two Top 5 albums.

A second show at the Bag O'Nails on January 11 was watched by a young electrical engineer named Roger Mayer, who was employed by the Royal Navy Scientific Service in sound analysis. Having heard 'Hey Joe' and seen Hendrix on television, the 21-year-old was keen to see him perform live. "I was involved in making guitar effects," says Mayer, "and some friends of mine who were in the business said 'You gotta see this guitar player.'"

After making his way to the Bag, Mayer was able to talk to Hendrix after the show, tell him what he did and that he had been working with the likes of Jimmy Page and Jeff Beck, friends from Surrey. "I told him I had a few sounds that I wanted to talk to him about. He said 'great' and we just hit it off. We spoke the same language about guitar tones. There was an instant synergy between us."

Also in the Bag that night was Beatles manager Brian Epstein, who was reported as saying that Hendrix and his band were the "most talented act since The Rolling Stones".

Interestingly, one of The Stones was also in the crowd that night, along with Paul McCartney, Ringo Starr and members of The Hollies and The Small Faces. Bill Wyman

JIMI HENDRIX MADE IN ENGLAND

recalls that "Hendrix's music and wild appearance personified the changing adventurous sounds." Wyman also claims to have seen Hendrix play a few days earlier, when he noted that "At the end of his set he set fire to his guitar on stage." As he listed the date as January 5, 1967, when The Experience had no gig, he might have been mistaken on both counts.

By this time, The Jimi Hendrix Experience set list had expanded to feature tracks such as 'Killing Floor','Can You See Me','Have Mercy On Me Baby','Like A Rolling Stone', 'Rock Me Baby','Third Stone From The Sun','Foxy Lady','Hey Joe' and 'Wild Thing'. The last-named was a song written by American Chip Taylor which UK group The Troggs had taken to Number 2 in the UK and to the top of the US chart in 1966.

Apparently Hendrix first heard The Troggs' version while driving to a gig in the band's van with his girlfriend and road manager Gerry Stickells. "Jimi immediately turned it up," recalled Etchingham, and wanted to know who it was. When Etchingham told him it was a group called The Troggs, Hendrix seemingly wondered, 'What sort of name is that?'"

Odd name or not, Hendrix was suitably moved by The Troggs' efforts and, according to Etchingham, went in search of the record as soon as they arrived back in London. "He bought a copy and played it to himself a few times, deciding to make a cover version which he could use in the stage show."

As 'Hey Joe' climbed the chart and his live shows attracted more interest, so Hendrix became the centre of attention for the music press, and in the January 14 edition of the NME, writer Keith Altham announced that Hendrix was the man "for whom the words 'wild one' were invented". He went on to declare that Hendrix was "a one-man explosion … what this man does with a guitar could get him arrested", and ended by quoting the man himself who, after recalling his adventures in the US music business, proclaimed, "Now I'm going to make certain I don't fluff it all up."

The Jimi Hendrix Experience performed 'Hey Joe' for a second Top Of The Pops show on January 18 before completing three nights in succession at the 7½ Club in Mayfair and then moving on to The Speakeasy. This club in Mortimer Street opened at 10pm and closed around 4am, making it a popular West End hang-out for musicians, record execs, journalists, DJs and a host of music industry hangers-on.

The 'Speak' became a regular haunt for Hendrix who, when he wasn't booked to play, would get together and jam with whoever was on stage. Future Faces and Rolling Stones guitarist Ronnie Wood recalled seeing Hendrix there one night and commented,

SOME PEOPLE THINK I'M GOOD

"There was Hendrix, the ultimate in black cool. Everything he did was natural and perfect." Stones frontman Mick Jagger went further and announced to the world that, "Hendrix is the most exciting, sexual and sensual performer I have ever seen."

For some, however, Hendrix's live performances left something to be desired. "I used to like to watch Jimi Hendrix," said The Who's Pete Townshend in 1968, adding, "Sometimes he worries me now because he often gets amplifier hang-ups and stuff. I can't stand that. It kills me." It might have been some consolation to Hendrix to read what Townshend had to say about the band which let him jam with them in October 1966. "I used to like to watch Cream until they got sad and fucked-up."

In the same week as he was finally granted a six-month UK work permit, Hendrix sat with a second NME reporter and this time, in the January 28 issue, he told John King about his music. "The approach is R&B [rhythm and blues], but that's just the way we happened to feel it. I never do a number the same way twice – quite often I change the words." He went on to offer his opinion of the competition he faced from Britain's finest. "You have a lot of groovy groups here in England but some of the sounds are just too clean. You can't expect deep feeling to come out of music put down on bits of paper with arrangements."

It was in this interview that he also answered people who took the view that, by wearing a military jacket, Hendrix was insulting the British Army. "Let me tell you I wear this old British coat out of respect. This was worn by one of those 'cats' who used to look after the donkeys which pulled the cannons way back in 1900. This coat has history, there's life to it. I don't like war, but I respect a fighting man and his courage."

Even though the record was already in the Top 20, the first advertisement for 'Hey Joe' (and 'Stone Free') was taken by Polydor in Melody Maker on January 21 and, looking back at the psychedelic imagery today, it seems that only the faces of Hendrix and Redding appear in the half-page advert. A week later, Melody Maker gave readers an insight into the mind of Jimi Hendrix with their 'Pop Think In' feature.

Invited to offer up a snapshot opinion on a host of topics, he came up with the following observations. Mexico – "I guess I think about open-air jails, 'cos man they have them there"; The Monkees – "Oh God I hate them! Dishwater. I really hate somebody like that to make it so big"; English food – "Mashed potatoes … I ain't gonna say anything good about that!"; California – "The best place in the world. I like the cars – beautiful cars. Not too many Volkswagens, which is good"; Vietnam – "After China takes over the whole world, the whole world will know why America's trying so hard in Vietnam";

English pop – "The only ones holding it up at the moment are the solid performers like Tom Jones, Dusty Springfield, Spencer Davis … The Who, they're solid."

Both British food and America's involvement in Vietnam were subjects that Hendrix talked about with Geno Washington during their times together. "We used to stop at the Blue Boar on the M1 all the time and I used to meet Jimi in there. For us it was just like lining up for food in the Army or the Air Force," says the 68 year-old singer, whose band took their name from the Ram Jam Inn on the A1 at Stretton in Rutland. "There was always a line at the Blue Boar where you stood with your tray to get your food. It was just like being in the forces in the US, except the food here was shit!"

The Vietnam War, in which America was embroiled from the early Sixties through to 1973 was an event both Hendrix and Washington managed to avoid. Washington got himself stationed in Britain – "Germany was my first choice 'cos I heard they partied big over there, then it was France and the UK was third" – while Hendrix was discharged from the Army on medical grounds.

"Jimi didn't like jumping out of planes too much, and if you have to do that in real life, while they're shooting at your arse, that ain't no fun. He told me that he pretended to be gay to get out of the Army. Lots of guys did that and some others pretended to be crazy or pee in the bed 'cos that would get you out," explains the ex-serviceman who was stationed in East Anglia. "But if Jimi wasn't in Vietnam, his music was."

One of London's most important club venues was the Marquee in Soho's Wardour Street. Having moved there from its original site as a jazz club in Oxford Street in 1964, it was at the heart of the capital's pop and rock scene. When The Experience made their debut Marquee Club appearance on January 24, the queue ran from Wardour Street along Shaftesbury Avenue to Cambridge Circus!

Future Yes bassist Chris Squire was a member of support act The Syn. "It was an incredible show that went down in history as the biggest night at the Marquee ever. All the people I was a fan of were in the front few rows waiting for [Hendrix] to come on and politely watching us! The Beatles, the Stones, the Who, Steve Winwood, Eric Clapton – anyone who was anyone was there to see that show. You can imagine it was pretty daunting being in the support band."

Squire, a technically gifted player even then, suggests he gave Noel Redding, a guitarist playing bass, some off-the-cuff help. "I spent the afternoon when we were loading in our gear watching Hendrix trying to teach him to play 'Purple Haze'! Which they didn't play that night because they couldn't get it together. I didn't know what to make of

4

them because I thought it's only a five-note riff and he can't learn it. And this is the headlining act?"

Before the end of the month, the band found themselves back down the Caves in Chislehurst for a return gig and once again Radio Caroline's Robbie Dale was host for the evening's entertainment. "Jimi always gave the impression that his performance and music was it all, but like all creative people he would have a deeper side. He smiled a lot, a bit boozed or stoned but always on the ball.

"After the show we would drive back to London and join Jimi in one of the 'in place' night spots in the West End. Chas was putting Jimi, Noel and Mitch about and they were going down a storm. All three of them worked really hard, but it was Jimi who made the band a very different proposition."

This show in Kent on January 27 was the night when Roger Mayer met Hendrix for the second time. "I had one new sound that I was developing and I had showed it to Jimmy Page, but he thought it was a bit too radical," says Mayer. It was the Octavia, and when Mayer travelled to Chislehurst to meet with Hendrix for a second time and backstage at the Caves the two men forged both a working relationship and a long-term friendship. "When I showed it to Jimi he loved it. We made some modifications and then I went to the Ricky Tick club in Hounslow (February 3) to show it to him again. We went back to Olympic Studios, which is where we overdubbed the solos to 'Purple Haze' and 'Fire.'"

Nashville Teens guitarist John Allen also has a memory of Mayer's latest invention. "I think I played with one of the bits and pieces that Roger was doing back then and I think the Octavia was the one that played a note above or below the note you're playing so you got these two notes coming together," recalls the man who bought his first fuzz box from Mayer for "about a fiver" before suggesting that the new invention was "very good but I don't think I was able to afford it".

Whether Hendrix could afford it or not was another matter, but Mayer remembers his reaction to the new effect which, as its name suggests (rather than John Allen's theory), produced a note an octave higher than that played. "Jimi loved the Octavia – it was instant fireworks. He could see in his mind's eye what it could do. He was the fastest man I ever met to recognize the right sound."

He had now met a man who knew as much about sound as he did, and Hendrix was keen to continue the partnership. "I dealt only with Jimi and I got paid expenses because you couldn't put a price on what I was doing. I got paid by Jimi and didn't work for his management company," says Mayer, who is quick to point out that, "Jeffery never crossed me and Kit and Chris from Track were always very nice to me. I was 'Jimi's friend who comes along with all these sounds for him', so they treated me very well.

"We were on the same wavelength in sound, in describing sound and pushing the boundaries further into what he could do with sound. Jimi was a complete innovator who had a vision in his head. Jimi always saw sound in colour and we had that in common."

For Hendrix, Mitchell and Redding, January 1967 ended on a high note as they found themselves on the bill at the Saville Theatre in Shaftesbury Avenue, in the heart of London's West End. Going on after The Koobas – a Liverpool group managed by theatre owner Epstein – and supporting The Who, this was a major stepping-stone for the band.

The theatre was part of impresario Bernard Delfont's showbusiness empire and Brian Epstein acquired the lease in April 1965. The Beatles' manager apparently glowed with pride and declared, "I want to present lovely things on Sunday nights. I want to make it marvellous."

While Epstein had seen Hendrix just a couple of weeks earlier at the Bag, it was Tony Bramwell who played the major role in booking the act for their theatre debut. "I ran the theatre from day one; Brian wanted Jimi on after I told him how good he was and then when he saw him at the Bag."

He was aware that The Experience had only done "a couple of gigs with the other two" when he booked them and also knew that "they only had around six numbers in their set", but Bramwell – and Epstein – saw something special. "He was just developing a stage personality. In those days guitarists either looked at what they were fingering or looked at their feet.

"His appearance was staggering – he was tall, with very long arms, masses of hair and a pock-marked face … it was like Little Richard meets Bob Dylan," says Bramwell. "Guitarists just stood there and certainly never did Elvis impersonations which Jimi did. He was very suggestive and fairly outrageous."

Joining Epstein in his box that night were Beatles John Lennon and Paul McCartney, but as usual George Harrison, the group's lead guitarist, was missing. "I don't think George did go and see Jimi ever. He was living happily in the countryside, learning to write and taking acid. John used to escape from Weybridge occasionally and go clubbing, but Paul was in St John's Wood and was always around and up to go clubbing."

SOME PEOPLE THINK I'M GOOD

Despite Bramwell's role in booking Hendrix, Chris Stamp has put forward his own version which suggests that he and his partner Kit Lambert "had a lot to do with who went into the Saville on Sunday nights". He says once they had booked The Who at the theatre, they brought in The Experience as support. Polydor boss Roland Rennie agrees. "They used The Who as a vehicle to promote Hendrix through Ready Steady Go! and with the first Saville Theatre show."

The Experience's set consisted of five songs which they performed at both the 6pm and 8.30pm shows, watched by Pete Townshend, who had some serious reservations about his management team allowing Hendrix on the same bill. "I thought Jesus Christ, what's going to happen? So he went on and he did his thing. He knocked the amplifiers over, he practically smashed it up. I'm not ashamed to say he blew us away."

The man who once explained that guitar smashing was all about the "visual effect" while admitting that "if the guitars exploded and went up in a puff of smoke I'd be happy", was not sure how Hendrix felt about his band. "I had a reverent attitude towards him but I don't think he took us [The Who] very seriously."

For Queen's Brian May, then a 19-year-old student at Imperial College, the release of 'Hey Joe' signalled the arrival of The Jimi Hendrix Experience. "I lived with a few guys at the time – we were all students – and one of them brought home 'Hey Joe'," he says. "We flipped it over and listened to 'Stone Free' and my jaw just dropped. I liked 'Hey Joe', but the B-side … I remember thinking to myself, 'No no no, he can't be that good. They've freaked in the studio, put the voice on afterwards and added all sorts of overdubbing.'"

May was involved with his first band, 1984 and, inspired by hearing both 'Hey Joe' and 'Stone Free', turned his attention away from The Beatles towards Hendrix. Then came the chance to see his new hero perform live on stage. "My mate Colin Cooper said that Jimi was going to play the Saville Theatre; they were all going along and he asked me if I wanted to go. So we all bowled down to see him.

"I remember that he only had about six inches of stage to work on. It was all very cheap-looking, but we all sat there and watched, and somewhere in the middle of the set he was suddenly doing 'Stone Free' and doing all the stuff we had heard on the record", says May. "Then my jaw dropped way, way further."

With just one Marshall amp to his name, which according to May "blew up the whole time", Hendrix was "still blindingly good" and set May thinking about how the top-of-the-bill act would cope. "I could sense that The Who were probably thinking, 'My God,

JIMI HENDRIX MADE IN ENGLAND

we didn't think we'd have to follow that.' Hendrix was just something else."

May had grown up with the likes of Clapton, The Yardbirds and John Mayall as his inspiration. "I thought I was a pretty fair guitarist but seeing Hendrix, I just thought you either have to give up or you have to go away and practice a whole lot more." He wasn't the only future member of Queen who was impressed. "Freddie [Mercury] was a huge fan of Jimi. He saw even more Hendrix gigs than I did – he followed him around avidly, he was a complete fan," recounts May.

So taken with Hendrix was the Queen singer, at that time a student at Ealing College of Art & Design, that he featured him in dozens of his own drawings and paintings, which he hung around the walls of his flat. "He didn't want to be a guitarist, but Jimi was still a great role model for him – it was the creativity, the freedom of the man that so impressed Freddie, who was truly a free spirit. That was inspired by Jimi Hendrix."

There was one thing about Hendrix's appearance that struck a final chord with May. "I had spent a long time feeling embarrassed about the way I looked because I had curly hair and it was very un-cool to have curly hair in the mid Sixties." In the same way that John Lennon felt relieved about wearing glasses when he first saw the heavily bespectacled Buddy Holly, May suddenly found he didn't have to worry about his hair any more. "I'd been straightening it for years using an iron. I went to endless lengths to not have curly hair and then suddenly, because of Hendrix, it was cool."

The day after the show at the Saville Theatre, The Jimi Hendrix Experience were given permission by Epstein to return to the scene of their triumph and make a promotional film for their next single, which was to be released in six weeks.

In the first week of February 1967, Melody Maker's famous Raver column informed its readers, "Stevie Marriott, Lennon and McCartney, Spencer Davis, Mike D'Abo, Klaus Voormann, Eric Clapton, Jeff Beck, Lulu, Terence Stamp [all went] to see Hendrix and The Who at the Saville Theatre." Meanwhile, Chris Welch's review of the show confirmed that Jimi Hendrix and The Who on the same bill was "a close battle … and fans will still be arguing about the winners". "Either way, two of Britain's most exciting groups thrilled the crowds with hard-hitting sights and sounds."

In the days between playing the Saville Theatre and MM's enthusiastic review, The Jimi Hendrix Experience made their way up north to Chandler's home region. A gig at the New Cellar Club in South Shields meant that manager and singer could stay with Chandler's mum in Newcastle. It was there that Chas found out about Hendrix's debut in the Top 10 with 'Hey Joe'. "I walked down the street to the phone [box] because

4

my mother had not had one put one in yet, to ring London and see how things were doing," recalled Chandler. On hearing the news that they now had a Top 10 hit, he said, "I knew we were really on our way."

It wasn't just the chart that featured The Jimi Hendrix Experience as the music press was also full of news about the latest pop sensation. Melody Maker carried a news story announcing plans for Hendrix to tour the UK with The Walker Brothers and Cat Stevens. Walker Brother Gary Leeds recalls a night out on the town when "Jimi asked me over to sit with him and he told me he was a fan. Then Chas, with the help of Keith Altham, who was our publicist, asked if I could get Jimi on tour. I said I'd do what I could."

On the front page of the same February 4 edition of Melody Maker, the premier pop paper proclaimed, "It's Jumping Jimi" in a banner headline above a story of how 'Hey Joe' had "… pushed aside The Rolling Stones [who dropped to Number 5 with 'Let's Spend The Night Together'] and taken over the Number 4 spot on the MM Pop 50".

The story went on to remind readers, "In the few weeks Hendrix has been resident in Britain he has broken box-office records up and down the country with his powerful Experience. Manager Chas Chandler says, 'Everything has happened as I hoped and believed it would. It's certainly a nice feeling. We are deciding now whether to release a new single or an album first.'" The story finished with a list of the group's UK dates in February.

Among The Experience's February dates were shows at the Ricky Tick clubs in Hounslow and Windsor, where owner/promoter John Mansfield had decided to up the ante. "We paid The Stones more money and Hendrix was around £25 for his first show, but for the next six shows the most he got was £100." Presumably Mansfield had agreed a fee with Dickins and was not about to change the money because of a hit record.

He also no doubt took into account the fact that, while his Ricky Tick clubs were immensely popular, they were not very big so the crowds – and the takings – were not particularly large. "In those days the fans were right up close to the bands and there was no room for moving or dancing," he says. "You stood still and just moved your head up and down to the music."

While Chandler had already booked a few top rock photographers to take pictures of Hendrix and his two bandmates, it was the turn of Gered Mankowitz in early February to focus his lens on the trio. Having met Hendrix at the Bag O'Nails in November 1966 and agreed to meet in the studio somewhere down the line, Mankowitz found himself booked for a session at the start of the second week, probably on the 8th before the group's gig in Bromley.

"I decided, after some consultation with Chas, that I would photograph Jimi in black and white, that we wouldn't use colour and there would be no instruments," explains Mankowitz. "I was convinced that this was going to be a dignified, serious, grown-up portrait of a serious musician. That was how I envisaged it and wanted it to be and I think I had Chas' support, although he wasn't at the shoot."

While Mankowitz remembers that he had no contact at all with Jeffery, and he can't remember who actually paid him for the session (ANIM, Track or Polydor), he does recall the band's arrival at his studio in Mason's Yard, close to the Scotch of St James.

"Jimi, Noel and Mitch each arrived with a little bag with a change of clothes. Jimi was wearing a military jacket and he had another one with him," says Mankowitz, who also made a habit of feeding the people he photographed. "I always used to feed them because it gave me an opportunity to look at them, talk to them and ease them into the experience."

One of the jackets Hendrix wore that day was, according to Mankowitz, very dark green with gold accoutrements, while the second one was blue/black and much plainer. "I don't remember which regiment the uniform came from but there was a story that it was in fact from a veterinary regiment.

"There have also been rumours that it was a facsimile and not a genuine jacket, but that is wrong. You could see the frayed embroidery work and marks where epaulettes had been removed. The overall quality of the material was too good for a copy. I think it's the jacket Jimi left at Stephen Stills' house before Woodstock and I think it remains there to this day."

The all-day session meant starting at noon and finishing at around 4pm, and a good two hours, says Mankowitz, was spent "having lunch and a puff and easing them into the background and the ideas I had".

Lunch for Mankowitz's clients would come from the nearby high-end grocers Jackson's of Piccadilly, where the photographer had some sort of a deal on prices. "I gave them nice food – very prim things like mini pork pies, good cheeses, ham, pate and French bread. It was all very laid-back but created a nice vibe and made a big difference," he says. "Musicians were always hungry and it was free ... and at noon they had just got out of bed and probably hadn't eaten."

Mankowitz knew from experience that people in general and pop musicians in

4

particular do not always like having their picture taken. He quickly discovered that Hendrix was an exception to that particular rule and he settled in to the task of having his photo taken with apparent ease.

"Jimi was fabulous, and like all young men he wanted to look mean, moody and sexy – that was all they seemed to be bothered about. Jimi was a very smiley person, but the pictures that were always used of him were the sullen ones and that was the look we were all going for. The session was great. He was very easy but he had no input as to what I shot. I told him where to stand and to look into the camera, but the key thing was not so much how he stood but really how he looked at me."

During the afternoon session, Mankowitz developed a genuine rapport with Hendrix, who was enjoying his time away from the pressures of the studio, the stage and perhaps even the music business as a whole. "He was very open, sweet-natured, very funny, and the best pictures were when he was smiling – even when he was smoking he has got a half-smile." However, it wasn't just Hendrix that Mankowitz was photographing that day. "The other two were also very sweet," he says. "Mitch was so funny. His efforts to look mean and sexy were so pathetic that Jimi and the rest of us would just crack up. He was the artful dodger, the pretty little kid who couldn't do snarling, while Noel was basically just a grump and a little embittered but always helpful."

For a man who acknowledges that at that time "my star was high" on the back of his many sessions with major pop acts and the recently released Rolling Stones album Between The Buttons, the Hendrix session was "just another shoot". He did, however, spot something about the subject that made him stand out from the crowd. "It is important to recognize that there was this charismatic, brilliant player who looked like nobody else on Earth. One knew he was special but I had no sense that we'd still be talking about him over 40 years later."

Both Mankowitz and Geno Washington knew the importance of image for a performer in the fashion-led swingin' Sixties and Hendrix was also aware of what he was and how he looked. "We talked about the uniqueness of him being a black guy in flower power," recalls Washington. "Being a black dude who is the front man in the band meant that he had no competition here or anywhere in Europe. He was called 'The Wild Man of Borneo' but he didn't care – it worked for him. He talked a lot about the value of the image he created."

Mankowitz was aware of how the majority of American black musicians appeared to the people in Britain on stage or on television. "The experience for all of us was of

4

black female singers wearing wigs and glittery clothes, while the male singers had their hair straightened and were wearing ruffled shirts and bow ties – or suits and ties.

"It was all very showbiz and theatrical. That was the idea back then. You put on your best clothes to get up on stage," explains Mankowitz. When Hendrix turned up at his studio, "he arrived looking exactly as he did in his pictures. He was completely un-groomed, which is what made him look wild. His look came from New York's Greenwich Village and its beatnik-y, mad, Bohemian freedom, which he embraced."

The hairstyle was a natural part of Hendrix's appearance. "He didn't have a tight perm and I never saw him use an Afro comb," says Mankowitz. "I remember him being exactly what you see and that was what made him so easy, plus he had a great willingness to work."

Hendrix's Afro also made an impression on Eric Clapton, who also submitted himself to the new craze for 'perms' as Cream took on Hendrix in a battle of the bands. "It was just what the market wanted, a psychedelic pop star who looked freaky," he said. Though he claims it was actually Bob Dylan's hairstyle that first caught his eye – "I liked Dylan's hair. I went and had my hair curled" – Clapton acknowledges Hendrix's influence. "Then Jimi came on with the curly hair … and then everybody else did it 'cos they dug Jimi and other people did it 'cos they dug me. It became quite a trend to have curly hair."

Mankowitz recalls that, at that first session in February 1967, "Noel and Mitch had natural hair that day – long and quite unruly", and was delighted with the results. "The shoot seemed to go really well and Chas loved the pictures. The one shot that has become a classic – the one on a white background with Jimi with his hands on his hips –was earmarked as the cover of the first album."

However, when somebody at the management office or the record company pointed out that the album cover should be in colour, Mankowitz's black-and-white collection was discarded in favour of a colour shot by Bruce Fleming, which might just feature the jacket Hendrix 'pinched' from under Geno Washington's nose.

Mankowitz has produced over the years a series of limited-edition prints of his Hendrix pictures in addition to exhibiting them in galleries around the world, but has no idea what became of them in 1967. "I was told that a 12-inch EP of four tracks from the album was put together for radio DJs, with one of my pictures on the cover. I haven't got one and have never seen it but that was what I was told at the time. I do know they were used as press and promotion shots, including flyers for his Saville Theatre shows."

SOME PEOPLE THINK I'M GOOD

Bruce Fleming was a former press photographer with Melody Maker who eventually became a personal photographer to the likes of Lulu, The Hollies, The Dave Clark Five and The Animals. That was where he came into contact with Chandler, who invited him to meet Hendrix, Mitchell and Redding.

According to Fleming it was Chandler who insisted that his session be shot in colour, although Stamp has gone on record to claim "I organized the cover artwork … with a photographer I trusted." Told he had to shoot the whole group as it was important to feature all three members on the cover of their debut album, Fleming did his work in one shoot on February 27 – not in two sessions spread over a week, as some people have suggested – and had a fixed idea of what he wanted to create. "This guy could fly, literally. That's what I tried to get across. Not Dracula, but as he wore cloaks quite a lot I thought it might be nice to incorporate the cloak."

Throughout February, The Experience got to know the byways and highways of Britain as they played shows in South Shields, Bristol, Stockport, Cambridge, York, Bath, Leicester, Southend and a host of places in-between. It was the band's busiest month to date, with a total of 23 shows plus TV and radio spots and with the odd recording session thrown in.

As Hendrix's flame burned ever brighter, so his new British fans found a unique way of showing their appreciation of the 'guitar hero' … by wearing badges produced by a British jam maker. Robertsons had introduced the 'golliwog' into their marketing of jams and marmalades back in 1910 when it was seen as an acceptable image of empire. By the 1960s the company had developed the logo into a series of metal lapel badges featuring the small black doll playing a selection of musical instruments.

It seems that fans of Hendrix quickly opted for the badge which featured the doll playing the guitar as an unofficial and even clandestine sign of their devotion to Hendrix. What would now be considered a wholly inappropriate and racist symbol, was seen in the UK during the swingin' sixties as a simple sign of being a fan.

At the same time the fee for Hendrix and his band went up as they became more popular, but neither Mitchell nor Redding immediately benefited from the increase in earnings. After he found out the band were earning up to £400 a night, Redding took it upon himself to write to Chandler to complain about the £25 he and Mitchell got each week. His ploy worked to some extent as they received a £200 bonus and their weekly salary was upped to £30.

The amount of work the band was doing was also taking its toll on Hendrix's guitars,

4

according to Dave Wilkinson. "He bought three or four from us around that time. I sold him a white Stratocaster for 162 guineas, which Chas probably paid for, although he probably talked to the manager to get a better price."

It's likely that Hendrix's sudden spending spree on new guitars had more to do with light-fingered fans than his own on-stage antics. At least one, maybe three, of the band's guitars were stolen after a gig at the Imperial Hotel in Darlington on February 2, prompting a simple line in Melody Maker's Raver column which said, "Jimi Hendrix guitar stolen". It seems a black Stratocaster turned up a few months later when it was bought by a local musician for £20. Hendrix 'lost' another guitar after a Roundhouse gig on February 22 when it was reportedly stolen from the backstage area.

The fact that Chandler may have done the deals for Hendrix's guitars throws into doubt a story told by a struggling wannabe musician who was working in the Selmer store back in late 1966. Sixteen-year-old Paul Kossoff recounted a story about Hendrix visiting the store and he described Hendrix as "looking and smelling strange". He went on to claim that he was the only assistant to step forward and offer his help, and they watched "wide-eyed" as the young American "took down a right-handed model, flipped it over and played it upside down with no problem". The London-born teenager then claimed that when Hendrix bought the guitar, he noticed that "the cashier put a 'c' for 'coloured' on the sales sheet".

However, veteran salesman Dave Wilkinson dismisses this account as a complete fabrication. "I have absolutely no recollection of anybody ever using the letter 'c' for 'coloured' on sales sheets. The only reason it could have been put there was to indicate a cash sale – we had cash and hire purchase sales – but I never put a 'c' on any sales sheets."

Situated in the heart of London's thriving music business surrounded by music publishers, record companies and a host of clubs, Selmer was used to black musicians calling in to try out and buy instruments and equipment. "We never had any instruction to identify anybody in that way. Kossoff got it completely wrong," says Dave indignantly.

In fact, the idea of Hendrix paying cash for any equipment in those days is pretty far-fetched. But Jeffery was undoubtedly the 'money man' who was financing the creation and setting up of The Jimi Hendrix Experience, with an eye on some sizable future returns on his investment. Chandler summed up his own financial situation when he told people, "I was flat broke so I had to sell my last guitar. I swapped my last bass for a new guitar for Jimi."

By now, Hendrix had already gained a reputation – alongside arch-rival Pete

SOME PEOPLE THINK I'M GOOD

Townshend from The Who – for smashing his guitars, although Experience roadie Gerry Stickells has claimed that in the early days, "We had a 'breaking-up guitar', nailed together with bits of wood, which I used to patch up after every show."

Somewhere along the line it seems likely that Hendrix progressed from using the 'breaking-up guitar' to actually wrecking newer and better guitars. "He did smash up a few guitars and he used to bring in the damaged ones – they might have a cracked neck or something – to part exchange against a new one," says Wilkinson. "He'd take a new Strat and Chas would usually pay the difference." It seems that Selmer then repaired Hendrix's damaged guitars and re-sold them in the shop but, as this was long before the days of celebrity memorabilia, they never advertised them as being 'ex-Jimi Hendrix'.

Hendrix remained a regular visitor to Selmer, even after he had hit the charts and begun to sell out club dates around the country. Wilkinson recalls he would still find his way to Charing Cross Road in order to pursue his very favourite pastime … practising and experimenting with music. "He would come in for an hour or even longer and play a guitar and he always asked very politely before he picked anything up."

Although The Experience was busy playing round the UK, they still found time to visit the London clubs, either to perform or just to hang out. Agent Dickins recalls that "it was a very social life" for Hendrix and his mates as they flitted between the Scotch, the Revolution, the Bag, Blaises and the Speakeasy. "It was somewhere different to party every night," he says. "They played their gig and then they went partying and some of the best gigs I've ever seen were at 11pm in the Speakeasy when there would be Hendrix jamming on stage with Clapton or Townshend."

For Keith Emerson, who was two years younger than Hendrix, hanging around in the Speakeasy was a necessary part of the scene in Sixties London. "I joined Jimi and Jeff Beck at a table one night when they were discussing guitar strings. I couldn't contribute to the discussion," he recalls, but also remembers that more than music was on the agenda. "Hendrix taught me to light a match from a book of matches with one hand … and I burned my thumb in the process of showing the trick to other people."

The teenage David Arden was another who caught Hendrix during one of his legendary jam sessions at the Speakeasy. "I saw him with The Brian Auger Trinity and singer Julie Driscoll and he was sensational," he recalls, before reflecting on Hendrix's influence on the British music scene. "He had a tremendous impact on other musicians. It was extraordinary that we had a black dude fronting a rock group – it was totally new."

For Joe Boyd, the idea of a black man fronting a rock band and being a rock act wasn't particularly memorable. "It didn't surprise me that much and didn't strike me as being that remarkable. Being American meant that I probably had a broader view of what Black American culture involved – which was as many shades as White American culture."

There was one significant difference between the US and the UK for Hendrix and his fellow Black American artist Geno Washington, as Joe Boyd recounts: "They could walk down the High Street with their arm around a white girl and nobody would try and kill them."

As for Hendrix's stage act, Boyd concludes: "He was great, but a lot of what he did was not as astonishing for me as it was for some people, because in 1964 and 1965 I'd been to a club in Chicago's West Side and seen Buddy Guy playing between his legs and behind his back. I thought to myself, 'Oh, he got that off Buddy Guy'. But Hendrix was far more interesting that Buddy Guy."

And the interest level in Jimi Hendrix was about to rise exponentially…

I WISH THEY HAD LET ME PLAY

5

'PURPLE HAZE' RELEASED – DEBUT OFFICIAL BRITISH TOUR –
PRESS INTERVIEWS – SETS FIRE TO GUITAR – CONTROVERSY
SURROUNDS 'SEXY' STAGE ACT

News of the long-awaited follow-up to 'Hey Joe' came in February 1967 when Track Records announced that 'Purple Haze', the song written by Hendrix while waiting around at the Upper Cut club on Boxing Day, was set for release in March. The label described the record as "a bit unbelievable. It's freaky and funky and with some great guitar but won't be too far out for the fans."

Paul McCartney was given an advance copy for his guest reviewer's spot in the February 25 issue of Melody Maker and straight away knew who it was. "Must be Jimi Hendrix. So Jimi freaks out and sounds all the better for it. This is a good record too. I don't really know whether it's as commercial as 'Hey Joe' or 'Stone Free'. I bet it is, though," wrote the Beatle before closing with the lines, "Fingers Hendrix. An absolute ace on the guitar. This is yet another incredible record from the great Twinkle Teeth Hendrix!"

Despite Jimi's growing fame, there were halls around Britain that were still managing to get his name wrong on the bill posters. In Cheltenham, for the February 11 gig, the group was listed as Jimmie Hendrix Experience, while at the Club a'GoGo in Newcastle, owned by the band's co-manager Jeffery, they were listed as Jimi Hendrix & The Experience.

The group's final show in February saw them in a one-off line-up at the Cliffs Pavilion in Southend, where they slotted in below Dave Dee, Dozy, Beaky, Mick & Tich and The Nashville Teens for the two Sunday-night shows – at 6.15pm and 8.30pm – which boasted ticket prices of 18 shillings and six pence, 15 shillings and seven shillings and six pence and were hosted by top DJ Pete Murray.

According to one fan who posted her memories on the internet, the venue was so empty that the management made a unique two-for-one offer. "The theatre was only

5

a third full and so the first audience were invited back for the second show and asked to sit at the front to make it appear fuller."

The fact the theatre was less than full on the night might explain why the two issues of the weekly Southend Standard newspaper leading up to the shows had carried larger than usual adverts on page two – one a prominent quarter-page and the other a four-inch strip across all six columns advertising the "Grand Pop Festival".

Nashville Teens singer Arthur Sharp's only memory of the night is seeing Hendrix backstage. "He was just there and we chatted, said hello and he was very polite, but I wasn't in awe of meeting Jimi Hendrix. I'd met Lennon and Ringo, we'd done tours with Bill Haley and Chuck Berry. I was very blasé about it all. We were The Nashville Teens and had had more hits than Hendrix. I was very arrogant in those days."

Sharp was also unmoved by Hendrix's guitar skills. "I wasn't a guitarist so I took no interest in his playing, but I can see why guys like Clapton, Beck and May liked him – and 'Hey Joe' was a cool record."

Ian 'Tich' Amey from the headline act made the effort to watch Hendrix and has recounted that he closed his act with 'Wild Thing'. "It included the whole works – squealing feedback and Jimi setting fire to his guitar in front of a family audience with frightened grannies and wailing babes-in-arms. The theatre staff didn't know what to make of it."

Like Amey, John Allen was a guitarist and was one member of The Nashville Teens who stayed to catch sight of Hendrix live. "I stood at the side of the stage and watched a great performance," he recalls 45 years later. "I remember him setting light to his guitar on the stage. It was the closing moment of his show and he had trouble getting it to light. The guitar was on the stage and he finally got it alight and then stood back and bumped into the Marshall amps, which began to topple over; then Mitch kicked his drum kit over and that was the end of the show."

Allen remembers it was a white Stratocaster Hendrix set fire to – and, while he has no recollection of him switching guitars before the flames, he is sure about what he saw that day in Southend. "He just had a natural ability to play the guitar, which was far beyond anything that anybody else had. No one could hold a candle to him – he was an extraordinary player. Sadly I never spoke to him that night. I chatted with Chas, who I knew, but he was being very policeman-like about Jimi, who was ushered away."

Whether Hendrix did actually set fire to his guitar at Southend on February 26 still remains something of a mystery. All reports – despite Bill Wyman's earlier-recounted recollections – point to a later date, and despite two guitarists who were there on the night both recalling the same incident, the local paper's reporter saw something completely different.

Confirming that the show was "sparsely attended", he went on to say, "Jimi Hendrix, who the audience had come to see, manipulated his guitar rather than played it. Dressed in orange velvet, he threw the instrument over the rest of the equipment, played it behind his back, between his legs and with his tongue! At the end of his set, as if in contempt of the whole business, he kicked over the amplifiers and walked off."

A report from an earlier Hendrix show in Essex – at the Grays Club in Tilbury – fails to mention lighter fuel, failed matches or a burning guitar, but suggests pyrotechnics. A local journalist wrote, "Jimi performs a ballet with his guitar … finally a terrific 'Wild Thing', during which the stage seems to burn, and at the end he throws his guitar on the floor."

Around this time, Les Fleur de Lys were undergoing a personnel change with Bryn Haworth joining as a replacement for guitarist Phil Sawyer, who had left to team up with The Spencer Davis Group. "When Bryn joined and he saw Hendrix, he began to be influenced by him, which was good for him and for us," says Gordon Haskell.

Another person whose life was influenced by Hendrix was Andrew Black, who joined Polydor Records in early 1967 as an ambitious artist and repertoire (A&R) man. "Roland [Rennie, Polydor MD] introduced me to Hendrix just after I joined, when 'Hey Joe' was a hit, and for some reason he gravitated towards me," he recalls. "One of the perks of being in A&R was that you got your own office where you could meet artists and talk to prospective signings and, most importantly, listen to what they were offering.

"He used to come in and hang out in my office. He would ask very politely, 'If you don't mind man, can I sit here?' It was something of a retreat for him and somewhere where he could use my phone without being interrupted," explains Black. Polydor, like many record companies, was pretty free and easy about artists using phones and also having drinks. "Each of the A&R guys had their own cocktail cabinets. The biggest in our department was the head of A&R's and Roland's was even bigger than that!

"Jimi spent a lot of time with me in those early days, although he never said very much. I always found him very reclusive when he was in my office," Black recalls. "Everything came out on stage, but off stage I got the impression that he didn't want people making demands on him and if he could escape somewhere – into my office for a drink and a cigarette – then he was happy."

JIMI HENDRIX MADE IN ENGLAND

5

As Hendrix's flame grew ever brighter, it was surprising that only the music press and a few local papers homed in on his stage antics. The national press was, it seems, happy to ignore the new movement in music and fashion, contenting themselves with stories about The Beatles, The Stones, Tom Jones and the latest arrivals from America … The Monkees.

The growing trend for freak-outs and all-night raves cut no ice with either the popular tabloids or the up-market broadsheets, and whatever Hendrix got up to on stage didn't warrant either a record or concert review. However, around the country one or two local journalists saw something worthy of mention in The Experience. One pointed out that "Jimi proceeded to show just how many positions it was possible to play the guitar in … he squatted on the guitar with both feet and rocked to and fro."

They stopped short of using phrases like "bumping and grinding" as he sat on his guitar, and made no reference to him playing it with his teeth and even licking the neck, but it was the sort of stuff that prompted a girlfriend of The Animals' Vic Briggs to tell him, "I've never seen anyone being so sexual on stage." Briggs, who joined the band in early 1967, reckons that because he was black and American, Hendrix was ignored by the media and the authorities. "There wasn't anybody doing stuff like that. You couldn't get away with it. It just wasn't done."

According to keyboard ace Keith Emerson, Hendrix brought a new dimension to British pop music in the mid Sixties, and it worked to his advantage in one particular area. "He was dangerous-looking," he says. "Young chicks were scared of him, but there were a lot of women around that wanted danger and Jimi took advantage."

On the first day of March 1967, Hendrix and The Experience went into their old haunt of De Lane Lea studios in London's Kingsway to work on a song that was never satisfactorily completed and never heard again as the tapes somehow disappeared. Dylan's 'Like A Rolling Stone' was tried time and again but, according to Chas Chandler, "Mitch could never get the time right … we both wanted to record it but we were never successful."

Then it was back to Europe – for the first time since the band's debut shows in October 1966 – for five days, during which the band flitted between France and Belgium to play gigs and record TV shows. One of these shows resulted in Melody Maker recording for posterity the thoughts of Chandler, who described as "ridiculous" the crowd's reaction at the Law Graduation Society Ball in Paris.

He went on to explain, "Jimi and the group played their very first gig at Paris L'Olympia

5

(not quite true, but it certainly was their first major concert) just three days after the group was formed. Obviously nobody forgot that first outing because there was a crowd of 6,000 at the Ball last Saturday."

On their return to the UK, Hendrix, Mitchell and Redding once again made their way to Gered Mankowitz's studio in Mason's Yard for a follow-up shoot. "Chas called saying we had to do another session and I was worried that there was something wrong with the first set of pictures," explains Mankowitz. "Then he said that Noel and Mitch had had their hair permed in order to look more like Jimi, so the group pictures were out of date." (He has no idea to this day if or when Chandler or Track used any of his shots from the second Experience session.)

As he began shooting, Mankowitz noticed something about Hendrix's hair. "The boys arrived with their new perms, but what was odd was that Jimi's hair had taken on a more uniform look. All three of them had begun to have this Afro roundness, not as wild, a bit more groomed. And that only took about six weeks to happen after the first session."

Mankowitz looks back at his time spent in the studio with Hendrix as special. "I think that was a particularly wonderful moment to have worked with him because I think he was very happy. This was a brief period when everything seemed to be coming together. The spotlight was on him, he wasn't in the back line any more and he was expressing himself in every possible way.

"He was much loved. He was really embraced by the music industry and the country as a whole. I think he was loving it and he and the band were having a great time," concludes Mankowitz, who never sensed any conflict or animosity between the trio. "They were enjoying each other's company in what was a fantastic moment, but I don't think that lasted too long because within a few months it was obvious things were changing."

Hendrix's love of Britain and being British was something that was noticed by both the English photographer and an African-American singer. "The things Jimi liked about being in the UK after the Deep South of the US were the things I liked about the UK and why I stayed here," says Washington. "It was exactly what we talked about – the pluses of being here as opposed to over there – and his mind was like a sponge soaking up what I was telling him about being in Britain."

The young American seemed to have found himself a new home across the Atlantic. "He certainly embraced the culture as it was – a curious mix of music, drugs, velvet, tea, plus the daintiness of aristocratic British-ness."

Whatever it was about Britain that Hendrix had adopted and taken to his heart, it

5

wasn't made clear in an NME feature headed "Life Lines Of The Jimi Hendrix Experience". The article, dated March 11, 1967, focused on snappy answers to a series of one-word questions and told the world the following news: Biggest break – meeting Chas Chandler and forming the group; Hobbies – reading science fiction, painting landscapes, daydreaming; Food – strawberry shortcake, spaghetti; Drink – chocolate milkshakes; Composer – Bob Dylan, Muddy Waters, Mozart; Dislikes – marmalade, cold sheets.

On Sunday March 12, The Experience made their way to Yorkshire to play a gig at the Troutbeck Hotel in Ilkley. On this night over 400 fans, encouraged by the success of 'Hey Joe', forced themselves into a ballroom which had a fire regulation capacity of just 200.

While the manager reportedly put the crowd's number at close to 900, the noise of Hendrix's group and the raucous fans proved too much for passing policeman Tommy Chapman. He forced his way through the mass and on to the stage, where he asked "the chap playing the guitar – I don't know who he was" to stop playing. When Hendrix carried on with the set, Sgt Chapman literally pulled the plug on proceedings and sent everybody on their way.

The events in Ilkley made headlines in the Yorkshire Evening Post, where they snappily proclaimed: "Chaos After Police Break Up Crowded Pop Show", and went on to report that "a door had been ripped off its hinges, pictures slashed, electrical fittings and furniture broken and glasses smashed". Hendrix's reaction was to simply say, "I wish they had let me play before emptying the club."

With the show in Ilkley brought to a premature end, Hendrix, his band and crew seemingly went in search of sustenance and, according to local girl Sheila Lilley, ended up in the world-famous Harry Ramsden's fish and chip shop. There she spotted none other than Hendrix in all his military glory standing behind her in the queue. After saying how sorry he was that the gig had been cancelled after just one number, he autographed a photo of himself that she had with her. She then took it home, framed it and hung it on her living room wall as a souvenir.

The first sign of the normally polite and reserved Hendrix having any sort of a tantrum came in Amsterdam on March 14 when the group played so loud in rehearsal for a Dutch TV show that plaster began to fall from the ceiling. Fearing for their safety, the production crew made a quick exit, and when the producer then asked Hendrix if he would mime the guitarist walked out in disgust.

"They said 'Play as loud as you like.' Then this little fairy comes running in and yells

I WISH THEY HAD LET ME PLAY

'Stop! Stop! Stop! – the ceiling is falling down.' And it was too," said Hendrix, who finally agreed to mime for the live transmission of the Fanclub show.

On March 16, some six months after they had first hatched their plans for Track Records, Chris Stamp and Kit Lambert were able to officially launch their new label with a lavish party at the Speakeasy. A host of pop celebrities in attendance included The Who, Mick Jagger and Marianne Faithfull, whom Hendrix optimistically attempted to lure away from The Stones' lead singer.

Despite funding the label, Polydor head Roland Rennie accepted from the outset that the two founders of Track were better qualified to make decisions about signings and releases. "I was 35 at the time [and] people in their twenties … knew a damn sight more about it than I did. Kit (Lambert) was an absolute character who had a genuine feel for things."

George McManus, who joined Polydor a couple of months later, was familiar with the habits of the two owners of Track. "Kit drank like a fish and was completely chaotic, while Chris was very organized and effectively ran the business. Kit had the flair but Chris made sure things happened."

The significant event for Track was the release of Hendrix's second single, 'Purple Haze', on the day after the label's launch. It was celebrated by the group at a press conference in Hamburg as they prepared for three nights at the Star Club, home to The Beatles for over 70 nights in 1962. During the conference, Hendrix asked Chandler, 'When am I going to get my money? Is there any money?' Little did he know that, within a few days, there would be a lucrative new deal on the table that covered the world's biggest record market – America.

Claiming that the label would debut on the UK chart with 'Purple Haze' on March 20, 1967, Track press officer Richard J. Green issued his first press release and confirmed that The Who and The Jimi Hendrix Experience were the first artists to be signed by Track. "The label does not intend to sign artists indiscriminately," said Green. Lambert added, "Our policy is to sign people who we consider to be unstoppable. Only artistes of the highest quality and Top 10 potential."

Green might have been a little premature in announcing Hendrix's chart debut on Track, as chart listings show that 'Purple Haze' entered the Melody Maker Top 50 at Number 43 on March 25, the NME Top 30 at 25 on March 29 and the then-definitive Record Retailer chart at 39 on March 23.

Reviews were coming thick and fast for 'Purple Haze', with Melody Maker proclaiming,

"Climbing to freakish heights, it contains all the stunning Hendrix characteristics with flashing, weaving guitar and a fat, churning sound from The Experience. If there's any justice in the world this will be a Top 10 hit." At the same time, NME was noting, "Mean, insidious R&B – the sort of stuff we rarely hear produced in this country. Not everyone's cup of tea but bound to make the charts."

Trade paper Record Retailer was equally confident that the record would be a hit as they listed it as one of their front-page Top 20 predictions with the words, "Another good showcase for an astonishing guitar talent. Slower but full of tonal qualities, with the two backing boys driving tremendously." A mention at last, albeit slightly begrudgingly, for Mitchell and Redding!

The same March 23 issue carried a special insert advert in its chart section. The 15-inch by six-inch advertisement featured a purple tinted photo of just Hendrix with the words 'Purple Haze' in out-of-focus psychedelic lettering.

Having ignored the group's debut single, the national newspapers finally caught up with the Hendrix phenomenon by the time 'Purple Haze' came out, but the Daily Mirror's Don Short dismissed it in seven words: "Purple Haze. And I'm still in it." Virginia Ironside, writing in the Daily Mail, was convinced of its hit potential and said, "Absolutely no question of this at all", while Anne Nightingale's pop column for the Daily Sketch on March 21, 1967 included producer Mickie Most's assessment of the new single. "It's a specialist record but it's a big hit. Top 10 definitely."

Despite the Mirror's dismissal of the record, 'Purple Haze' duly swept into the Top Ten in all the charts that mattered, peaking at Number 8 in the NME, 4 in Melody Maker and 3 in Record Retailer.

From the atonal two-note intro through to the signature riff, 'Purple Haze' was an uncompromising track, and Hendrix's performance rewrote the rock-guitar rulebook. Jimi's Strat was run through a Fuzz Face distortion pedal to thicken the sound, his vocals heavily echoed, and the sound was like nothing ever herad before.

The initial draft of lyrics was much longer than required but, with Chas Chandler's help, Jimi edited these down to suit. Chas was crucial in the early days of the Experience, acting as a sounding board for Jimi's ideas, reining him in where his natural instinct was to go beyond the limits of the format but allowing his imagination to run free where appropriate.

As with its predecessor, 'Purple Haze' was very much at odds with the unthreatening singles-chart fodder of the time. Engelbert Humperdinck, with 'Release Me', Harry

Outside his home in London's Montagu Place

At London's Marquee Club in 1967

In the studio with Noel Redding

Shopping in the capital's trendy clothing stores was part of the London scene in 1967

Accepted by rock's aristocracy: Hendrix relaxes with Eric Clapton and friends

The pose is unmistakable as is the guitar played upside down

Posing with the members of The Who in 1967

Leaving on a jet plane – about to depart from London's Heathrow Airport in 1967

I WISH THEY HAD LET ME PLAY

Secombe and Vince Hill made it a middle-of-the-road Top 3, while the Seekers, Frank and Nancy Sinatra, Petula Clark and Val Doonican lurked not too far below. Pink Floyd's 'Arnold Layne' plus The Beatles' classic 'Penny Lane'/'Strawberry Fields Forever' were the rockiest exceptions to a moribund listing.

In the midst of their success with the second single, news was released of a delay in the recording of the group's debut album. A story in the March 18 edition of Melody Maker announced a possible six-month delay due to "a fault", while Chandler added that Hendrix had written a further 15 songs which were to be recorded as well. "It's starting from scratch all over again," he said.

In the same edition, Chandler's former bandmate in The Animals, organist Alan Price, told the world that Hendrix would "do well if he takes notice of what Chas says", while road manager Gerry Stickells, asked how Hendrix got on with his management, suggested, "Pretty well in general. But no rock artist ever gets on that well with his manager. Either side is always bitching about something. Jimi didn't come around to the office unless he wanted some money or some studio time."

Roger Mayer reckons that Hendrix and Chandler had a pretty amicable relationship. "Chas was very generous to Jimi. They were friends but they didn't hang out too much together. In fact Chas didn't have very much in common with what Jimi was doing musically."

Assessing his own relationship with Hendrix's manager, electronic wizard Mayer explains, "We never had an argument and he was always very nice to me. The only question Chas asked was whether we could do what Jimi wanted to do and I said we could, then that was OK. Very rarely was there any question about how much it was going to cost. Chas was very cool and he knew that Jimi was breaking new ground and you don't want to stop that."

In 1967, German-based Polydor had branches around the world but had yet to make the move into the lucrative American market. This meant that the chance for Hendrix to make it in North America came via a record-breaking deal, negotiated by Mike Jeffery, with an unlikely and relatively new label which had been launched by the world's most famous crooner.

Frank Sinatra launched Reprise Records in 1960 and signed family and friends – daughter Nancy Sinatra, Dean Martin and Sammy Davis, Jr. – to the label before selling out to Warner Bros. in 1963. Label chief Mo Ostin then saw the need to expand the roster to cover pop and rock music and added the likes of Trini Lopez, Sonny and Cher and The

JIMI HENDRIX MADE IN ENGLAND

Electric Prunes to a list that already included UK acts such as Petula Clark and The Kinks.

He signed The Jimi Hendrix Experience as a result of his habit of running his eyes over the weekly UK chart in Melody Maker and noting which acts did not have US deals. When rivals Atlantic passed on Hendrix – they dismissed him as "a second-rate B.B. King" – Ostin swooped and signed the group to a five-year deal worth a reported $1 million. The deal gave Hendrix an estimated $50,000 advance – the highest amount, Reprise announced, ever paid by any record company for a new artist.

According to then Reprise employee Stan Cornyn, the deal was a reasonable one. "The early risk of $50,000 is the only firm payment involved. This is something of a fair number for Reprise, especially since it's getting an already-doing-well album in England and Reprise bears no recording costs for this album."

Cornyn points out that when The Everly Brothers signed to Reprise in 1960, "it cost a lot more than $50,000". In fact, brothers Don and Phil signed a ten-year deal worth a million dollars; after that, according to Cornyn, "I don't think the Hendrix cost staggered us."

Although he wasn't party to the deal when it was signed – he couldn't get a copy of the contract – bass player Redding made it his business to check out the press reports of the US deal and later make them public. "… I have heard that the advance was $150,000 with 8% artist royalties and 2% to Jeffery as producer. The advance never showed up in the accounts but there was money around," he recalled.

Insiders at the label were apparently aghast when they heard Hendrix's 'Purple Haze' played at their weekly new releases meeting. Talking to Cornyn for his book Exploding, the history of Warner Bros. Records, a Reprise accountant said, "When Mo brought in Jimi Hendrix I thought, 'Oh My God, we're paying forty thousand dollars!' We listened to the tape. Nobody – nobody – could understand. It was a bunch of screeching and screaming. We looked upon Hendrix as one of the strangest things to happen."

One of the people in the Reprise Records "Monday meeting" after the signing of Hendrix was Cornyn, and he recalls that the assembled company "didn't know how to react to the new screeching" but that the record 'Hey Joe' was sent out to the company's promotion team for delivery to US radio. "I don't think any of the promo men would have reacted badly [to the single]. They're used to facing rejection and moving on to the next disc. 'We'll give this one a listen then' was their attitude," he says.

Hendrix's on-stage antics and banner headlines would have made no difference to the boss of Reprise once he had noted the success of 'Hey Joe' in the UK. "Mo [Ostin] liked that single for its sales record in England. He saw something on that single, saw it on the English charts and that was good enough. Chart equals sales," explains Cornyn.

Reprise made it clear that they intended to promote Hendrix, in his native US, as "the greatest talent since The Rolling Stones", while a company spokesman announced, "We shall introduce a completely new conception in promotion which should put Jimi right at the top in a very short time."

Sadly, however, Reprise's "new conception in promotion" didn't result in any immediate success. Their first campaign included full-page adverts in the US music press for 'Hey Joe' with a photo of just Hendrix – no bandmates – with the oddly-worded slogan 'Become the psychedelic single of this year … ANY Year!' The record failed to make any sort of impression on the American charts.

"I can only guess that our star was Hendrix plus a couple of back-up boys," says Comyn, "so the full emphasis on Jimi in any photo made marketing sense," he explains, while adding that what Hendrix and his Experience stood for was "out there on a bit of a limb for the label's staff". The overall feeling was that Hendrix was fundamentally an English act with his own management and not an artist they had signed and nurtured in their own backyard.

Meanwhile in England, as the first month of spring drew to a close Hendrix found himself re-booked by John Mansfield – not at one of his Ricky Tick clubs this time, but the larger Assembly Hall in the Buckinghamshire town of Aylesbury on March 28, 1967. With hundreds of fans milling around the theatre, Hendrix's driver was forced to park the car away from the hall and then accompany Hendrix on the walk to the stage door – where a 'bouncer' tried to send them to the back of the queue. When they explained they were with the group, the driver was told, "OK, you can come in but that bloke with the fuzzy hair's not getting in."

The driver, a friend of Mansfield's, went up to a high-ranking policeman on duty outside the hall and, pointing to Hendrix, asked, "Do you know who this is?" The officer replied, "My daughters are on about him all the time. It's Jimi Hendrix." The driver explained the situation and pronounced, "There's going to be a fucking riot if he doesn't get in and play." With that, the officer ordered the security man to let Hendrix into the hall – but that wasn't the end of the band's problems.

"The Experience had to use the hall's resident DJ and PA system in addition to Jimi's own PA," says Mansfield. "When Jimi was doing his destructive bits with the speakers, the DJ wanted to go on stage and tell him to be careful because it was council property. And right at the end there was a lot of feedback and sparks before Jimi stormed off

5

stage. The DJ was going back on stage to end the show but Chas said to him, 'No, that's part of the act. He'll go off and come back and do the James Brown routine.'"

The following night, The Experience made their way to the BBC Studios in Lime Grove for a performance of 'Purple Haze' on Top Of The Pops. They shared the bill with former Animal Alan Price, who was riding high in the chart with 'Simon Smith And His Amazing Dancing Bear'. Unfortunately, a sound recordist hit the start button to run the tape of 'Purple Haze' only to play Price's effort. An unamused Hendrix told the studio audience, "I like the voice, man, but I don't know the words."

March ended on a high for Jimi Hendrix as his group was booked to start their first major UK package tour. Two shows a night on 24 dates covering the length and breadth of the country – from Bournemouth to Cardiff and Liverpool to Glasgow – was good exposure, even it meant appearing with such unlikely artists as Cat Stevens, Engelbert Humperdinck and the bill-topping Walker Brothers.

John Walker, talking in 2010, recalled the issues they faced adding the guitarist to their show. "It was the first tour promoted by our own management company, so we were very involved with the bill. Gary had seen Jimi play and said, 'We need this guy on the tour, it would be great to have him on.'

"But the management wasn't too happy about it all, having this outrageous guitar player on tour with us, but we just said, 'Excuse me, we like this guy and that's the way it's going to be.' In those days we were real powerful, and if we said that was what we wanted, then people kinda had to do it."

According to Chandler, the tour opportunity was down to the band's agent. "Dick Katz got the tour for us. They [The Walker Brothers] were supposed to be the big sex idols of the time but we knew Jimi would cop all their reputation, so we worked on this big, flamboyant sex act."

Barry Dickins, Katz's colleague at Harold Davidson, reflected on the financial benefits of what he called "a bizarre package … It was sold out and Hendrix was going to be seen by a lot of people, and most of them would not have seen anything like him ever before When you became a star on a package tour you went from £25 a night to £50 a night and that was what happened to Hendrix."

Looking back, John Walker acknowledged that it was an odd collection of acts. "Jimi was very happy to do the tour, even if it was the weirdest bill you could think of. To be honest, Engelbert was not our first choice but there was some give and take and he did have a big hit with 'Release Me.'"

I WISH THEY HAD LET ME PLAY

Before the tour started there was, according to Walker, an artists' get-together where the pecking order was established. "The first time I ever saw Jimi was when we all met up before the tour – us, Jimi, Cat and Engelbert all got together just to say 'hello'. What I liked about Jimi was that he never displayed any kind of 'I need attention' attitude. He was reserved but you knew something was going for him. It was like, 'I think I'm good but we'll see.'"

The tour also featured a Wolverhampton band called The Californians, along with comedian/compere Nicky Jones and a group called The Quotations, who opened the show and then backed Jones during his spot. According to Californians bass player Peter Lee, they got the gig because their manager knew The Walker Brothers, they were "a young band with the right image" and their blend of Beach Boys/Four Seasons-type material fitted the bill.

The running-order had The Quotations opening, followed by The Californians and Hendrix and The Experience, with Humperdinck closing the first half. Jones (with The Quotations) opened the second half, followed by Stevens, with The Walker Brothers closing the show.

Hendrix's set would consist of just four songs – 'Hey Joe', 'Purple Haze', 'Like A Rolling Stone' and 'Wild Thing' – and in the programme notes, alongside a shot from Fleming's session for the first album cover, fans were told, "Jimi has rejected the accepted image of coloured American artiste, i.e. processed hair, slick silk suits, meticulously rehearsed, rather stereotyped dancing on stage." The article ended with the pronouncement that, "His already large band of fans sees him as a sort of Bob Dylan, lyrically, but generating the excitement of, perhaps, Mick Jagger."

The first night of the tour at London's Finsbury Park Astoria – later re-named the Rainbow – has gone down in history as the night when Hendrix first set light to his guitar, despite Bill Wyman's assertion and what others claimed had happened at Southend a month earlier. Kathy Etchingham doesn't seem to be sure either when she says, "Finsbury Astoria doesn't stand out to me as the first time he did it."

According to Chas Chandler, it was part of a plot to ensure Hendrix made an impression on his debut UK tour. "We were sitting around the dressing room trying to think of something new to put in the act," he said after the event. "I think it was Keith Altham's idea (the NME writer who had become the band's publicist) to set fire to the guitar. Jimi had a song called 'Fire' and Keith said wouldn't it be great if he could start one."

Altham's recollection is that a variety of things were discussed, and his suggestion

5

of setting fire to his guitar appealed to Chandler and Hendrix. "We tried a couple of experimental runs in the dressing room. It worked, and Jimi later used it on stage."

Lee recalls watching the drama unfold during the afternoon as everyone prepared for Hendrix's show. "I remember them practising with lighter fuel in the afternoon. They had a yellow can of fluid, sprayed it on the guitar and set fire to it to see what happened. It was dangerous, but in those days nothing was dangerous to any of us."

Californians guitarist Mickey Brookes was at the side of the stage when Jimi did his new party trick. "I saw Hendrix just before he went on and he had two guitars with him – one he played on stage and another one which had the end of the stock broken and only a few strings," he recounts. "He was stuffing a piece of cloth under the strings and pouring lighter fuel on it and then, during the last number, he picked up this other guitar, went back on stage and just struck a match while he was playing it. When it caught fire, he chucked the guitar down and then it set fire to the curtains and caused a real panic."

Gary Leeds has also recounted his reaction to the events that took place in north London that night. "Jimi had set fire to his guitar and the place was in panic. That was Keith's little idea to set fire to the guitar, a trick that would become part of the Hendrix legend."

Hendrix's main guitar man Roger Mayer knew exactly what was going to happen. "I knew he was going to set the guitar on fire because he'd got the can of lighter fuel in his back pocket. He changed to the 'sacrifice' guitar and poured fuel on it and lit a match but the first time it didn't light so he put a bit more on and then it went up in flames."

Despite both Brookes and Mayer recalling that Hendrix set fire to his guitar using a match, Leeds is on record as saying, "He [Jimi] said to me, 'Can I borrow your lighter?'", while Altham, the instigator of the plot, has suggested that he himself borrowed the lighter from the Walker Brothers' drummer and gave it to Hendrix.

Mitch Mitchell remembered seeing Hendrix "mucking about in the dressing room with lighter fluid and a lot of giggling going on", and that, at the end of the group's set, "Suddenly this can of lighter fluid appeared and suddenly it was squirted everywhere and then this lighter appeared and suddenly things were on fire."

The fall-out from the burning guitar involved promoter Tito Burns threatening both Hendrix and Chandler. "You're never going to work for me again if you pull a stunt like that", he apparently raged, while Brookes recalls things getting more violent. "The tour manager gave Hendrix a right bollocking over it and then they got to fighting and Hendrix hit him. If it had been anybody else they would have been thrown off the tour, but I don't think he did it again while we were on tour."

While he didn't see the incident, John Walker was left to pour water on the conflagration. "I just said to his people that if he's going to do that every night, just let us know because we need a fire marshall. That was our only reaction."

Concerned that some of the theatres they were playing were old and potential fire hazards, Walker recalls discussing the issue with Chandler. "I said that if Jimi is going to do that it's no big deal but we need to make sure everybody is safe. Whether he did or not didn't really matter. It wasn't a question of being up-staged. Jimi Hendrix was not going to upset The Walker Brothers and he was good enough not to need to set fire to his guitar to get noticed. What Jimi did was all showmanship and kinda interesting to watch."

If the idea was for Hendrix to capture the newspaper headlines with his flaming guitar stunt, it was only a partial success. Most of the nationals managed to ignore the incident completely, while two papers did carry a report on their front page – albeit only three lines long.

The Daily Express had a down-page paragraph which said, "Pop star Jimi Hendrix was burned on the hand last night when his electric guitar burst into flames at the Finsbury Park Astoria. The show continued after the blaze was put out." The Daily Mail reported that "Guitarist Jimi Hendrix, 21 (sic), was taken to hospital with a burned hand after his instrument burst into flames on the first night of the Walker Brothers tour at Finsbury Park, London." The alleged trip to hospital might just have been a further piece of PR hype from the Hendrix camp.

Melody Maker covered the event as its front-page lead story on April 8 under the headline "Hendrix: clean act." The report focused not on the fire but on concerns that his act – full of pelvic thrusts and suggestive guitar movements – needed to be toned down. They claimed that Hendrix had been warned to clean up his act after the first night of the tour, reporting Chandler as saying, "I was told he had to change his act. The tour organizers said it was too suggestive." Hendrix himself said, "I play the way I play and I can't understand the situation at all."

Chandler later recalled an all-important detail of his run-in with the promoter. "I distinctly remember Tito Burns waving a fist at me and shouting, 'You can't get away with things like this, Chas. If we find that guitar I'll have you prosecuted.' Underneath his overcoat I could make out the charred end of an electric guitar."

Chris Welch, reviewing the show in the same edition of Melody Maker, wrote somewhat bizarrely that, "Hendrix was lying on the stage playing the guitar with his teeth when it suddenly burst into flames." He went on to report that Jimi and band fled the stage before "an attendant rushed on stage with a fire extinguisher and put out the flames which were leaping ten feet into the air".

Even stranger was a report in the NME written by Altham, who was seemingly doubling as journalist and press officer. He wrote that the finale to Hendrix's act "came when his guitar burst into flames, by accident we are assured, and precipitated the entrance of a security officer who sprayed detergent from a canister all over compere Nick Jones".

After the events of the opening night, Chas Chandler went on record to complain that not everything on the tour was perfect for Hendrix following his opening-night shenanigans. "There was a lot of ill feeling backstage. They would screw up the lights or put the house lights up on the audience during his act. It was quite a tour … and a great tour for the audiences."

It seems Chandler arranged for the tour organizers to give him the nod when anybody from the theatre circuit was likely to be 'in the house' and Hendrix would change his act accordingly. He confirmed that his star act not only enjoyed his first major UK tour but also gained something important. "Jimi had a ball, he loved it. It was then it dawned on him he could be successful. It was then he got his confidence."

Hendrix's fellow support acts found the guitarist a little distant. "He talked very little, mumbled a bit, but was a nice guy," says Lee, while Brookes recalls, "It was a four-week tour and in that time he hardly said anything. But then the rest of us were all from a similar background. We were English and worked on the scene for years but he was American and came from a completely different background."

John Walker, too, recalls the two sides of Hendrix. "The most interesting thing was that he was opposite on stage to what he was in person. Quiet, shy, polite, and then when he was on stage it was like someone had lit up a firecracker." He had fond memories of the time they spent together. "When we sat and talked he had a lot to say … about music and where he was going from here. But it seemed to me that he was a little bit lonely and wanted to have a family of some sort around him. He was definitely looking for something and that was maybe why he got so deep into music."

Travelling on the tour bus with Hendrix and his band (The Walker Brothers and Humperdinck went by car) gave Lee a very different memory. "The atmosphere on the bus was thick with drugs and there was great camaraderie between us all." Recalling a particular night when the tour came close to London, he adds, "Hendrix invited us all to stay at his flat. We all went to the Speakeasy. He suggested we go there for a 'nice night, and then you can stay at my flat'. There were four of us plus our road manager, Noel Redding and Hendrix."

The regular use of cannabis on the tour bus was never an issue, Brookes recalls, until one night, the police decided to pull the coach over for speeding. "All the spliffs went into the little plastic holders on the seat backs and we had to shout to the driver not to let the police on to the coach."

Brookes also remembers fondly the night the tour arrived in The Californians' home town of Wolverhampton for two shows at the Odeon cinema on April 13. "After our local show we played a gig at one of our regular spots, the Kingfisher Club. John Walker turned up and started to play and then Jimi turned up and jammed with us. So now it's there in the history books that Jimi Hendrix jammed with The Californians."

Hendrix spoke to both major music papers about the tour midway through the trek, telling the NME (Keith Altham was again the writer), "Most will come to see The Walkers. Those who come to hear Engelbert sing 'Release Me' may not dig me but that's not tragic. You've got to gentle people along for a while until they are clued in on the scene." He told Melody Maker's Chris Welch that it was not all roses on the road. "The bosses on the tour are giving us hell … but we refuse to change our act and the result is that the amplifier gets cut off at the funniest times."

After they had opened the show and done their 20-minute set, The Californians were free to watch the rest of the entertainment, which, according to Lee, they did most nights. "The Experience was a bit of a rabble – Mitch used to hit anything he could and Noel wanted to prove to everybody that he could play the guitar. It was all incredibly loud and Hendrix would do all his tricks, playing behind his neck and with his teeth. But he did pull the plug and stop the show more than once when he felt he wasn't going down well with the audience."

It seems that Redding's determination to prove himself as a guitar player rather than a bassist – and perhaps earn some welcome cash – involved him working with some of the other acts … even though nobody ever saw him. "Noel would get himself a little extra money on the tour by playing for other artists from behind the curtain, which meant he still got to play the guitar," recounts Mayer. John Walker claims that "Noel was very bitchy about the control Jimi exerted over the group. His biggest bitch in life was that Jimi told him what bass lines he should play, and he had to do it that way even if he didn't like it."

JIMI HENDRIX MADE IN ENGLAND

5

Guitarist Brookes might have been expected to be in awe of Hendrix, but he recalls having reservations. "I didn't particularly like what he was doing on stage. The tour was timed to the second and he would stop halfway through the first number and start playing 'Star Spangled Banner', which he hadn't rehearsed and the other two didn't know what was going on. He was searching around the fingerboard for the notes and obviously didn't know it. Whether he was half-stoned I don't know."

It seems that by this time Hendrix was quite open about his drug use and made no secret of it on the road. "His drug consumption was quite frightening," says Lee. "It was all day, and even on stage he used to have a joint on his guitar. It wasn't that rife in the mid- Sixties and nobody really 'smoked' in public, but he didn't seem at all bothered."

Brookes recalls another show when Hendrix went off script. "He was halfway through one of his own numbers and he just said, 'I've had enough of this crap' and started playing 'Wild Thing'. It was all very undisciplined."

Californian Peter Lee was surprised and impressed with some of the new-found partners Hendrix turned up with at the acts' roll-call each morning. " Hendrix would come to the coach – rarely alone – and some of the girls he had with him were absolutely stunning. It would take hours to do 100 miles in those days and there were no TVs or videos on the bus. There were no card games or gambling on the bus but lots of drugs and fun and games … and we slept a lot."

Arriving in a new town meant a trip to the nearest cafe for food and drink – and, according to Lee, "some strange looks from the regulars and locals" – while the road crew set up the gear for the next show. Once the musicians got into the venue – usually a cinema or theatre – there was an opportunity for them to see a different side of Jimi Hendrix the guitar player.

Sitting in the stalls of the venue, Hendrix was apparently happy to play guitar for hour upon hour. "He used to practise for hours just fingerpicking," says Lee. "He rarely rehearsed his heavy stuff, just sat down with a cigarette on the go and played stuff he didn't do on stage. Seeing him in the afternoon, you could tell he was a fabulous guitarist. And his stage show was exactly that – a stage show with just volume, feedback and all sorts of different sounds."

During his afternoon practice sessions, Hendrix was often joined by an unlikely playmate in John Walker. He recalled that, during one of those impromptu jam sessions, Hendrix turned to him and said, "How come you got blue eyes?" According to Walker, this was his way of saying, "You're white and you shouldn't be able to play the blues."

"What he was doing during those jams was coming up with some really weird kinds of things, using the kind of chords Mickey Baker was using," explained Walker, adding that American jazz guitarist Baker's obsession with "manipulating a 12-bar into more than 12 bars with lots of interesting chord structures" was an inspiration to Hendrix.

Their jamming took in some familiar tunes. "When we were playing, Jimi was working on a new song called 'The Wind Cries Mary', trying out different chord structures and running them past me every day to see what I thought. At the same time he was working on a recorded version of 'Wild Thing', and he told me that this was the song that always made him laugh. Every time he practised it, it always cracked him up."

As this unlikely collection of artists progressed around the UK, there were the usual highs and lows associated with a package tour. John Walker and London-born singer-songwriter Cat Stevens, riding on the back of two Top 10 hits, did not enjoy the best of relationships. "I became quite friendly with Engelbert but was never overly friendly with Cat Stevens. He spent a lot of time trying to impress everybody and there was some friction between him and everyone on the tour – not just Jimi, who wasn't particularly impressed by him."

Brookes recalls that Stevens – who had peaked at Number 2 in January 1967 with 'Matthew And Son' – finally left the bus midway through the tour in order to travel alone. "Everybody else including Hendrix stayed on the coach where we had a good rapport going. He was very polite and always called people 'sir' but said very little. He seemed like a bit of a loner to me."

The relatively unknown Californians didn't warrant much media attention and consequently had plenty of time on their hands. "We had this thing about water pistols," explains Brookes. "In those days they put chicken wire over the orchestra pit to keep the fans off the stage. We used to sneak into the pit with water pistols and squirt them at the audience, who hadn't got a clue what was going on."

After a few weeks, the band turned their attention to their fellow artistes. "We finished up spraying Jimi, Noel and Mitch during their set and then Noel and Mitch would spray us when were on. Jimi took it OK when we did it but we couldn't do it too often or the tour manager would have chucked us off the tour," recalls Brookes.

While The Experience – all fuzzy hair, military jackets and decibels – clashed style-wise with the smooth Walker Brothers, the elegant crooning of Humperdinck and the somewhat reserved Cat Stevens, they went down well with the audience. So well, in fact, that, as the tour progressed, the organizers were forced to move Hendrix up the

5

bill from his first-half spot as a section of the audience had started to leave after he had finished.

Jimi later shared a few home truths with the NME about life on a package tour. "It was all wrong. That Engelflumfluff hadn't any stage presence, he never got anything going", before turning his attention to the media. "There are still a few who have obviously been sent to get me. They come to the dressing room with a kind of 'let's strip him naked and hang him from a tall tree' attitude."

The tour came to an end at the Tooting Granada in south London on April 30, 1967 after a total of 54 shows in 27 different locations. Despite mixed reviews – Leeds, Chesterfield and Slough were less than enthusiastic while Bedford, Wolverhampton, Leicester and Birmingham found something favourable to say – John Walker took away only positive memories of Hendrix.

"He said it had been such a great opportunity for him and he appreciated the chance to play to people who had not come to see him. His focus every night was that if he could impress just a few people ... that would be good."

Walker went on to reflect on what being in Britain meant to Hendrix, just seven months after his arrival. "I think he had started to feel comfortable in Britain because Britain made him welcome. In fact he was so welcome that he ran off with our fan club secretary – she was very blonde – and we didn't see her for nearly three weeks. Our management went nuts."

David Arden understands what made Chandler take a chance and put Hendrix and his group – the emerging heroes of psychedelic guitar-rock – on the bill with an American pop trio, a British ballad singer and an up-and-coming singer-songwriter. "The idea was always to get your act in front of a big audience and the theatres and cinemas were the only places where you could get a good size crowd in the days before stadiums and arenas."

Fellow American Geno Washington believes Hendrix was still evaluating this new country he had flown into. "He wanted to get information as to whether he had bitten off too much, was he in the right place. I was trying to give him confidence and telling him that he was in the right place. He was a cool dude and his mind was set on taking advantage of the chance he had."

That chance was about to be taken with both hands.

WHERE'S THE STAGE, MAN?

'THE WIND CRIES MARY' RELEASED – FIRST ALBUM
FINISHED – BAND FEE BREAKS THE £1,000 MARK –
RETURNS TO STATES TO PLAY MONTEREY – US PRESS
UNIMPRESSED – DRUG USE STARTS TO TAKE TOLL

The end of Hendrix's first British tour coincided with the release of The Experience's third single, 'The Wind Cries Mary', and around that time Chandler talked to Record Retailer and explained the reasoning behind the decision to release a new single while 'Purple Haze' was still in the Top 10. "There's big demand for Jimi Hendrix and we feel that it's quite possible that both records can be in the Top 20 at the same time. If you listen to the new disc you will realize that it is completely different from anything Jimi has ever done before and should appeal to a family audience."

Chandler was proved correct as 'The Wind Cries Mary' reached Number 15 on May 18 while 'Purple Haze' was still at 10. A week later it was at Number 9 while 'Purple Haze' slipped to 16 after a 14-week stay on the chart.

Released more or less simultaneously with their first album but not included on it, 'The Wind Cries Mary' displayed a softer, more lyrical side to Hendrix the songwriter that would be explored more fully on the forthcoming Axis: Bold As Love LP.

Astoundingly, given its place in the guitraist's canon, it was knocked off in 20 minutes' spare time at the end of a day's recording at de Lane Lea studios just before the move to Olympic. Mitch and Noel played it without prior rehearsal, and Jimi made four or five more guitar passes as overdubs to complete what had only originally been intended as a rough demo.

Rock was, as ever, in short supply in the singles chart in the Summer of Love; although Procol Harum's anthemic 'A Whiter Shade Of Pale' was on its way to the top, only stablemates The Who's 'Pictures Of Lily' truly rocked. Most bizarre of all was Jeff Beck's

JIMI HENDRIX MADE IN ENGLAND

'HI Ho Silver Lining', a record company-inspired vocal outing from the master guitarist so blatantly commercial he would spend decades disowning it. At least Hendrix's releases were true to his musical spirit.

Back in London at the start of May, Hendrix made his way back to the Selmer shop in Charing Cross Road, where Dave Wilkinson was still serving. "He would come for an hour or maybe longer and his favourite to play was a Strat, but if something new came in he was always interested in trying it out. He played Les Paul guitars in the shop but never bought one," says the former guitarist turned salesman. "Hendrix was interested in sound as well as technique, so he wanted different guitars for different things."

With a major tour and two (soon to be three) hit singles under his belt, Hendrix's fame and reputation were catching the attention of the biggest names in pop. Rolling Stones leader Mick Jagger was moved to announce, "Since the peak of The Beatles and The Stones there have been a lot of big groups but none with any real flair – except for The Who and The Jimi Hendrix Experience."

Pink Floyd manager Peter Jenner also saw something special in the new guitarist who was taking the business by storm. "It was quite interesting that he was a black rock star leading a band and that was why he was so embraced by the rock world. We all liked black soul music but here was Hendrix playing 'our' rock music and doing interesting things with it. The rock world really embraced him and the fact that he was black was a positive and he had less problems being a black guy in England than he would have had in America in those days.

"From the outset Hendrix would never have been taken as a rock star in America," Jenner concludes, while Selmer's Tom Wilkinson put his finger on what he saw as the reasons for Hendrix's success in the UK. "He looked different to every black act we had ever seen in this country up to then. He was outrageous and went with all the weird stuff that was around at the time. If he'd turned up in a suit and tie and just played his guitar we might never have noticed him."

According to Roger Mayer, Hendrix held a different view when it came to colour. "Jimi didn't consider himself to be black – he was mixed race – but he suffered in the US as a coloured person and it was total racial freedom for him when he came here."

Musically, Mayer believes England meant so much to Hendrix "because The Beatles came from here. All the hot sounds were coming out of England and he had nothing to lose by coming here." Other musicians he rated highly included "Bob Dylan, because he enjoyed the soul in his songs and the fact that the songs were saying something. He

6

enjoyed Dave Mason's [Traffic guitarist] acoustic playing and we used to hang out a lot together and go round each other's house to jam."

Mayer also reveals a number of musicians were intimidated by Hendrix. "Mama Cass and Paul McCartney used to come by the flat or the studio. Jimi was a very generous musician who just wanted to sit down and play, jam with people. But there came that time when the top guys didn't want to play with him, which he didn't fully understand."

Ironically, as far as singing went, Jimi was initially daunted by having backed such stars as Little Richard. His comment 'I want to do with my guitar what Little Richard does with his voice' said it all. But hearing Bob Dylan's gruff delivery on such well-received albums as Highway 61 Revisited (whose 'Like A Rolling Stone' found its way into the Experience's live set) gave him the belief that he could step into the spotlight as a vocalist as well as an instrumentalist. "If this guy can sing," he reportedly said, "then so can I."

Recording the songs for The Experience's debut album, under the guiding hand of manager-turned-producer Chandler, had begun way back in December at CBS Studios. These initial sessions were followed by time spent in De Lane Lea in January, February and March 1967. Visits to Olympic Studios in Barnes during February and April added the finishing touches to an 11-track collection that would be called Are You Experienced – without a question mark.

The decision not to include the group's hit singles was one that stemmed from Stamp's work with The Who. "We were already working on the idea of 'album' albums. We hated that there were things called 'album tracks'."

It was at Olympic Studios that Jimi first met recording engineer Eddie Kramer. Kramer was able to get the best sound out of the recordings already made, and help Chas and Jimi obtain the studio sound they wanted. He would prove a recurring figure in the Hendrix story, worked closely with him on 1968's Electric Ladyland and would be a key figure when Jimi opened his own studio in New York in 1970.

In the weeks leading up to the release of his first album, Hendrix had time to visit some of his favourite London haunts, including his regular hideaway in Andrew Black's office at Polydor. "Jimi came in one day and when he couldn't find me he came down to our in-house studio where he sat in on the session I was overseeing."

Black was working with a three-piece he had signed to the label called The New Nadir, a 'freakbeat/R&B' band which featured American guitarist Ed Carter alongside Gary Thain and Peter Dawkins. Sitting in Polydor Studios in the basement of their

6

offices off London's Oxford Street, Hendrix paid particular attention to the music he heard.

"He got very animated at a tape of Carter," explains Black, "and said he loved his guitar playing. When Carter came in…I introduced them and it started a real friendship and mutual admiration society." So impressed was Hendrix with The New Nadir and Carter in particular that he began to work on the band's tracks alongside Black. "I offered him a credit on the record but he turned it down. There was still a chance that Jimi might produce their album but nothing ever came of it as Carter left to join The Beach Boys."

That was not the end of the story, as Black explains. "The New Nadir got a gig at the Speakeasy one Saturday night and when I told Jimi about it he asked if he could come with me. I picked him up and we drove off to the club, where he sat through the gig and then asked if he could go backstage to see Carter."

Hendrix and Carter hatched a plan for Jimi to make a surprise appearance during the second half of the London-based trio's show – and it would come with an added hint of mystery. "The band's manager was delighted and Jimi walked on with his back to the crowd and then he suddenly turned around," recalls Black. "There was a long silence before people realized who it was, and then when he started to play it went crazy. It was an amazing evening."

In early May 1967, the first reviews appeared for 'The Wind Cries Mary', which Hendrix wrote as an apology to girlfriend Kathy Etchingham (whose middle name is Mary) after a row over her cooking. She recounts that when she returned to their flat a day after she "stalked out", Hendrix gave her a piece of paper with 'The Wind Cries Mary' written on it. "Mary is my middle name, and the one he would use when he wanted to annoy me," explains Etchingham. "I took the song and read it through. It was about the row we had just had, but I didn't feel the least bit appeased."

Top DJ David Jacobs was Melody Maker's guest reviewer in their May 6 'Blind Date' feature and was seemingly baffled ."Jimmy Witherspoon giving an impression of Mick Jagger? Could be Long John Baldry. I really don't know." After being told it was Jimi Hendrix he added, "He is an experience I have never experienced. Not as good as 'Purple Haze'."

Over at the NME, Derek Johnson was telling the world that it was "A beautiful record – the best showcase yet for Jimi's inherent feeling for the blues." It seems the public was also taken with the track as 'The Wind Cries Mary' stormed up the UK chart throughout May before finally settling in the Top 10 in June 1967.

Just as his third hit record was taking off, Hendrix – the new psychedelic god of UK pop – was an unlikely guest of honour at the traditional Variety Club of Great Britain's Tribute to the Recording Industry, held at the upmarket Dorchester Hotel in London's Park Lane on May 9. The showbiz charity was formed in the UK in 1949 to help young people and Hendrix followed an appearance by John Lennon and Paul McCartney in 1963.

Two days earlier he and The Experience had returned for their second stint at the Saville Theatre – supported by Denny Laine, The 1-2-3 and Garnet Mimms – and Hendrix recalled the significance of that night's shows in terms of his development of the band's special effects. "When we were at the Saville ...I had this gadget on the guitar that every time I hit a certain note, the lights would go up."

In the midst of all this activity in Hendrix's life, a bunch of aspiring young musicians known as The People gathered in London's Covent Garden to support Procol Harum at the Middle Earth club.

The line-up included guitarist Henry McCullough, who recalls two people who were there in the crowd to see their set (which started at 3am). "Chas Chandler and Mike Jeffery were there, and after the gig they came up to us and asked us to sign with them. They changed our names to Eire Apparent and then sent us off to Spain for three months to write songs," says McCullough. "We only wrote one, and that was put on the B-side of our first single."

Those early days of being managed by the ANIM team were not great fun, according to the Irish musician. "I found Chas to be a little bit off-putting, to be honest. After we signed, every day all four of us had to go down to the office and just sit there from eleven in the morning until four in the afternoon looking for money to go and buy a beer."

On May 13 – one day after the official release date of their album – The Experience were booked to play at Imperial College London. Future Queen guitarist Brian May was a member of the entertainments committee which forked out £1,000 – "quite a lot in those days," says May – for the trio to perform in the 'top hall'.

Agent Barry Dickins also recalls the importance of this and other bookings around that time. "Hendrix was the first act I got £1,000 a night for. He was really well paid in the mid-Sixties and made a lot of money but I don't know whether he kept it or not."

Earning the magical figure of 'a grand a night' also had an impact on Noel Redding, who, after threatening to resign months earlier over his weekly wage, was quick to re-negotiate new figures for himself and Mitch Mitchell. "I found out we were earning £1,000 a night and that was a lot of money. We split it 50 per cent to Hendrix, 25 per cent between me and Mitch and 25 per cent to Mike Jeffery and Chas."

Breaking the four-figure barrier also represented a change in attitude from Dickins' boss at the Harold Davidson agency. "I started right at the beginning of it all when Hendrix was unknown, and then, when he exploded, my boss Dick Katz took over," says Dickins. "He said, 'You're a nice kid but I've got the experience,' and he probably wasn't wrong."

May's interest in Hendrix quickly influenced the music his band 1984 were playing. "We covered all sorts of people and music, but as soon as Hendrix arrived I leapt on it," recalls the guitarist. On the night Hendrix played his college, his band were also on the bill – but in a different hall. "I actually played 'Purple Haze' during that show. There was also a rumour that Jimi came down and saw me do it, nodded to himself and smiled," adds May. "But it is sort of apocryphal. I don't know for sure if it happened or not."

Over 1,000 people crammed into the top hall to see Hendrix and it seems that the college, despite the fee, still turned a profit. "We all crammed in to see him and it was magical beyond belief," said May in May 2011. "The hugeness of his sound was just mind-blowing."

That was also the night May got closest to actually meeting his hero. "I was walking from the jazz club room in the college – which had been turned into the changing room – to the stage and there was Jimi coming out of his dressing room in a cloud of smoke. He said, 'Where's the stage, man?', and we all sort of dumbfoundedly nodded our heads in the direction of the stage and off he went."

While Hendrix was entertaining the students in west London's Exhibition Road, Eric Clapton and Cream were on stage at Wembley Pool as part of the high-profile NME Poll Winners' show, despite not winning a prize of any sort. They joined award-winning acts such as The Beach Boys, Cliff Richard, Dusty Springfield and Steve Winwood, plus top DJ Jimmy Savile, in front of 10,000 fans.

Show over, Clapton and friends, including The Move's Trevor Burton, adjourned to their favourite watering hole in the heart of London. "Afterwards Eric went to the Speak for a drink as it was somebody's birthday," recalls Burton. "Then in came Jimi Hendrix and Eric called him over and said, 'I hear you've made an album.' Jimi said 'yes' and asked if we wanted to hear it."

Then, according to Burton, "We went to Jimi's place and he played us a demo of his album – and, as our jaws dropped, he just sat there with a huge grin on his face. It was extraordinary sitting next to Eric and seeing the look on his face as Jimi played each track. We were both gobsmacked. It was like the Martians had landed."

The debut album by The Jimi Hendrix Experience was officially released on May 12, 1967, the same day as 'Hey Joe' was issued in America. While the US managed to ignore the band's debut single almost completely, the album brought universal praise from the British media. Still writing for the NME, Keith Altham exclaimed, "The only sounds I have heard comparable to those produced on Jimi Hendrix's first LP are those electrical storms received by [satellite station] Jodrell Bank", while Melody Maker announced, "Although it may sound very weird and freaky to some, you can be assured that this album is, repeat, is the real Hendrix Experience."

MM reader Derek Lister was less impressed. He wrote to the paper to say that Clapton was better than Hendrix, before adding, "Hendrix is artificial and his new LP is just a fuzz-box nightmare." Brian May didn't feel it represented the live act. "I guess that when I first heard the first album, which was after I had seen him play most of it live, I wasn't that impressed with the sound of it." But, adds May, "There was a lot more sort of fuzz-boxy sound on the album than there was live."

Guitar effects supremo Mayer recalls his part in the proceedings. "I was just a friend who was in charge of the sound, together with Jimi. Chas was in control of producing the record, which meant he had to pay for it, get everybody there, book the studio and then sit there and provide another viewpoint."

There was, in Mayer's mind, an obvious line drawn between what he did with Hendrix and Chandler's role as producer. "When it came to the technical aspects of getting the guitar sounds, this was down to Jimi and me. The major decision we made after 'Purple Haze' was that we were really ahead of the curve and we had to be very careful not to go too far out or too far forward at that time," he explains, before confirming that it didn't always take a long time to get things right. "We cut the solos for 'Purple Haze' and 'Fire' in the space of two or three hours and then went down the Speakeasy. You can't call that expensive."

Although he describes Are You Experienced as "piecemeal with bits and pieces from different sessions fitted in while the band were on the road doing gigs", Mayer recalls time spent debating which version to issue. "After the songs were recorded there would be discussions about different versions. Jimi was conscious of creating a radio-

JIMI HENDRIX MADE IN ENGLAND

friendly single, a pop single, and we knew when to draw back and not go too far with the sounds."

The plan was to "feed the ideas and sounds to the public very slowly. Jimi was getting an extreme reaction to the way he looked and we had to be careful about how he sounded and what the reaction might be if he went too far," Mayer says. "We were aware that you had about eight seconds to capture people's attention, hence things like the intro to 'Purple Haze'. He was conscious of making things sound commercial but I think he was more concerned that he enjoyed the end result than how successful a record was in the charts."

Speaking to Keith Altham just weeks before his death in 1970, Hendrix looked back at his early work. "I heard that just recently and it seemed like I must have been high or something. When I heard it I said, 'Damn, I wonder where my head was at when I said all those things.' I don't consider that the invention of psychedelic music. I was just asking a lot of questions."

In another interview given in Stockholm just after the album's release, Hendrix told the press the secret ingredients that made up his debut album. "You have all these different sounds, but all were made from just nothing but a guitar, you know, bass and drums, and then our slowed-down voices."

The album kicked off with feedback slowly building before slamming into the now-familiar stabbing riff of 'Foxy Lady'. Guitar and bass interlocked to punch home the riff while the sexually charged lyrics about Jimi's 'sweet little lovemaker' and Jimi and Noel's whispered 'Foxy' asides only added to the lecherous overtones. The guitar used distortion – a dirty word in British studios at this time – to thicken the sound of the trio and add to the sleazy ambience.

'Manic Depression' featured an unusual, for rock at least, time signature of 3/4, the Experience making the waltz-time track swing along. Jimi then began to build the excitement by introducing a series of guitar licks between the sung verse lines, while still doubling the main verse riff with Noel's bass as Mitch began pushing, probing and sparring with the guitar.

Jimi returned to his first love with the 12-bar blues of 'Red House'. The song was to remain a concert favourite throughout his career, often exceeding ten minutes. Nevertheless, in this relatively compact version of just under four minutes Jimi had sufficient time to reel off a series of fluid blues licks while Noel played his bass part on the lower strings of a regular six-string guitar. The Experience taped another version of the song at a later Olympic session, and this was the one included on the US release of Smash Hits.

'Can You See Me' was an early staple of the Experience live set and played at Monterey, so was obviously highly rated by Jimi. His vocal was double-tracked to good effect and, for a singer who was chronically self-conscious of his vocal abilities, was left quite naked at the end of each verse as the backing dropped away.

'Love Or Confusion' would have made a fine single, with lead-guitar licks behind the vocal throughout creating an almost otherworldly texture. For a recording realised on four-track equipment (as was the rest of the album) this track remains today a fine technical achievement and demonstrates how hard Jimi, Chas Chandler and Eddie Kramer were working to push technical boundaries.

'I Don't Live Today' was a regular in the Experience set right up to 1969, and often a vehicle for extended improvisation. Jimi dedicated the song live to 'the American Indians' and, while the lyrics do not directly refer to them, the song's theme is one of repression. After this downbeat fatalism, the psychedelically-tinged ballad 'May This Be Love' was the perfect antidote. Mitch's tom-tom rolls, a single rhythm guitar and an understated bass combined to create a spacious quality. The cymbal crashes sounded like splashing water droplets, echoing the lyrics (the song's working title was 'Waterfall'). This was the lyrical side of Jimi that was to feature more heavily on Axis: Bold As Love.

'Fire' was a tour de force from Mitch Mitchell, whose drumming totally dominated. A deceptively simple series of riffs, ironically including a staccato vamp of the kind typically reserved to accompany a live drum solo, were perfectly executed, while Jimi's double-tracked guitar solo was brief and to the point.

The predominantly instrumental 'Third Stone From The Sun' was the first example of Jimi breaking out from the three-minute single format. Begun at one of the early CBS Studios sessions with overdubs and mixing effects added later at Olympic, it became heavier as it progressed. The slurred, half-speed vocals were actually a communication between a visiting alien and his mothership – the alien judging chickens to be the most intelligent life form on earth!

'Remember' harked back to Jimi's days backing R&B artists on the 'chitlin circuit' and was probably the most conventional song on Are You Experienced. Mitch, while, relatively restrained, still managed to insert a playful feel through a 'skipping' drum pattern. Lyrically Jimi used typical soul vocabulary such as 'mockingbirds' and 'singing for his supper'.

JIMI HENDRIX MADE IN ENGLAND

6

If 'Remember' was conventional, then 'Are You Experienced' took Jimi and the boys back into the experimental sound lab with a vengeance. Obviously indebted to the Beatles' pioneering 'Tomorrow Never Knows'. backwards guitars and drums churned as a single piano note played four to the bar, anchoring the song while the music headed into outer space.

Totally recorded at Olympic Studios, the track was one of the last to be recorded and was a fine closer to an album which opened up a wealth of possibilities Jimi was to explore on subsequent releases.

Geno Washington pinpoints the role played by Chas Chandler as both manager and producer as crucial. "He was always confident that Jimi was going to be the biggest thing since sliced bread … Jimi wasn't no piece of cake or easy to work with and he drove Chas fucking crazy at times. It was OK for Jimi to spend hours in the studio getting it exactly right because the shit worked in the end, but it got Chas real frustrated."

The ever more confident Jimi would frequently butt heads with Chas, leading the manager at one point to lose his rag. 'He wanted to record louder and louder and we just couldn't get it on tape, so he threw a tantrum. I had his passport in the studio…and took it out. It had his airline ticket in it as well. I said "Well there you are, go and fuck off then"'. Fortunately, Jimi for once ignored his mentor's advice. "He started laughing and that was the end of it…"

Chandler's skill as a producer was not lost on former Animals colleague Hilton Valentine, who reckons, "He was very good. He made Jimi Hendrix a star and those records still sound great today – 'Hey Joe' and so on." Brian May had been a tad disappointed by the first album, but "liked the showmanship of Hendrix's stage act and the fact that he used the guitar as a voice."

Gerry Stickells, who had cut his teeth driving the van, humping the gear and generally shepherding The Experience around the UK and Europe, went on to be Queen's road manager at the height of their fame. "When he was drunk at night on the road he used to tell Hendrix stories, and one of them was about Jimi being in the studio and refusing to sing unless they put screens around him so nobody could see him sing," recounts May. "Apparently he was so upset and so embarrassed by the sound of his voice."

Stickells, who described Hendrix as "an easy guy to get along with", particularly in the early days when he was "very keen and seemed to know what he wanted", was at the heart of an ugly situation that developed in Stockholm during the trio's 13-day visit to Germany, Denmark, Finland and Sweden.

6

After appearing on the Popside TV show and performing in Stockholm, Hendrix and his bandmates were refused hotel rooms in the Swedish capital. Reflecting that the whole pop scene in Europe was being "made up as we went along", Stickells recalled that they were often excluded for no reason. "Even if you booked something it might not work out. We often got thrown out of hotels either because Jimi was black or they just generally didn't like the look of us."

Whatever the reasons, Hendrix found himself room-less in Stockholm on May 24, 1967 and told reporters, "It seems people in Scandinavia just aren't ready for the way we look", before switching into positive PR mode and adding, "The kids are great and the concerts have been much more successful than we could have expected for a first visit."

The near-overnight success of his first album had whetted Hendrix's appetite for studio work, and this made Stickells' job slightly more difficult. "He enjoyed a show, but it was a case of getting him on stage. To him it was much easier going into the recording studio. But once he was out there he was fine."

In less than a month after its release, Are You Experienced had settled in the UK Top 10, reaching its peak position of Number 2 by mid-June, where it loitered behind The Beatles' masterpiece of a concept album, Sgt Pepper's Lonely Hearts Club Band. In fact, Hendrix's first album release was unable to dislodge The Beatles, The Monkees (who, incredibly, had three albums in the Top 10) or the soundtrack to the film The Sound Of Music from top spot during its 33-week stay in the UK album chart.

At the time of Hendrix's death in September 1970 Are You Experienced was still his best-selling release and would remain so for nearly 20 years before being surpassed by the Smash Hits compilation. Certainly, in July 1967, at the supposed height of the Summer of Love, it had more right to a place in the UK Top 10 album chart than the likes of easy-listening bandleaders James Last and Herb Alpert who inhabited it. Retrospective histories do not reflect the fact that Hendrix brought rock to the best-selling LP listings in a way few bar The Who, Cream (their first album) and Rolling Stones had before.

The States could at least boast the debut album by the Doors and Jefferson Airplane's Surrealistic Pillow in their long-playing Top 10 of July 1967. But with Andy Williams and the Dr Zhivago soundtrack keeping them company, it was clear the rock revolution had yet to ensnare the record-buying public, let alone the mass media. It is against this conservative background that Hendrix's groundbreaking music must be viewed.

6

The Jimi Hendrix Experience's final date in May was at the Barbecue '67, held in the unlikely setting of the Tulip Bulb Auction Hall in Spalding, Lincolnshire, on May 29. Boasting 'non-stop dancing 4pm to midnight', admission was £1 and Hendrix appeared alongside Geno Washington, Cream, The Move and Pink Floyd.

Over 4,000 people were reported as being crammed into a warehouse which had a stage at one end and a caravan parked outside which acted as a dressing room. But Washington, who closed the show with his Ram Jam Band, reckons the crowd was bigger than that. "The security guys who were supposed to watch the fence and make sure people didn't get in for free, they had money sticking out of their pockets from where they were taking bribes to let people in."

According to Washington, Hendrix's group was never suited to share the bill with The Ram Jam Band: "Jimi went on before us and what he did wasn't working on my shows, although it worked when he played to his own audience. He often had some doubts about the reaction he got." The people of Spalding's thoughts on the night were seemingly no different.

Hendrix was plagued with tuning problems in the swelteringly hot conditions, which Australian writer Germaine Greer was moved to describe as being "...underneath the corrugated iron roof in the stink of cattle shit and sweating English youth." The more Hendrix struggled to get his guitar in tune, the more the crowd jeered, which eventually led him to exclaim, "Fuck you! I'm gonna get my guitar right if it takes me all fucking night."

Writing for the underground magazine Oz, which had been launched in the UK earlier in 1967, Greer reported that the crowd was not the least bit bothered whether Hendrix was in tune or not. "They just wanted to hear something and adulate. So he did it and fucked with his guitar and they moaned and swayed about..." Hendrix finished his act by tearing the strings off his guitar and smashing it against the bank of amplifiers which toppled over, causing an electrical short-circuit and plunging the entire hall into darkness. He made his point and also an unforgettable exit.

Pink Floyd manager Peter Jenner looks back on the event as a positive career move for his band, who were fast moving towards the chart with second single 'See Emily Play'. "Geno was a big live act in those days and sharing the bill was a good move for us, and it was always a pleasure to see Hendrix. We were not best mates but we knew each other. He would always say 'hello' and was always very affable." Jenner has another, more personal memory. "I subsequently discovered that Hendrix spent some considerable time that day pursuing my wife, which I thought was something of a feather in the cap."

The Barbecue '67 gig gave Geno Washington to catch up with his fellow American artist. "We talked about the times on the road and the different groupies we both knew and ran into around the country. We'd say, 'Have you seen Weekend Betty from Manchester lately?'" The singer is adamant that, on all the times they met up, Hendrix was always coherent and in good spirits. "I never saw him out of his crust. He had a drink and the occasional joint but he was never out of it and just rambling on – he never did that. His mind was seriously focused on his career and building up a following."

Fresh from a major UK tour, a string of British club dates and a headline tour of northern Europe, Hendrix was on the brink of the big time. Three Top 10 singles and a best-selling album had pushed him, Redding and Mitchell to the forefront of the Sixties pop scene. "Within six months he was the biggest act in England," says Dickins, "and he came from nowhere." Photographer Mankowitz agrees that his rise to stardom was extraordinary and based around one major decision. "It was a stroke of genius to bring him over here, and if they hadn't then Jimi Hendrix would not have happened. The instant recognition he received here was a revelation."

As a man who was at the heart of the scene in swingin' London, Mankowitz would regularly catch up with the biggest stars of the day. "The world wasn't that big back then. The Pheasantry, the Ad Lib, the Scotch, the Crazy Elephant, the Speakeasy, Blaises, the Bag were all the places you went to and if you saw Jimi or Paul [McCartney] or Mick [Jagger] you'd say 'hi', have a quick drink and a chat. There was no big deal about it."

Hendrix was quick to make an impression on Mankowitz, a man with a keen eye for image and presentation. "He was always vibrant. Brian Jones used to take him to Granny Takes A Trip and he was also introduced to the Portobello Road and Kensington markets," he says. "And he took to that look of the day – velvet, silk lace, ruffs and scarves – without ever looking effeminate."

Interestingly, the colourful look that Hendrix, The Stones and even The Beatles were sporting – as they discovered flower power at the first stirrings of the hippy movement – was largely ignored by Britain's mass media, and so was the music that was being wrapped up and delivered under the heading of psychedelia.

Peter Jenner recalls that, when Joe Boyd needed a last-minute replacement band at the UFO club, "I rang up the agency and asked them to get another group and they sent down The In Crowd. I was pretty nervous at the thought of a group called The

6

In Crowd playing the UFO, but when they arrived they told me that they had changed their name to Tomorrow. So they played – and blew everybody's minds! Jimi leapt up on stage and played bass and it was all very amazing."

Despite Hendrix impressing Boyd both on record and on stage, the co-owner of the UFO never actually booked The Experience to play at a club where commercial success was seen as a sell-out. "When we opened, Hendrix was a pop act and we were an underground club ...it wasn't until Pink Floyd sort of graduated to being a bigger act, followed by Soft Machine, that the two worlds met," he explains.

"We were coming up and merging into the world of pop music, which was taking more acid, and coming down to merge with our world," reflects Boyd, who also faced a business decision in the spring of 1967. "By that time we wouldn't have been able to afford him, and when we could have afforded him we didn't want him. He was from another world in the early days."

When it was pointed out to him that Dickins was booking out Hendrix for around £25 a night in the early days of 1967 after 'Hey Joe' came out, Boyd admits he might have had second thoughts. "If I had known he was available for £25 I might have tried to book him," he says, while recalling the reaction of his clients to other pop acts he booked. "I got static from our hard-and-fast fans for booking Tomorrow, The Move and Procol Harum."

Though fans of underground music were filing into the UFO – once described by Paul McCartney as "a trippy adventure playground" – there was a distinct lack of interest in the wider world. "It was only the kids who were into psychedelia and the music," says Jenner, "and the kids didn't count for much back then, which was why the mass media ignored all the new music." During the first six months of 1967, none of Britain's major national newspapers were moved to include a report that even mentioned the likes of Cream, Hendrix or Pink Floyd, despite their records crashing into the upper reaches of the charts.

The first major feature relating to this counter-culture appeared in the Daily Mirror on Saturday June 24, but it was all about hairstyles! Under the heading "Now It's The Wild Freakout", the article focused on "frizzy mops" and noted that "there are quite a lot of these hairdos around at the moment". After suggesting that it all started with Bob Dylan ("who bizarrely had naturally curly hair"), the story reckoned that it caught on in Britain thanks to Eric Clapton ("who had a perm") and ended by saying, "If your television screen is big enough you may have noticed Jimi Hendrix's [frizzy mop] the

6

other week", a reference to his recent Top Of The Pops appearance.

At the same time, the UK's leading music business publication Record Retailer decided to run a feature warning the record-shop owners of Britain about underground music and drugs. Under the heading "Psychedelic Music Craze: Does It Bring New Problems For Dealers?", they gave retailers a few useful hints about the shopping habits of drug users. "Drugs do have enormous dangers. But a heavy junkie is likely to be too dozy to want to hang around a record store making a nuisance of himself. And anyone under the influence of LSD is unlikely to be able to co-ordinate sufficiently to even enter a shop."

The same paper's analysis of the British charts during the second quarter of 1967 – from April to June – saw The Jimi Hendrix Experience top a chart for the first time. Thanks to the success of 'Purple Haze', they were Number 1 in the Singles; Artist/ Groups section, ahead of The Monkees and The Mamas & The Papas, while 'Purple Haze' was at Number 8 in the overall singles section.

On June 4, The Experience returned to Epstein's theatre for their second appearance on a 'Sunday At The Saville' bill. This time they performed alongside Procol Harum (who had just hit Number 1 with 'A Whiter Shade Of Pale'), The Chiffons and Denny Laine's Electric String Band.

The theatre's general manager, Tony Bramwell, had given Hendrix's manager an advance copy of The Beatles' Sgt Pepper album in the week before it came out. "Brian [Epstein] had some copies which he shared out and I gave one to Chas, who played it to Jimi at the flat in Montagu Square. I knew Jimi had heard it and just thought he might do something at the show."

Somebody else who heard the advance copy of The Beatles' eighth studio album – and their eighth consecutive UK Number 1 – was Roger Mayer. The man who helped create Hendrix's unique guitar sound was with him on the day he got the pre-release version and recalls, "I remember listening to the acetate in the flat and Jimi kept saying, 'Listen to that.'" Mayer also knows what went through the guitarist's mind as he listened to the latest offering from the world's biggest group.

"He loved to have fun and tongue-in-cheek fun for him was going out on stage knowing they [The Beatles] were in the audience and starting out with a few bars of 'Sgt Pepper' ... but doing it his way," said Mayer. "Giving it a few bars and letting people know, 'I could have made that song my own.' It was a little bit of brinkmanship."

Bramwell's suspicions of what was going to happen on the night proved correct

6

when it came to the afternoon run-through at the Saville. "He rehearsed it in the afternoon and painted his guitar in rainbow colours backstage during the afternoon."

Among the audience in the theatre that night was folk singer Donovan, who recalls a huge turnout of stars – "The Beatles and The Rolling Stones sat in opposite boxes over the stage" – and gave his reaction to what was happening. "The Experience performed 'Wild Thing' and an amazing version of 'Sgt Pepper's Lonely Hearts Cub Band'. Both blew us all away as Jimi took the tunes into the stratosphere on his Stratocaster guitar."

Watching from one of the boxes as Hendrix stepped through the curtain and walked forward across the stage playing 'Sgt Pepper' was Paul McCartney, and, as one of the creators of the band's critically acclaimed concept album, he was overwhelmed by Hendrix's tribute. "That was like the ultimate compliment", he said, before adding, "to think that the album had meant so much to him as to actually do it by Sunday night, three days after the release."

As well as Hendrix's opening salvo, Bramwell was also forewarned about the guitarist's finale. "I knew he was going to set fire to his guitar because he had done it at the Astoria and warned us that he was going to do it again. It was all very strict in those days with theatre regulations, so we had to have a fire blanket on the side of the stage and a theatre fireman in attendance. If he hadn't warned us we would have been in big trouble."

Having paid Hendrix and his band £25 on their Saville debut in January, Bramwell doubled their money to £50 for the 30-minute show in June, but points out that "there were no backstage riders in those days, not even for The Beatles, although I might give an act a bottle of Scotch if they had a good show. I can't remember whether I did for Jimi that night!"

Aware of Hendrix's future overseas touring plans, Epstein threw an after-show supper party at his London house in Chapel Street, where McCartney was apparently on the door to welcome Hendrix, Mitchell and Redding. And he was seemingly still bowled over by the performance. "It's a pretty major compliment in anyone's book. I put that down as one of the great honours of my career."

While Epstein was hosting what he saw as a "farewell and good luck" party for Hendrix, the man himself told the Saville Theatre crowd, "This is our last gig here for a long time, so we're gonna make it nice." A week later, just before playing his first ever concerts in his homeland, Hendrix told the NME, "In America people are much more narrow-minded than they are in Britain. If they do like us – great! If not, too bad. I don't

6

really think we'll achieve as much success there as we have done here."

The opportunity to return and perform in America came in a large part from Paul McCartney who, even before hearing 'Sgt Pepper' at the Saville Theatre, had been a fan. And when American record producer Lou Adler and John Phillips, founder of The Mamas & The Papas, got together to organize a pop music festival in Monterey, California, he had the chance to recommend acts for the three-day event.

McCartney nominated The Experience as one of the most important UK acts, recalling that, "John Phillips and some others came to see me in London, asking if The Beatles would perform. I said we couldn't but recommended Jimi Hendrix. Jimi played it and he was great." Despite the fact that it wasn't going to be a well-paid show, manager Chandler still saw the festival as a major opportunity. "We all realized something big was going to happen. It was such a good idea and it could only have been done through the goodwill of the artists."

Armed with first class air tickets, The Experience travelled to California to join a bill that featured The Mamas & The Papas, Otis Redding, The Grateful Dead, Buffalo Springfield and The Who. According to Adler, who launched Ode Records in 1967, the ethos surrounding Monterey was simple. "Nobody got paid at Monterey, except for Ravi Shankar, who had a contract [with the original festival organizers]. Our philosophy was do everything for the acts that the acts and their representatives have been screaming about for years. We provided the best sound system, first-class transportation, good food, good rooms – everything for the artist."

The festival, set for June 16-18, 1967, had been taken over from the previous organizers by Adler and Phillips in exchange for $50,000. Part of the plan to recoup some of the costs was a US television broadcast via the ABC network but, according to Phillips, that deal fell apart thanks to Hendrix. "When this southern gentleman (ABC president Tom Moore) saw the footage of Hendrix banging his amplifier and balling his guitar he said, 'I'm sorry, ABC cannot be part of this.'"

Just before he left the UK, Hendrix apparently told girlfriend Kathy Etchingham, "I'm going home. Home to America again." He recognized who was responsible for the opportunity to play his homeland. "Paul McCartney was the big, bad Beatle, the beautiful cat who got us the gig at the Monterey Pop Festival. That was our start in America."

Hendrix found himself facing rivals The Who on the final night of the festival, and the running order was the subject of some discussion. "I said, 'OK, let's toss a coin,'" recalls

6

Pete Townshend. "So we tossed a coin and we got to go on first." There was no doubt in Mitch Mitchell's mind that they were going to follow a class act. "They [The Who] were incredibly good, as usual, but we were too on edge to enjoy it. When Pete broke up his guitar … we thought how do you top this?"

Monterey was going to be a first chance for the Reprise label's record executives to see exactly what they had signed up for – and for veteran producer and Atlantic Records founder Jerry Wexler it was a shock. "I'd known Jimi since his back-up days with King Curtis. There he was, however, a veteran of the soul circuit, in crazy feathers and psychedelic gear. 'It's only for the show' he whispered in my ear before going out."

To get proceedings under way, Rolling Stone Brian Jones had flown over to introduce Hendrix and his band to an estimated audience of 90,000 fans and he did so in glowing terms. "I'd like to introduce a very good friend, a fellow countryman of yours … he's the most exciting performer I've ever heard – The Jimi Hendrix Experience." With that, the trio went into a nine-song set which featured 'Hey Joe', 'Purple Haze' and 'Like A Rolling Stone', where Hendrix moved from the second verse to the fourth, commenting, "Yes, I know I missed a verse, don't worry". He then set his guitar alight during closing number 'Wild Thing'.

According to Mitchell, the excellence of The Who forced the band to "roast the Fender again" as they strove to outdo their British rivals and impress the US fans. "He wanted to pull out all the stops. It was a hard job after The Who," added Redding, while manager Chandler recalled (and claimed), "The audience went berserk. We let off fireworks and his guitar caught fire."

"I'm gonna sacrifice something here that I really love," Hendrix told the Monterey crowd and film cameras, adding 'Don't think I'm silly doing this 'cos I don't think I'm losing my mind.' The instrument he incinerated during the performance of 'Wild Thing' was a red rosewood neck Strat it's said he borrowed especially for the purpose. He'd painted it white, then decorated with his own artwork.

The iconic pic by Ed Caraeff of Hendrix summoning the flames higher with his fingers will forever summon up Monterey for those who were there and the majority of Hendrix fans who weren't.

Watching all this from the side of the stage was Pete Townshend. He was seated with Mama Cass, who turned to him and said, "Isn't this guy stealing your act?" The Who's lead guitarist replied, "Yeah, but you see he's so fucking great, who cares?" Bizarrely, the men from Reprise seemed to care, with chairman Mo Ostin apparently none too

WHERE'S THE STAGE, MAN?

impressed by what he saw.

"He told me he was a little embarrassed by the lighter-fuel spectacle," recounts Reprise executive Stan Cornyn, who himself still had moments of doubt. "Clearly Jimi Hendrix was for all of us an acquired taste and I'm not sure that many finally acquired it", although he accepted that something was about to change. "The feedback, the eerie modulations, those changed rock the way 'The Rite Of Spring' changed classical."

In fact, Monterey was the first time anyone from Reprise Records actually saw Hendrix in the flesh – either for a meeting or on stage – and Cornyn still recalls the show as being "Exceptional for all of us. And we were the ones who signed The Grateful Dead too! Now this?"

For Hendrix, playing in northern California, just down the coast from his home town of Seattle, was a new pinnacle in his career. There were press reports that his Monterey set had made him the biggest star in the US – "45 minutes earlier he was unheard-of, and the burning of the guitar made the headlines" – while the man himself simply said, "When we're on stage it's all there is in the world – that's your whole life."

Hendrix took the festival stage still largely unknown to the American audience compared with fellow acts the Beach Boys, the Animals, and Simon and Garfunkel. He left it having burned his name into his country's psyche – and, thanks to the film that followed in 1968, rock fans across the globe.

The Experience's appearance at Monterey brought them a varied reaction from the media. The NME reported that "the areas around the backstage area filled up faster with musicians than for any other acts", and concluded, "For a man yet to have a big record in the US, Jimi created a fantastic response", but there was a less enthusiastic response from renowned American journalist Jann Wenner. Writing for Melody Maker, the man who would launch Rolling Stone magazine five months later concluded that, "Jimi Hendrix made a memorable return to America. Although he handled his guitar with rhythmic agility and minor drama he is not the great artist we are told. His real art is in his presence."

US music trade paper Billboard was also less than convinced by Hendrix's return to perform in his native land, dubbing it "sensationalism, not music". It then concluded, "The Jimi Hendrix Experience from Britain, making its American debut (although Hendrix is from Seattle), proved to be more presence than music, pop or otherwise. When he sings, Hendrix has trouble with phasing and his modal-tuned chicken-choke handling of the guitar doesn't indicate a strong talent either."

JIMI HENDRIX MADE IN ENGLAND

6

These comments were a step up from the Daily Mirror's report of the festival, which managed to completely ignore Hendrix (and The Who) and focus on the worrying appearance of hippies, flowers, peace and love and drugs! But for festival organizer Phillips, Hendrix's Monterey moment stayed with him long after the show had ended. "I think Jimi's gonna be remembered for centuries, just like Lead Belly and Lightnin' Hopkins. He's really a folk hero."

The Jimi Hendrix Experience remained in America throughout June, with pioneering West Coast promoter Bill Graham booking them in for six nights at the Fillmore West in San Francisco. For Mitchell, this represented a major upswing in the band's fortunes. "We came out of that gig [Monterey] with nothing. We had no gigs. We were saved by Bill Graham, who picked us up for the Fillmore, and by John Phillips, who booked us to open for The Mamas & The Papas at the Hollywood Bowl."

Promoter Graham paid The Hendrix Experience $500 a night for their Fillmore shows – plus, according to Chandler, "a bonus of $2,000 each … also engraved antique watches". Graham recognized Hendrix's ability as a performer – "He was supreme" – and acknowledged that the guitarist played another role. "He was also a fashion leader. He came to San Francisco with a scarf tied around his knee. When he left there was one on the elbow and one around the head. All of a sudden, everyone else was doing the same."

Despite mixed reviews and less than sell-out dates, Hendrix was still moved by his return to America in the middle of 1967. "I felt like I was coming back to reality after a tab of acid. For a few minutes I wondered if I had ever been to England at all." Seemingly less enamored by it all was bassist Redding, who recalled, "I was completely disillusioned with America at first."

Henry McCullough was in America playing club dates with Eire Apparent when Hendrix returned. "That was when I first saw him play, on those mid-1967 US dates, and I recall that Buddy Miles came and jammed with him on one of the shows. He was a very skilled player and he did fool around a little on stage and change the numbers without telling anyone."

McCullough recalls that "We did meet Jimi in Chas's flat back then, but none of us had any idea what was going on with him except for 'Hey Joe' and 'Purple Haze.'" Those two records had been enough to convince him that Hendrix was something special. "They were like something else, like turning a page in a new book."

After their month-long tour together through April 1967, John Walker and Jimi

WHERE'S THE STAGE, MAN?

Hendrix met up a few times around the London club scene. The American singer, who had his only solo hit with 'Annabella' in July of the same year, was candid about the socializing that went on. "We were all big drinkers in those days but I don't think the Scotch and the dope was as bad as the damn sleeping pills – they really screwed us all up."

While extolling the virtues of Hendrix the musician – "He was such a talent, a great player who just wanted to perform and excite audiences" – Walker also saw the human side of the man. "There was nothing inside of him that was bad and I really cared about him." And Walker was concerned as the 23-year-old returned to his homeland, "It broke my heart because America is the land of plenty and I'm not talking about good stuff. He didn't have somebody who cared enough about him to keep the crap away from him, and like most musicians he didn't have any real self-discipline."

While he was concerned for Hendrix's well-being, Walker also recognized how important the country of his birth was to the young man from Seattle. "I think America was the beginning of the end of his life, though to become a huge star there meant an awful lot to him." Although one performance at a pop festival and 13 follow-up shows in San Francisco were hardly the stuff to make you a headline act, Hendrix's star was in the ascendancy and throughout the summer of 1967 The Experience did their best to crack the US market.

According to Hendrix, it was a simply a case of "Now they're starting to catch on to us so it's the right time", but two men in the UK who spent time with him knew that America represented something more. "It was great for him to go there and see that he could be accepted," says Roger Mayer. "But it was never a do-or-die ambition of his."

Geno Washington nevertheless recognized a sense of pride in his fellow countryman. "Jimi was proud of breaking America. He knew he had created history after Monterey and that made me very, very happy because he was from the chitlin' circuit and had come a long, long way," explains the soul singer, who took the opportunity to remind Hendrix of an earlier incident. "He knew he had created history and I told him he did it 'with my fucking jacket'. He always laughed at that."

John Walker was not the only person who was worried about Hendrix in 1967, but it wasn't what might be on offer in America that concerned Kathy Etchingham. "Acid was just starting to be introduced into London and there was a lot of gibbering from people like Jimi and Brian [Jones] about how they were expanding their minds and seeing new insights into the meaning of life."

6

While this aspect of Britain's rapidly expanding drug culture "bored her", Etchingham looked on as Jimi got more into drugs. He took to keeping his store of LSD in the fridge of their flat in Upper Berkeley Street and even meeting the press while 'under the influence'. "I would sit and listen to Jimi giving interviews, spouting this most ridiculous acid-inspired stuff, which the journalist would soak up as if it were timeless wisdom," she explains.

Reports were coming back from America than Hendrix was spending time with the ultimate 'rock chick', Janis Joplin. She and her band Big Brother & The Holding Company had been on the bill at Monterey and then supported The Experience on dates at Fillmore West. According to one of her closest friends, Joplin – who died of a drug overdose in Hollywood in 1970, aged just 27 – "was in love with Jimi and they were doing heroin together".

As Hendrix was playing his first dates back in America, Eric Clapton, in conversation with Disc magazine's Penny Valentine, explained that Cream's "great popularity" was due to the fact that Jimi was out of the country. "That's our real competition," declared Clapton before admitting, "We're always getting compared, and when he's around we knuckle under."

During the time he spent in California – between June 17 and July 1 – Hendrix made a visit to the offices of Reprise Records, located on the Warner Bros. film set in Burbank. And Stan Cornyn was there to greet the young guitarist. "I met him when he came solo to my office in the old building we had in Burbank," he recounts. "Hendrix came in the door wearing his regalia, boa included, to shake my hand. 'Shake' puts it too strongly as his proffered hand was limp and it was like his body that morning was without bones." Hendrix made no real effort to make conversation and it was left to Cornyn to make the running. "We spent a few minutes together, politely I said a few admiring sentences, then he moved off. 'What was all that about?' I wondered. Hendrix seemed utterly dazed."

The next thing on the agenda was a booking which upset Hendrix and enraged Chandler. When Jeffery called to say that he had got The Experience "on the hottest tour in America", Chandler was curious to know who the main act was. "When he told me it was The Monkees, I dropped the fucking phone. I couldn't believe it."

When he asked Hendrix what he thought, the guitarist apparently replied, 'What's Jeffery doing?' Chandler, meanwhile, told his partner in no uncertain terms that he wanted nothing to do with the proposed 29-date US tour with Davy Jones, Micky

WHERE'S THE STAGE, MAN?

6

Dolenz, Peter Tork and Mike Nesmith. "I said it would be a fucking disaster and I told the boys that I wouldn't go with them on the tour."

Bizarrely, Hendrix was only invited on the tour because The Monkees were fans of his music. Dolenz had seen him in a club in New York at a time when they were on the lookout for an opening act for their tour. "Micky comes to me and says he has heard this trio in a club and the rock'n'roll was unlike anything any of us had ever heard," recalled Nesmith. "Micky says he wants the trio and I say fine."

The American guitar player then went off to a London club, where he met up with John Lennon, Paul McCartney, George Harrison and Eric Clapton. "This was like me with the Vatican, the pop priests of the time." When Lennon pulled out a small tape recorder and played Hendrix's 'Hey Joe' to the assembled supergroup, Nesmith "made a mental note of Jimi Hendrix".

Months later, at the Monterey Pop Festival, Dolenz and Tork caught up with Hendrix and The Monkees drummer saw a similarity in the two acts. "The Monkees were very theatrical in my eyes," commented Dolenz, "and so was The Jimi Hendrix Experience. It would make the perfect union."

As million-selling headliners with two American chart-toppers – 'Last Train To Clarksville' and 'I'm A Believer' – in their pockets, The Monkees could call the shots, and it was they who proposed to promoter Dick Clark that Hendrix should open the summer tour.

For seven nights, as the tour made its way from Florida through North Carolina and up to New York, Hendrix put up with teenage Monkees fans screaming for the made-for-TV pop group. Tork, who made a point of going to see Hendrix play "because he was a world-class musician", felt bad for the trio from Britain. "There's poor Jimi and the kids go 'We want The Monkees!' It didn't cross anybody's mind that it wasn't gonna fly."

Nesmith, too, made a point of getting to the side of the stage – sometimes in disguise – to watch Hendrix play. "It was the most exhilarating, the most majestic, the most entertaining, the most fulfilling music I'd ever heard," he later explained. He also recalled being "the only one of 10,000 people shrieking and yelling", while all around him he saw "pink, clean-cut fourteen-year-old girls who were absolutely nonplussed" by the sight of the man Dolenz described as "this black guy in a psychedelic Dayglo blouse playing music from hell, holding his guitar like he was fucking it".

The furore that accompanied the tour is something Kathy Etchingham still remembers today. "I recall that there was a hoo-ha about The Monkees tour and the fuss when all

6

the mothers complained about Jimi's stage act. But he wouldn't have been bothered about all that. He didn't worry what they thought, but just got on and did what he wanted to do."

Finally, at the Forest Hills Stadium in New York on Sunday July 16, 1967, Hendrix lost patience with the audience as they drowned out his set by shouting for The Monkees. "The yelling got so bad that he walked off stage," recalls Nesmith. "He was in the middle of a number, threw his guitar down, flipped everyone the bird (America's middle-finger salute) and said 'fuck you' and walked off. I turned to Micky and said 'Good for him.'"

Dolenz later recalled that even if the fans didn't appreciate the sight of The Experience, The Monkees had a good time. "Jimi was really one of the nicest people I've ever known. We all had a lot of fun in the hotels. The Monkees were into chicks and being drunk and stoned and so was Jimi's band," he said. "The little kids didn't understand their music but we all had such a good time off stage."

For Experience drummer Mitchell, the tour with The Monkees was a case of déjà vu. "We thought, 'Here we go again.' After The Walker Brothers and Engelbert, we get The Monkees." Nevertheless, he did find something positive in the tour. "We did a couple of days on Greyhound buses and we discovered that Peter Tork could play banjo, Mike Nesmith could play guitar, Micky Dolenz was one hell of a nice guy and Davy Jones was extremely short!"

US music magazine Billboard had carried a story which predicted that The Monkees' largest gross earnings from the tour – reckoned to be over $300,000 – would come from the three dates at Forest Hills, which is where Hendrix decided enough was enough. He told Melody Maker, "They gave us the 'death spot' on the show, right before The Monkees were due on. Some parents who brought their young kids complained that our act was too vulgar. We decided it was just the wrong audience. I think they're replacing me with Mickey Mouse."

One man who found some joy in Hendrix's aborted attempts to entertain America's teeny-pop fans was Stephen Stills. Then a member of Buffalo Springfield, he later told writer Dave Zimmer about the effect it had on him. "Jimi was my guru, man. Some people thought we were fags or that I was a groupie, but hey, it wasn't like that at all. I was going to music school, learning how to play the lead guitar."

Stills reveals he "followed Jimi Hendrix all around the country for a year learning how to play." He and Hendrix began jamming in clubs with other musicians like Buddy Miles and Johnny Winter. "Jimi and I played for fourteen hours once at my house in Malibu.

WHERE'S THE STAGE, MAN?

We must have made up fifteen rock'n'roll songs, but forgot them all, because it wasn't taped. We just played for the ocean."

Jeffery's plan to put his act on tour with the biggest pop act in the world had seriously backfired, and it was left to Chas Chandler to get the group out of that situation. There had been talk before the tour began that putting Hendrix on a bill with The Monkees was a publicity stunt dreamed up by Chandler and that the plot to get him fired was hatched before the first date in Jacksonville, Florida, on July 8.

That seems unlikely in view of Chandler's reaction to the tour and the fact that he was left to meet up with tour promoter Dick Clark – the host of American's earliest pop TV show, American Bandstand – and explain that it was "not a compatible combining of talents".

In an attempt to save face, Chandler and his PR team came up with a story that the right-wing Daughters of the American Revolution had waged a campaign to get Hendrix banned because his act was 'obscene' – this despite the fact that, as far as anyone knew, nobody from the organization had ever actually seen him on stage.

This fiction created for the music trade magazines and the industry to persuade them that Hendrix had "not been jerked off the tour" soon became a news story with an extra dimension. "We did expect to get sued by the Daughters of the American Revolution and we never were," Chandler recalled, adding that his partner was less than happy with the outcome. "When I told Mike what I had done, all hell broke loose. He said I was a stupid idiot and shot off to Majorca for seven months." Jeffery's non-appearance was nothing new to Mitchell, who once noted, "We only ever saw Jeffery about twice in the first year, any of us. You never knew what he was up to or where he was."

While Chandler's 'story' failed to make any impression with Britain's national newspapers – not a single line about him leaving The Monkees tour appeared anywhere –the music papers went along with what they were told. Melody Maker's front page on July 29 carried the headline "Hendrix In US Tour Ban", with the story that his act had been deemed "too erotic" for the young Monkees audience. The NME also reported that Hendrix had been sacked after protests from the Daughters of the American Revolution, but threw in the possibility that the musician had "quit in anger" after being asked to open the shows.

Despite the fiasco, Hendrix held no malice towards the four young American musicians. While he got on with his career and they continued on their US tour, he

6

reflected that despite being like "plastic Beatles", the individual members of the band were good company. "Don't get me wrong, I liked The Monkees themselves. The personal part was beautiful," he said.

The day after ending his association with the tour, Hendrix – seemingly without his two bandmates – entered Studio 76 on New York's Broadway to record with Curtis Knight at the behest of Ed Chalpin from PPX. Hendrix was reported as saying that Curtis had wanted them to record together for "old time's sake", while Chalpin was apparently "causing problems at Track".

In an effort to "cool everybody out", Hendrix dropped into the studio and played on two tracks with Knight, 'Flashing' and 'Hush Now', which he understood were being recorded but were later described as "a jam session". While Chalpin stressed that there was no way Hendrix could not have realized they were recording the session – "Hendrix entered the control room to hear the results in order to judge whether they had been recorded correctly," he explained – Hendrix himself went on record to say, "I said I'd play on some tracks for Curtis but that they couldn't use my name. Curtis agreed."

Elated by his Monterey triumph, he would record his next single, 'Burning Of The Midnight Lamp', on his way back to London. Hendrix visited another studio in New York in late July, this time with Mitchell and Redding in tow, to record the track that was both The Experience's third Hendrix-penned and their fourth British single release. The lyrics were mainly written while aboard a plane in the US and were melancholic ("The morning is dead and the day is too"), dealing with loneliness and isolation with a hint of lost love.

Notable for Hendrix playing harpsichord and the presence of Aretha Franklin's backing group The Sweet Inspirations, 'Burning Of The Midnight Lamp' used the eight-track facility of New York's Mayfair Studio to its fullest. It would be the band's last single release of the year outside the US, where Reprise were still trying to catch up with the success story.

If Jimi Hendrix's career had been made in the United Kingdom, he was now intent on bringing it back home with a vengeance…

I CAN'T REMEMBER ALL THE THINGS I DO

7

The Experience continued to make their way across America, from New York to Washington, D.C. and on to Los Angeles. Mitch Mitchell, for one, was "knocked out with the reaction … We went out unknowns, but on every gig there were fans who knew our LP tracks. It's like a status symbol to own an English LP. We went out on a three-week promotion trip and it lasted two-and-a-half months."

It was at the Fifth Dimension Club in Ann Arbor, Michigan on August 15, 1967, that Hendrix was first photographed on stage playing his new Gibson Flying V guitar, which he had painted in a psychedelic design. At some time he also went on record to talk about his guitar-smashing – "We just try not to bore ourselves and hope the audience likes it" – and his playing. "Sometimes I grind the strings up against the frets. The more it grinds, the more it whines. Sometimes I rub up against the amplifier. Sometimes I play the guitar with my teeth or with my elbow. I can't remember all the things I do."

Whatever he was doing, Hendrix was making a major impact across America as he played the Gaslight, Café Au Go Go and Salvation clubs, plus the Ambassador Theatre and the Hollywood Bowl. Along the way he was played with the likes of B.B. King, The Mamas & The Papas, Moby Grape and Natty Bumppo and found time to jam with Frank Zappa, John Hammond and his old mate Eric Clapton. "On return visits to New York, I used to go down to the [Greenwich] Village with Jimi and we'd go from one club to another just the two of us," says Clapton. "We'd play with whoever was on stage that night. We'd get up and jam and just wipe everybody out."

With all the attention focused on his stage presence, the level of volume – "I didn't see how anybody could inflict that kind of volume on himself, let alone other people," observed Frank Zappa – and his playing, Hendrix was once moved to analyze his own

7

technique. "I think I am a better guitarist than I was. I've learned a lot, but I've got to learn a lot more about music," he confessed, "because there's a lot in this hair that's got to get out. I want other musicians to play my stuff. I want to be a good writer."

Hendrix also found time to indulge not just his love for cars in general but for one car in particular – the Corvette Stingray. During his lifetime – and despite poor vision – Hendrix actually bought six of them, but this first one was a rainbow-painted psychedelic dream machine which reached a top speed of 160 mph. At some time he took esteemed American rock critic Jane Scott on a shopping trip, as her 2011 obituary records the fact that she went to help him "buy a new blue Corvette".

One-time roadie James 'Tappy' Wright recalls the guitarist's love affair with his first multi-coloured sports car. "This car was his baby, beautiful and fast and for his use only, despite his terrible eyesight, which prevented him from achieving a licence to drive it." The fact he never actually passed a driving test did not stop Hendrix from taking his sports car out for a spin and then leaving it as close to his destination as possible – but rarely in a designated car park.

Hendrix's car was often towed away and impounded but that didn't bother the singer, who would simply take a cab home. For Gerry Stickells, who had been given a spare set of keys, it meant a constant round of rescuing the Stingray, paying the fine and returning it to wherever Hendrix happened to be.

With America over and done with for a while, Hendrix and his crew returned to the UK around August 21, 1967 and, with the new single 'Burning Of The Midnight Lamp' to promote, they immediately stepped back into the swing of things. Dee Time, hosted by ex-radio DJ Simon Dee, was a prime-time BBC-TV entertainment show and this appearance was followed two days later, on August 24, by the obligatory performance on Top Of The Pops.

These shows helped push the new single into the charts, although it would end up being a blip in the annus mirabilis, peaking at a modest Number 18 in a UK chart topped first by off-the-shelf hippie anthem 'San Francisco' (Flowers In Your Hair)' and the dreaded Engelbert Humperdinck's 'Last Waltz'. It was the group's first release not to reach the UK Top 10.

Reviewing the singles in Melody Maker's Blind Date feature at the end of August was Kinks' guitarist and singer Dave Davies, whose conclusion was less than entirely positive. "An instant hit. Horrible song but a fantastic production." Davies' sentiments coincided with some other less than enthusiastic reactions, but Hendrix remained unmoved by the first set of indifferent reviews he had suffered. "I don't really care what our records do chart-wise. Everybody round here hated [that record], but to me it was the best we ever made."

Phil Swern, now a highly respected radio producer, worked for Strike Records as a 17-year-old runner. The label was based in Upper Berkeley Street, in the same building as the flat shared by Hendrix and Kathy Etchingham. It was there, in 1967, that Swern first came across his neighbour.

"I used to see Jimi Hendrix in the lift quite often. He used to frighten the life out of me with the way he looked – the wild hair and the outlandish clothes." While he recalls one specific occasion when Hendrix was dressed in leather and all in black, he points out, "As it was his home I also saw him in sweaters and other casual things."

One of Strike's signings was the up-and-coming folk singer Roy Harper, who released his debut collection of poetry and songs, Sophisticated Beggar, in December 1966. It was a record Hendrix heard but was seemingly reluctant to buy. "One day I go into the lift on the ground floor and Jimi was in there," explains Swern. "He asked if I worked 'for that lot upstairs' – Strike was in an office above his flat – and when I said 'yes' he explained that he knew we had released an album by Roy Harper and that he would really love a copy. He said, 'Do you think you can get me one?', and I told him I was sure I could."

Within a few days, Swern had 'borrowed' a copy from the Strike cupboard – "I didn't dare ask for one" – and made his way to Hendrix's flat. "One afternoon during my tea break I went down and rang his doorbell. He opened the door and invited me in.".

Swern's arrival at Hendrix's door some time in the late summer of 1967 coincided with the musician preparing afternoon tea. "He had just made some tea and some sandwiches and he asked me if I wanted some. I was very nervous, which he obviously noticed because he said, 'You're really nervous, aren't you?' Then we sat and chatted, mainly just about music."

The pair of them swapped stories about songs, singers and new styles of music. "I told him I remembered the original version of 'Hey Joe' by The Leaves, so we talked about that," recalls Swern, "and also about some of the early psychedelic music that was just coming out of America, and we chatted about James Brown for a bit."

Swern was impressed with Hendrix's attitude to a teenage record-company junior. "He was very charming and very quietly spoken, but I have to say that I was too young and innocent to know whether he was stoned or not. He did seem very normal. I was there for well over 15 minutes because I got into trouble when I got back for taking too long over my tea break. The Strike people were not impressed with me spending time

7

with Jimi Hendrix when I should have been looking after their artists."

The office boy and rock star met a few more times in the lift. "He did invite me back for tea but it never happened as he was off on tour a lot after that. But he did sign a copy of his first album for me, which I still have," says Swern proudly.

Being back in Britain meant Hendrix could once again spend time in the Speakeasy – either relaxing or jamming with whoever was on stage. According to Roger Mayer, who believes he saw Hendrix play live close to 90 times, the trip always prompted one question: "When we were going to the Speak, sometimes I'd say, 'Shall I put a guitar in the car?', and Jimi would just say, 'Yeah, you never know.'"

The opportunity to play with other musicians was something Hendrix cherished, recalls Mayer. "I have never met anybody who wanted to play the guitar more. He just liked to be around people who had fun. He never wanted to intimidate anyone and was always very polite. He was a very nice guy."

Remembering nights spent in dark and smoky clubs, Keith Emerson reckons he never saw anything other than great mutual respect between the guitar greats. "I never saw any jealousy. Jimi had the fondest respect for Eric Clapton and all the guitar players wanted to learn from him [Hendrix]," he says. "There was an aura and confidence about Jimi that just drew others. 'Hey, Jimi just walked in the room.'"

One group who found themselves sharing the stage with Hendrix at the Speakeasy in the late summer of 1967 were Les Fleur De Lys, complete with the two former flatmates Gordon Haskell and Keith Guster plus guitarist Bryn Haworth. "Jimi didn't seem to be aware that he was once in a flat with us," recalls Guster. "He never said a word about it and we never got a chance to say anything about it."

On the night in question, Hendrix apparently sat through the first set by Les Fleurs before spotting the band's guitarist. "He invited me over to his table for a drink," says Haworth. "He was there in his big black hat and he got me a rum and coke and then told me he really liked the solo I had played on a Sharon Tandy record called 'Hold On'."

The track was the B-side of the South African singer's Atlantic release 'Stay With Me', and one reviewer concluded that it "featured the band in stunning form with Haworth's guitar solo helping fashion one of the most memorably neglected moments to emerge from the late Sixties UK scene".

What astounded Haworth was that Hendrix, who had spent the summer in America, had even heard the track. "It was quite stunning. I thought, 'How did he ever get hold of that?' And then I was struck by his humility. He was really just another musician and

7

the conversation was totally all about music. We talked about nothing else. He was just an ordinary man who loved playing the guitar and he didn't seem to reckon much of himself either."

Hendrix surprised Haworth further by announcing that he had a plan to produce 'Hold On' with a group called Eire Apparent. "Then I asked him if he wanted to come up and jam and he said 'yeah'. I always used to take two guitars – a Strat and a Telecaster – just in case somebody like Clapton or even one of The Beatles wanted to get up and play."

For both Haskell and Guster it was, and still remains, a memorable moment. "We just did a blues jam with Jimi on guitar. He took the white Strat, turned it upside-down and played it. That was a sign of his genius," says Guster, while Haskell has a similar memory. "He played it amazingly upside-down, back to front – that did blow our minds."

Standing on stage next to one of his guitar heroes as he played a borrowed guitar also left a deep impression with Haworth. "He played 'Blues In E' with us and he played with the same dexterity as if my guitar had been strung left-handed. He just turned my guitar upside-down and whacked away and you would not have known any difference."

Guster, seated behind his drum kit throughout this unrehearsed showcase, remembers vividly what went on in front of him. "It went on for about 15 minutes, with Jimi and Bryn sharing a legendary Vox AC30 amp, and after I recall that Jimi asked if he could play bass. So we did another thing with Jimi on Gordon's bass but I don't know where Gordon was during that."

While Haworth has a similar memory to Guster – "I'm sure he played bass as well and he was scarily good on that too" – Haskell can't remember where he was either. "I do recall Jimi asking me to sing 'a blues', but I didn't know what he meant and was just stood there laughing. I was probably the worse for wear by then."

Keyboardist Pete Sears believes the event was recorded in sound and vision and claims Hendrix "was seen filming us on stage with his home video camera. We were playing at the Speakeasy, kind of out of it at the time, more out on the edge then we usually were musically, very strange stuff. I'm playing the organ and then, all of a sudden I looked up; Hendrix somehow appeared on stage with a guitar and started playing a solo; it just came out of the blue, really. It was a pleasure to see. And we were recording it on reel-to-reel in the bar, someone had a reel-to-reel machine, I have no idea what happened to the tapes, no one tried to track them down."

Felder's Orioles were another band of young hopefuls who played around the London club scene in 1967 and eventually found themselves on stage in front of Hendrix

7

during one of his nights out. Their young manager Chris Morrison remembers the band's appearances in the capital, which included both the Marquee and the Speakeasy.

"Felder's Orioles used to get paid £17 and ten shillings a night for two 45-minute sets at the Speakeasy and that was where I used to come across Hendrix," says Morrison. "They'd be up on stage and Jimi would be in the audience. After a bit he'd get up on stage, nudge the guitarist out of the way, pick up a right-handed guitar and play it upside-down, and then Noel Redding might get up too and play bass."

Morrison also recalls that his band, which featured drummer John Halsey – later to find fame in the Rutles TV show – were not always overjoyed about Hendrix's intrusion. "They'd go, 'We fucking hate playing here.' At first they were impressed with the idea of playing with Hendrix, but after a while it became too much of a regular thing and they sort of resented it a bit. It was their gig, after all!"

Someone who would have given his eye teeth for the chance was Welsh guitarist Deke Leonard. His band Lucifur (sic) and the Corncrackers were playing the Speakeasy which, he said, "paid peanuts but, if you wanted to be spotted it was the place to play. The playing times were half-hour on, half-hour off, all night from seven until four. People didn't start coming in until eleven, so the first three sets were played to a virtually empty club. We viewed these as paid rehearsals.

"On our first gig we started at seven on the dot. There was only one person in the club, a man sitting way back in the gloom. We played our first song and, when it had finished, the figure in the darkness applauded enthusiastically. We turned toward him and bowed ostentatiously. We played another song and once again the figure in the darkness applauded. We told him he was a wonderful audience and invited him to clap along with the songs.

"After our set, on the way back to the dressing room, we took a detour past our audience's table to thank him personally. All the tables were lit by candles in transparent orange glass bowls and, as we approached, our audience leant forward into the amber light. My heart stopped, my mouth went dry, and I broke out into a cold, cold sweat.

"It was Hendrix. He was dressed in the black, military jacket. He stretched out a huge, bony hand, with beautiful fingers like telegraph poles. 'Far out, man,' he said.

"In a state of shock, we made our way to the bar and tried to compose ourselves. Half-an-hour later, we were back on-stage. The place had filled up a little but Hendrix watched our second set from the same table. This time, I pulled out all the stops. Well, you would, wouldn't you?

I CAN'T REMEMBER ALL THE THINGS I DO

"By the fourth set, the place was packed and you couldn't turn around without falling over somebody famous. There were a brace of Kinks present and Graham Nash held court near the bar. We ignored them and played for the benefit of one man. He was no longer at his table but we caught the odd glimpse of him, doing some serious mingling.

"At the end of the night we packed up our gear as the crowd thinned out. Hendrix, apparently by tradition, was the last to leave, accompanied by a tall, Nordic blonde. As he walked out of the door he turned and waved goodbye to us. Grinning like synchronized swimmers, we waved back. We picked up our money and drove back down to Wales."

On their third visit to Epstein's Saville Theatre on Sunday August 27, The Experience were supported by emerging fellow Track act The Crazy World Of Arthur Brown, The Cryin' Shames and Tomorrow. During the early show, they performed Eddie Cochran's classic 'Summertime Blues' for the first and, seemingly, also the last time and gave a live debut to 'Red House' from their first album.

This was a show Joe Boyd remembers fondly. "I thought Hendrix was great live and I thought his records were great. I was a keen fan by now and he was kind of remarkable even then when there was a lot of remarkable stuff around."

Overseeing their appearance once again was the theatre's general manager Tony Bramwell, but his recollections are less positive. "The roadies had become a bit cocky and Mitch and Noel were a bit lippy, so it wasn't nearly as much fun as the earlier shows." Before the night was over, Bramwell would hear news that shocked the pop world – his boss Brian Epstein had died.

As a mark of respect, The Times reported, "The 8.30pm pop concert at the Saville Theatre headed by The Jimi Hendrix Experience last night was cancelled as a tribute to Mr. Epstein, who owned the theatre's lease."

Bramwell felt it was his duty to let Chas Chandler, a personal friend, know when his top-selling act was in danger of pushing things too far. "About that time I sat Chas down and told him that Jimi was getting a bit out of hand, hanging around with John and Paul and Brian Jones – the acid heads as we called them," Bramwell recounts. "Chas was a whisky man and he never knew about acid, but I sat him down in the Speakeasy and told him about the LSD trips and he just said, 'What? He lives with me and I never knew.'"

For his part, Redding also acknowledged the role drugs – and acid in particular – were now playing in the lives of The Experience. "We were spaced constantly. Chas stayed straight. He leaned towards whisky, which was his cure for anything."

JIMI HENDRIX MADE IN ENGLAND

As summer moved into autumn, Reprise decided the time was right to launch The Jimi Hendrix Experience's first album on the American public. At the same time, the band were embarking on a two-week tour of Europe, which featured one appearance in West Germany and ten shows in Sweden.

The show in Berlin marked the first colour transmissions on West German television and also featured Traffic, with Steve Winwood, Dave Mason, Jim Capaldi and Chris Wood. Realizing that the show's producer's knowledge of pop was limited, the musicians, it seems, switched between bands without anyone ever knowing. After this fun-filled moment it was downhill into Karlstaab in Sweden, where The Experience shared the bill with an unlikely support act.

Road manager Stickells later told people that he had asked the promoter who the opening act was, but his request was met with silence. "He couldn't even explain. Then I went out and saw this ramp and then these seals went on. They weren't even any good. Hendrix thought it was hilarious."

As The Experience made their way across northern Europe, their American label began taking adverts in the US music magazines to alert the 'trade' to what was coming. Once again the focus was on the band's frontman, with the advert in Billboard on September 9, 1967 featuring a single photo of Hendrix repeated and superimposed to create a suitable 'trippy effect'. There was no mention of either Mitchell or Redding, although the US album cover was featured alongside the arty tag line, "Another Chart imperative From Reprise Records".

The same magazine featured the new release on their important back-page Pop Spotlight section, with a brief review which read, "One of the wildest new groups around musically, The Jimi Hendrix Experience proves an exciting experience on the trio's debut album."

Despite this rousing endorsement from the leading music-business publication in the US, Reprise was not overwhelmed with orders for Are You Experienced. The leading distributor in Detroit ordered 175 copies (and got 25 of those for nothing), while in Charlotte, North Carolina, the top order was for six plus one free copy. As Stan Cornyn says, "Reception to this new Experience was cool. This was not what Reprise needed."

The arrival of Hendrix at Reprise was part of the label's effort to re-invent itself. "1967 was a major breakthrough year for us in many ways," says Cornyn. In 1966, the label had released albums by artists such as Dean Martin, Frank Sinatra and Nancy Sinatra, while sister company Warner Bros. had offered Petula Clark, comedian Bill

I CAN'T REMEMBER ALL THE THINGS I DO

Cosby, Peter, Paul & Mary and The Marketts, who hit with 'Batman's Theme'.

A year later, Hendrix sat on the roster alongside the established singers plus The Electric Prunes, Arlo Guthrie and British hit-makers The Kinks, while The Grateful Dead and Harpers Bizarre appeared on Warner Bros. According to Cornyn, this new A&R policy made "us where acts wanted to be."

For its release in America, Are You Experienced was given both a new cover and a new track listing. The British photograph by Bruce Fleming, with the band against a black background, was replaced by a shot taken by US photographer Karl Ferris, whose work would feature on the cover of all three of the band's US albums.

He used the hugely popular Sixties fad of a 'fish-eye' lens for the centrepiece shot of the trio – taken in London's Kew Gardens – which was placed on a yellow background alongside distinctly 'flower-power-hippy' lettering for the title 'areyouexperienced', which was joined together in lower case type to create just one word. Cornyn doubts that the label's art department had any say in this, believing it more likely to have come from Jimi's management "somewhere in this next step in Hendrix's career."

While Reprise may not have been responsible for the new sleeve design, they were entirely behind the decision to change the album's tracks. Out went 'Red House', 'Can You See Me' and 'Remember' to make room for the three UK hits, 'Hey Joe', 'Purple Haze' and 'The Wind Cries Mary', while the song 'Foxy Lady' was rendered as 'Foxey Lady'.

Years earlier, The Beatles had suffered a similar fate when their first seven UK albums were changed for America, getting new titles in some cases and suffering track changes on every release. This enraged both The Beatles and their producer George Martin, and Track executive Chris Stamp was no less upset when it came to Hendrix's album.

A furious Stamp declared, "They [Reprise] did exactly the sort of bullshit that record companies do. He [Jimi] didn't have control over it. Jimi always related to Track. He would always come personally with his records to Track. And he always gave his masters to Track before Reprise."

Despite, or perhaps because of the new cover and re-organized track listing, Are You Experienced made its way into the US chart at Number 100 in the first week of September 1967, a week before 'Purple Haze' first featured as a 'bubbling under' hit at Number 110. Interestingly, when the tapes of 'Purple Haze' were delivered to Reprise Records for US release, there was a note which urged the label execs to leave well alone by stating "deliberate distortion, do not correct".

Both single and the album climbed up their respective charts until the middle of

JIMI HENDRIX MADE IN ENGLAND

October, when Are You Experienced peaked at Number 5 during what would be a 19-week stay on the chart during 1967. October 14 was also when 'Purple Haze' hit its highest spot on the Billboard Hot 100, peaking at Number 65 before completing an eight-week stay. The Experience was now a hit act in the biggest market in the world.

It wasn't all rock music, gigs and parties for Hendrix, as David Arden, a kid-about-town in those days, recalls. "I used to love to be with Jimi and people like Keith Moon down at the Speakeasy, but oddly Jimi never really got involved in the big party thing." When The Who's notorious wild man drummer said, "Come on everybody, back to my place", there was one man who didn't always go. "Jimi would sort of mumble and sort of shrug and then never turn up," says Arden. "He seemed to like to be quiet and be with quieter people."

Hendrix liked to relax by playing some of the Sixties' most popular board games. "If we were at home at Chas's place we used to play Monopoly and Risk and other board games," says Roger Mayer, who was a regular visitor to the flat. While he preferred the US version of Monopoly, it seems that Risk, the game of world domination, was his favourite. "Roger was a close personal friend," confirms Kathy Etchingham, who describes the guitar technician as "one frequent and welcome caller" to their flat.

Hendrix's love of science-fiction was matched by the enjoyment he got from humour. In addition to being a fan of the US magazine Mad, he also enjoyed British comedy. "He loved listening to The Goons on the radio," explains Mayer, who lists the other things they talked about as music, food, fashion and movies, but "he wasn't into sport of any sort."

During September 1967, The Beatles started filming their TV film Magical Mystery Tour in Teignmouth in Devon. The venture was described as "a four-day coach trip of the south of England picking random locations and filming an hour-long TV show", and among the passengers on the bus were a fat lady, four dwarfs, an accordionist, a courier, a starlet and an amateur photographer.

Also there alongside the four Beatles were McCartney's brother Mike McGear, Lennon's infant son Julian, Apple electronics wizard Alexis Mardas, Liverpool actor Victor Spinetti and pop star Spencer Davis and his family, but one guest was absent. "We were supposed to be on the Magical Mystery Tour," claimed Hendrix. "The Beatles used to come and see us sometimes. Paul told me about this little scene he had. He wanted us to be in this film. He was trying to help us but we got a nice break before they got the movie together." Hendrix and his band were in Stockholm on September 11, the day filming began.

I CAN'T REMEMBER ALL THE THINGS I DO

Four days later, Hendrix and Mitch Mitchell turned up at the Bluesville 67 club in the Manor House public house in north London to join in with Eric Burdon and The New Animals. In the audience was journalist David Hughes, who had reviewed the first Experience single nine months earlier for his local paper, but who was now a writer for the music paper Disc. "It was interesting that he had been around for over six months and had hit singles and an album, played Monterey and was still playing pubs." Although he didn't review the show, Hughes recalls "It was packed out."

Such was Hendrix's standing by the autumn of 1967 that Melody Maker, in September, chose to run a half-page feature headlined "The Magnificent Seven", which assessed and compared the various merits of the country's leading 'axemen'. Writer Chris Welch opened the piece by declaring, "Guitar-slinging heroes with sideburns, wild and wooly clothes, blazing away on all six strings are a phenomenon peculiar to the rootin' tootin' British pop scene.

"These young men of the groups who beat up towns the length and breadth of the country every night with a barrage of note-bending, feedback and fuzztone" were Eric Clapton, Jimi Hendrix, Pete Townshend, Jeff Beck, Jimmy Page, Steve Winwood and Peter Green.

While five of them got worthy mentions – Townshend for being the first to use feedback; Beck as the enigma of the seven; Page for being the dark horse; Winwood as best and youngest blues player; and Green as the newest, toughest and meanest – it was the remaining two who took top honours.

Clapton was identified as "King of Britain's blues guitarists and is raved about in America, home of the blues", while Hendrix was nominated as chief competitor: "If anyone can claim [sic] to Clapton's crown, is it American Jimi Hendrix, who has settled in Britain, or rather stirred up Britain with the sensational Experience."

Melody Maker was not the only one assessing the qualities of guitar players or the state of the music business at that time. Hendrix too spent time contemplating what lay in store for both himself and other musicians. "I started thinking. Thinking about the future. Thinking that this era of music, sparked off by The Beatles, had come to an end. Something new has to come and Jimi Hendrix will be there."

While Hendrix wondered in late September 1967 what the future might hold, the present was all about awards. The Melody Maker Readers' Poll put him in top of the list as Best International Musician, ahead of his pal and hero Eric Clapton, although bizarrely the positions were reversed by the same readers when it came to Best British Musician.

JIMI HENDRIX MADE IN ENGLAND

Although Hendrix only won the one prize, he did figure prominently as fifth Best International Brightest Hope and third Best British Brightest Hope, while Are You Experienced was named fourth Best International Album and second Best British Album, with 'Hey Joe' coming in as fourth Best British Single. In its editorial comment, Melody Maker told its readers that this recognition had "set the seal on one of the fastest success stories that even the British pop scene has ever seen".

Hendrix was at London's Europa Hotel on September 16 to collect his prize from top disc jockey Jimmy Savile – the photo was Melody Maker's front-page picture the following week – and the music paper reported that Hendrix "wowed everyone with his clothes and his quiet charm". To celebrate, ANIM Management and Track Records took out a half-page advert in the music papers proclaiming, "All Hail King Jimi."

The issues which arose from Hendrix's 1965 recording session with Curtis Knight, which he did under a contract signed with Chalpin and his PPX Productions company, refused to go away, even after the guitarist had done the second set of sessions in July 1967.

Newspaper reports in September under the headline "American Producer Sues Jimi Hendrix" said that Chalpin claimed he had a valid contract with Hendrix and was intent on suing the musician and the companies "associated with him in America and Britain". For his part in the row, Stamp claimed, "This man … has a contract but we do not believe it is valid. If it goes to court we believe we have a very good chance."

However, lawyers advising Hendrix and Jeffery suggested that the New York-based producer could possibly keep Hendrix out of the studio and off the road until the problem was resolved. While various agreements were reached during the ensuing years, the legal issues would drag on into the 21st century.

The Experience's final concert of September was an unlikely, not to say strange, outing for the psychedelic three-piece on the final Monday of the month. They joined an assorted bill featuring leading folk player Bert Jansch, classical guitarist Sebastian Jorgensen and flamenco star Paco Peña at the Royal Festival Hall on London's South Bank. A "Guitar-In" had been organized to showcase different styles, with admission prices running at between five shillings (25p) and a guinea (£1.05p).

Jansch, a veteran of Britain's folk music scene for over 40 years, went on record in his biography to recall his personal highlight of Hendrix's appearance. "I enjoyed the sound check more than anything else," says the former Pentangle member who died in 2011. "He walked on, plugged into one of his pedals, turned the whole volume up as loud as possible, smashed [a chord on] the guitar once and that was it."

I CAN'T REMEMBER ALL THE THINGS I DO

The evening then became even weirder as Liberal Party leader Jeremy Thorpe was also on hand to garner some publicity for his party. He succeeded in having his photo taken with Hendrix, including one shot with the MP holding Hendrix's multi-coloured Stratocaster.

At the end of the band's US tour, Hendrix turned his attention to what his second album would sound like. He was conscious that he and his group were being judged on just ten months together and "one album and perhaps one or two concerts" and was keen to show that The Experience was much more. "I think it's time for these people to understand that we are not always in the same bag with each performance," he said.

Work on the new album began in London in Olympic Studios on October 2, 1967 with Hendrix insisting, "We have other sounds to make, other singles and LPs to cut." During the month and between gigs, the band spent 11 days recording plus extra pre-session rehearsals in both De Lane Lea and Regent Studios.

The dozen Hendrix-composed tracks, plus Noel Redding's 'She's So Fine' (an olive branch to the disgruntled bassist), were produced by Chandler, with American Eddie Kramer as engineer, with Roger Mayer on hand. "The secret of my sound," said Hendrix, "is largely the electronic genius of our tame boffin, who is known to us as Roger the Valve. Whatever incredible sounds we think up, he manages to create them. He has re-wired my guitar in a special way to produce an individual sound."

Mayer's importance is confirmed by Etchingham. "He and Jimi were on the same wavelength, talking about the sorts of sounds, feedback and distortion that Jimi wanted to achieve and adapting all sorts of electronic equipment to make the guitar sound different."

Hendrix's girlfriend's role in the proceedings was not always that of passive onlooker. "I had to stand for hours with my foot on the pedal while they fiddled about with knobs and switches," she said. "Every now and again they would tell me to press the pedal but I could never work out what they were talking about."

According to Mayer, Hendrix's work in the studio to create the new album was genuinely inspirational. "Nothing was ever written down – he had a vision which controlled what he was going to play with no preconceptions." The release of The Beatles' Sgt Pepper album in June had a major influence. "We linked up two four-track machines at Olympic to get multi-tracking," says the man whose work has bizarrely never been credited on any of The Experience's three albums. "We had more tracks and Jimi wanted to get into 'spatial movement and echo'. His studio music was something different to his live work. It was to be listened to."

JIMI HENDRIX MADE IN ENGLAND

Manager-cum-producer Chandler was, as before, responsible for the recording costs. "If you left Jimi in the studio, he would just keep playing because that was what people like him were like and I never stopped him because I wasn't paying the bill," admits Mayer, who confirms that Hendrix "chopped the second album out in about six weeks." If Hendrix was indirectly paying the bill through recouped recording costs via his contract it wasn't something that caused him any particular concern. "The money doesn't make any difference to me 'cos that's what I make the money for", he once said when asked about recording costs. "I wanna have stereo where it goes up: the sound goes up, and behind, and underneath, you know. I'm willing to spend every single penny on it, if I thought it was good enough."

Drummer Mitchell also observed something new during the making of the second album. "[It] was the first time it became apparent that Jimi was pretty good working behind the board as well as playing and he had some positive ideas of how he wanted things recorded." Acknowledging that this departure could have caused some friction with established producer Chandler, Mitchell was relieved to note, "Chas was fair, though, and realized that Hendrix knew what he was doing."

Mitchell reveals the layers of overdubs and effects that were put on the tracks did begin to cause some unrest in the band, with Redding apparently disappearing to the pub during sessions. Despite the incessant re-takes, the band's bass player still had positive things to say about the album. "The first one [album] was very raw. The second one was still raw but refined. We'd really progressed on our work in the studio."

Despite the quality of the new album, Mitchell still spotted the first signs of disquiet creeping into the trio's relationship with their manager and producer. "The strain was certainly showing between the band and Chas by the time we did the track 'Bold As Love'," he observed. "Jimi had started to find his own feet and Noel and I wanted some kind of impact with regard to our sound. Chas did his best to put up with us, which can't have been easy. Chas's patience definitely started wearing thin."

The likes of Roy Wood and Trevor Burton from The Move, The Hollies' Graham Nash and Walker Brother Gary Leeds lending support on various tracks. Mitch Mitchell had shared a flat with Nash in London during 1967 and they all spent time together, according to Mitchell's book The Hendrix Experience. Nash sang on a couple of choruses and stomped his feet for extra rhythm on 'If Six Was Nine', while Mitchell revealss "Graham and Jimi would often play together at the house, and there would be some thought given to them writing together, but I have the feeling that it was officially discouraged."

I CAN'T REMEMBER ALL THE THINGS I DO

The new album was finished by the very end of October, when proceedings suffered a major setback. Hendrix left the final mixes in the back of a taxi, which meant some serious overtime. "It was mixed beautifully, but we lost the original mix so we had to re-do it," said Hendrix. Chas and I and engineer Eddie Kramer, all of us, had to remix it the next morning within 11 hours and it's very hard to do that."

Replicating the mix for one song, 'If Six Was Nine', proved elusive, so a rough mix reel-to-reel tape which Noel had taken home to listen to was eventually utilised – after ironing to remove tape crinkles caused by a malfunctioning domestic machine! Several other songs were cut during the October sessions for the album, including an explosive instrumental, 'Driving South', which was ultimately left off the final album running order.

The October recording sessions were interrupted by shows and television recordings including a return to both the Saville Theatre and L'Olympia in Paris on consecutive nights, beginning with the London date on October 8, 1967.

Tony Bramwell put him on top of a bill with Track labelmates The Crazy World Of Arthur Brown, The Herd and fellow ANIM artists Eire Apparent. Hendrix reportedly played a set which included 'The Wind Cries Mary', 'Burning Of The Midnight Lamp', 'Foxy Lady', 'Hound Dog', 'Can You Please Crawl Out Your Window', 'Purple Haze' and his regular finale, 'Wild Thing'.

Over a year into a career which began in London in September 1966, Hendrix was in charge of his recordings and, thanks to a non-stop touring schedule of venues in Britain, around Europe and across America, he had also perfected his stage show. "Jimi had a very organized show and worked out in advance which part of the stage he was going to be using at any point during the set," recalls Bramwell. "It was all very orchestrated. We even arranged for the legs of the drum rostrum to be weakened so when Jimi whacked them with his guitar the whole drum kit collapsed – but he could only do it during the second show as we didn't have time to re-build it between houses."

Among the audience at the Saville was BBC producer Jeff Griffin, who had seen Hendrix at the very start of the year. "Hendrix started playing behind the curtain and all you heard were 'wah-wah' guitar notes and it sent a tingle down your spine," he recalls. "Then the curtain opened and there he was, this wild-looking person very flamboyantly dressed but such an amazing musician as well. The whole thing is just one of my best musical experiences ever."

As a man who saw and worked with the finest musicians of the day, Griffin still believes that Hendrix was something special. "He was possibly the most innovative musician I

7

have ever seen, and having a lead guitarist as the lead vocalist was unusual at that time. He was certainly less structured than even … Cream." Griffin was determined to find a slot which would allow him to work with Hendrix and it arrived ten days later in the shape of the Alexis Korner Show for the BBC World Service.

The BBC Playhouse Theatre was one of 14 studios used by the BBC for session recording, almost all being converted cinemas or theatres, and Griffin recalls the October day when Hendrix, Mitchell and Redding arrived there with fondness. "Jimi was such a lovely guy to work with. Absolutely charming and not in the least bit loud." He was also much more relaxed when in the privacy of a recording or radio station studio and working with the people he knew and respected, and on this session he brought his own entertainment. "He brought in this 'Froggie' bean-bag which he and his girlfriend were messing about with – just throwing it around to each other in the studio," says Griffin.

He reflects that Hendrix was "in really good spirits and you can hear that on the recording" and also forced a change in the show's usual routine. "We sometimes did artists right through with Alexis adding in the links after, but with Jimi we more or less did the programme right through," he says. It was obvious to everyone that Hendrix was enjoying the session, and the fact that he was working with Korner, whom he had met and hung out with around the London club scene, was a big help.

"It was Jimi who suggested that Alexis play on 'Hoochie Coochie Man'. He played slide guitar, although he never mentioned it on air, and for years people were surprised, thinking that Jimi had played slide." The session in fact started with Hendrix's version of Dylan's 'Can You Please Crawl Out Your Window', and for Griffin it remains one of the most notable moments from the session. "To my knowledge it was the only time he ever recorded it."

The final number in the session was 'Driving South', and Griffin again has a special memory of the song written by Hendrix's sometime colleague Curtis Knight. "It was the last track and I'm not sure to this day if they put the right version on the BBC Sessions album because the original was finished with something that had to be faded out to allow up to a minute for the different World Service time slots and announcements," he explains. "We'd gone past that point on the track when Jimi broke a string and you can hear him scratching on his guitar while Mitch goes on drumming. I decided to fade it out on the drum solo."

The recordings made with the British Broadcasting Corporation during the Experience's first full year of 1967 added much to Hendrix's recorded legacy. Six sessions of music were commissioned for broadcast during the year. Some of the performances were of otherwise available songs, but others were stage favourites or covers from earlier in his career that might otherwise have been lost to coming generations.

The 'session' phenomenon was an attempt to get around the restrictions on playing records insisted upon by the Musicians Union. Typically four songs would be recorded in a working day – two periods of three and a half hours, including setting up and miking instruments. The primitive recording equipment available at the time meant that sophisticated results were impossible. Extra vocals or guitar solos could only be achieved by bouncing tracks, meaning that what went don on tape was literally unrepeatable. There was no opportunity for re-takes.

On one occasion at the Playhouse Theatre, the Experience reputedly met Stevie Wonder. The Motown star was waiting to be interviewed by BBC Radio 1 DJ Brian Matthew, but slipped behind the drum kit as Mitch Mitchell took a comfort break. The resulting jam, plus an attempt at Wonder's 'I Was Made To Love Her', was captured on tape, but made disappointing listening.

The night after their final show at the Saville Theatre, which was turned into an ABC cinema in 1970, Hendrix returned to Paris for The Experience's second appearance at L'Olympia, where they were supported by the Belgian group The Pebbles, and stage manager Jean-Michel Boris was still there for the return visit. "Between his first gig when he supported Johnny Hallyday and October 1967, he had become a big star and this time people came to see him."

The French theatre executive also recalls one other change in the year between shows. "Hendrix used our house sound system on his first show, but when he came back he came with his own sound system. The L'Olympia system was not big enough for him," he explains. "The sound at the first show in 1966 was loud but not too loud, but by the second show we had to rent equipment for him in order to get the level of volume he wanted."

Booker Barry Dickins, who travelled across to France to see his act, was equally amazed to see the sound system which was set up on stage. "Boris said he had never seen anything like it, and I looked up at the stage – and it was a big stage like the London Palladium – and Jimi had these stacks right across it. It was full of amps – about 30 feet of amps all across the stage and this pretty big drum kit," says Dickins. "Boris was astounded by it all and I had never seen so many amps in my life. It was just fantastic."

JIMI HENDRIX MADE IN ENGLAND

7

For an act that had achieved four Top 20 hits in Britain plus a Number 2 album and was supposedly commanding £1,000 a night for major dates, The Jimi Hendrix Experience were still, in October 1967, playing some odd shows and venues. While The Beatles had retired from the live circuit in San Francisco in August 1966 and The Rolling Stones had said goodbye to provincial club dates in 1964, Hendrix played the likes of the Starlight Ballroom in Crawley, Hastings Pier and the California Hall in Dunstable, where admission prices ranged from 12 shillings and six pence (62½p) to 15 shillings (75p) and the support acts included the likes of Orange Seaweed and Modes Mode.

Hendrix passionately believed ticket prices "shouldn't go any higher than ten shillings … after all it is music and they have to pay twice as much or three times as much to buy the LP." He would have been happy that people who came to his show on November 8 at Manchester University's Union club were charged just seven shillings and six pence (37½p) on the door to see The Experience plus Tamla Express and Radio Luxembourg DJ The Baron.

On Tuesday October 24, 1967 Hendrix played his second and final appearance at the Marquee Club – exactly nine months after his debut on January 24. The Experience chose The Nice as their support act, as their Keith Emerson recalls. "Jimi specifically asked for us. We did jam that night but it was far too noisy. In fact it was so loud that I couldn't even hear myself playing."

After hearing Jimi and Keith Emerson jamming together, Chas Chandler briefly wondered about the prospect of recording a 'super session', but 'I was under the gun to finish the album and we couldn't spare the time.' Success had made Jimi Hendrix a hot property.

Emerson also remembers that Hendrix had acquired a movie camera and used it when The Nice's flamboyant keyboard player performed his famous knife-throwing assault on his Hammond organ. "He filmed me jumping and stabbing … I'd love to know what happened to Jimi's home movies."

Emerson only heard about years after the event, that he had missed out on playing on Hendrix's second album. "I didn't learn about Chas's idea until John McDermott's book [Ultimate Hendrix] stated that Chas said that Jimi wanted me to play on Axis. It was quite a surprise to me."

Another vaguely Hendrix-related story that did make the pages of Melody Maker appeared on November 4, 1967 which asked the question, "Why Do Customs Men

I CAN'T REMEMBER ALL THE THINGS I DO

Pick On Pop Stars?" While Customs & Excise denied that pop stars were given any 'special attention' as they entered the country, a spokesman for Hendrix offered up a different scenario. "He's been gone over by Customs so often he gets worried flying to Manchester," they quipped, before adding, "I suppose it's because he's American and a bit far out."

A week after they had finished work on the album Axis: Bold As Love, the three members of The Experience trekked round to Chandler's on November 7 to hear the end product which, as Redding recounts, was up to standard. "Thankfully, when we sat down to hear the test pressing it sounded good."

Hendrix returned to London from a couple of gigs and a TV show in Holland just as the newly launched but hugely influential magazine Rolling Stone ran its first feature on him. Completed during his time in America in July and August, the article by Sheila Walker was published on November 15.

Hendrix was asked about Bob Dylan and he reminisced about his one encounter with the man who was among his greatest influences. "I only met him once about three years ago, back at the Kettle of Fish [in New York's Greenwich Village]. That was before I went to England. I think both of us were pretty drunk at the time, so he probably doesn't remember it."

Hendrix admitted that his show did have a certain risqué appeal when he said, "I guess there is some sex but I don't plan it. I just do what I feel at the time. Gimmicks? Sure, but we don't work things out, we just let it happen." Manager Chandler, unsurprisingly, leapt to his artist's defence, telling people, "Jimi is also a showman and a bloody good one. I've never thought of him as a freak attraction and I'm sure he doesn't. Jimi is a phenomenon."

The feature also caused Hendrix to reflect on his audience's suggestions that his frenetic stage act was a gimmick and a distraction from the music. His response was to say, "I don't want to be a clown any more", before adding for good measure, "I don't want to be a rock and roll star."

Jimi Hendrix was now an undoubted major star in the worldwide rock firmament … but, unknown to anyone, the debut UK package tour he was about to headline would also be his last.

7

COME IN, BUT YOU GOTTA GET INTO BED

8

FIRST HEADLINE TOUR OF UK SUPPORTED BY PINK FLOYD AND
OTHERS – PLAYS ROYAL ALBERT HALL – SECOND ALBUM RELEASED
IN UK – SUCCESS IN US STILL ELUSIVE

Almost a year after he had booked him into a club date in Hounslow for £25, booking agent Barry Dickins' last throw of the dice with Hendrix came as he organized a package tour of the UK with The Move, Pink Floyd, The Nice and Amen Corner in support. It was an indication of how far and how fast the American had progressed in his adopted country.

Hendrix was now a seasoned performer and a high earner – "He would have got £1,000 a night for shows before the end of 1967" – but Dickins can't remember the exact financial details of the 15-date, twice-nightly tour that began on November 14 in London. "You didn't get £1,000 a night for package tours. You usually got just a fee and no percentage but I think for that tour Hendrix might have got 15 per cent and a fee.

"You turned up, played the gig, got in the van and went off to the next one. There was no backstage stuff at all and it was two shows a night – and sometimes it was three shows. These days you could go to Gordon Ramsay's finest restaurant for dinner for the cost of some of the riders – they can be up to £5,000 a night."

Host of the tour around Britain was newly appointed BBC Radio 1 disc jockey Pete Drummond. "I had to introduce each act but I'd never done anything like it before. I had to work out how to introduce each act and Barry [Dickins], who was the tour manager, just told me, 'You introduce the band, then after they've finished come on and say thanks. Then, after we've shifted things around, I'll bang on the floor twice and you introduce the next band.' I had to stay on stage for five minutes while the gear was shifted and do something entertaining, but it was very tough."

Pink Floyd manager Peter Jenner recalls what the tour meant to his band. "We were really pleased to get that tour and we played our three or four songs each show night. We were

8

down the bill … but it was a good opportunity to play to his audience on a twice nightly basis all round the country."

As pioneers of sound and light shows, Floyd were chosen to open the second half of the show, recalls Jenner, "because we could use the interval to set up our on-stage screen. Even now, 45 years on, it was one of the best-organized tours I have ever been on and Barry did an incredible job to get six bands [in fact there were seven groups on the tour] on stage every night for two weeks, although I do remember arguing with him about whether we could have more than our allotted minutes and him saying to me, 'No, it's 17½ minutes – that's it.'"

David Arden had taken over booking the dates for The Move and wasn't in the least bit worried about their fellow headliners. "We had no concerns that The Move would be blown off stage by Hendrix. We always believed that our act was the best, but my father was always concerned about positioning on the bill and there were times when we would insist that our act closed the first half rather than open the second half. It all depended on who was on after you or before you."

Hendrix's second package tour of the year opened at London's prestigious Royal Albert Hall, but things did not get off to a smooth start. "On the first night, Outer Limits didn't even get on because there wasn't enough time as everything was running late," according to Drummond. "They had to wear long-haired wigs because their hair was too short for a Sixties rock band on a tour like that."

Chas Chandler recalled this tour as pivotal in the success story. "Everything seemed to move so fast, but I think it was the first major tour here with The Move … that really hit them," he explained. "Noel and Mitch were shaking like leaves and even Jimi was petrified to go on stage. They realized they were part of something bigger than themselves and I had to get a bottle of Scotch in to restore some courage."

Reviews for the opening night were not entirely glowing, which was perhaps surprising given the status of the bands. "The bill seemed as if it would never get off the ground," reported Nick Logan for the NME. "Thank goodness for Hendrix, the untamed and unchained, swinging down from the trees through Knightsbridge to set the masses on fire in an ectoplasm of sound."

Chris Welch's appreciation in Melody Maker read as follows. "The Hendrix-Move tour thundered off on its trip round Britain with a deafening start … Pink Floyd gave one of their colourful and deafening displays of musical pyrotechnics … Eire Apparent practically damaged my hearing system for life … The Nice played some exciting new music … the

COME IN, BUT YOU GOTTA GET INTO BED

Amen Corner raved like a show band… and The Move thundered along in a shower of 'Flowers In The Rain' … Jimi was great and deserved the ovation, but really Mitch and Noel shouldn't make announcements. Sorry lads, but Jimi sounds better with the chat."

Over at Disc, Hugh Nolan's rave review read, "… Hendrix's hysterically exciting act provides what must be the most crashing, soulful, thrilling finale any pop show could hope for – short of, perhaps, The Beatles."

The show's programme notes confirmed that "excitement" was the watchword when it came to Hendrix. "Excitement over the type of songs he's going to hit us with next. Excitement at the way he, Mitch and Noel put it across. Excitement at the fact that, within seconds, we realize that here's a real performer – musician, showman, personality-plus."

The tour made its way around Britain with Amen Corner, The Nice, Eire Apparent and Outer Limits allocated a total of 45 minutes each night and Floyd going through their 17-minute-plus set, while The Move got 30 minutes and Hendrix a whopping 40 minutes, during which time he raced through 'Sgt Pepper', 'Fire', 'Hey Joe', 'The Wind Cries Mary', 'Purple Haze' and 'Wild Thing'.

With such a choice selection of the country's loudest, wackiest, freakiest, most colourful and potentially most destructive musicians on the road together, it's no surprise that the industry decided to tag the whole event as "the Alchemical Wedding" in homage to the amount of drug-influenced music produced. "Sheer madness" was how Mitch Mitchell summed up the proceedings. "It was that sort of tour."

Pink Floyd drummer Nick Mason recalls that the pick-up point in London after the opening night was the London Planetarium in Baker Street. "All the groups [with the exception of The Experience and The Move] were on one coach. It was rather like the Cliff Richard film Summer Holiday," he stated, while explaining that the camaraderie was no bad thing for him and his bandmates Syd Barrett, Roger Waters and Rick Wright.

"What was great was that we actually met some other musicians. We'd led a pretty solitary life as a band until then and suddenly we were hanging out with Hendrix. It was an opportunity to wallow in a bit of all-musos-together," he says, before reflecting, "I think it was the last big tour of that time."

While the 'lesser acts' were on their coach trip round Britain, the headliners were travelling in better style. "The rest of the bill used to have a coach but The Move and Hendrix had their own cars," says Trevor Burton, who spent some quality time with Hendrix. "I got to know him quite well on that tour. I used to travel with Jimi in his motor quite a bit because most of The Move used to go home after the gigs but I used to travel on."

JIMI HENDRIX MADE IN ENGLAND

8

As the tour wandered its way up and down the country – one night Bournemouth and then on to Sheffield and Coventry, followed by Blackpool, Nottingham and Newcastle – there was plenty of time for Burton and Hendrix to enjoy each other's company. "It wasn't a very coordinated tour and there wasn't the road system you have today so it took hours," says the Birmingham musician. "If you travelled in the daytime you tried to go to sleep 'cos it was so boring."

The refreshment stops during the journeys were usually truckers' cafes or greasy spoons which, according to Burton, had a certain appeal. "They were great with the old Wurlitzer jukeboxes – we all used to love those. But us lot walking in was a bit of a frightening sight for some people. We did get the cold shoulder quite often."

After the major music papers had reviewed the opening night of the tour in London, it was time for the provincial press to get a taste of the action. A Portsmouth reporter reckoned, "Never has a pop show been so deafening and lacking in variety and good presentation. The exception was Jimi Hendrix, as loud as any of the others but twice as talented and a superb showman." Two nights later – on November 24 – the local paper in Bristol reported "guitar smashing on stage… and glass smashing off stage," going on to say, "the incident did not spoil the triumphant return of Hendrix."

Reflecting on the tour and the finances, Move agent Arden reckons it was a case of flat fees for everybody, despite Dickins' memory of Hendrix taking a percentage. "The Move would have been paid a set fee and I don't think anyone took a share of the gate. You always took guaranteed money and there was no such thing as a per diem covering day-to-day living expenses – they came in the Seventies – so it was a case of the bands paying for everything out of their wages."

On the subject of money, Pete Drummond recalls that he was probably "the richest guy on the tour after Hendrix" as he was earning £25 a night while all the other acts had to split their fees. "I had to pay for a curry for the bands like Amen Corner on that tour." Although they were only added to the tour after the US group The Turtles pulled out, the Welsh group had racked up two Top 30 hits and were fast building something of a reputation as teen idols.

"Amen Corner was the biggest band at the time of the tour and they got all the screamers," says Jenner. "Andy Fairweather Low was a pretty boy, very much the teen crumpet, and he got more screams than Hendrix."

Nevertheless, the Pink Floyd manager admits the sight and sound of Hendrix was utterly memorable. "If you were in the guitar game you had good reason to be terrified of Hendrix

COME IN, BUT YOU GOTTA GET INTO BED

at that time. We all admired Hendrix, including Syd [Barrett], and my recollection is that everybody watched every show on that tour – both shows – because Hendrix was just so stunning," recounts Jenner. "And it was different every night. He did the same songs but he didn't play them the same way from one night to the next."

Syd Barrett, who died in 2006, would tell people after the tour was over, "I toured with Hendrix, you know", before adding, "We never really spoke. He'd lock himself in his dressing room with a TV and wouldn't let anyone in." Still, the man who was soon to leave the band he had formed in Cambridge just two years earlier, was full of admiration for Hendrix the musician. "He was better than people really knew. Hendrix was the perfect guitarist. That's all I wanted to do as a kid. Play guitar properly and jump around."

Sadly, Barrett went missing so many times that manager Jenner and his band members were forced to sit and wait for him to return either just minutes before their set or, on other occasions, not at all. That was when the band called on The Nice's David O'List to stand in. "By the end of that tour we were frazzled," said drummer Mason, while Move man Trevor Burton recalls "They used to stand him on the stage and make sure he didn't move or fall over!"

The show had to go on and, according to Jenner, it went on in a most civilized, organized fashion. "They got those bands on twice nightly and the show was tight at about two hours and ten minutes. Everybody had their own gear but all the roadies helped each other to dismantle and set up," he says. "Then we'd all meet up at the Blue Boar on the M1 or other places around the country – including Jimi, who never gave out any bad vibes. He was a lovely guy, and throughout that tour he was never anything other than a friendly geezer."

Interestingly, according to The Experience's Mitchell, the 'package' description was something of a misnomer. "In a way it was more absurd than the previous tour because none of the bands on this one was package-tour material. Sheer madness – it was that sort of tour, but at least it was our sort of audience."

Keith Emerson's overriding memory is also that it all went off pretty well, despite the number of acts and potential rivalry. "Just fun and camaraderie" is how he recalls the whole thing, but with one notable exception. "It was really great, but Pink Floyd weren't very sociable – and probably I wasn't at that time either. But I don't recall that anyone was uncomfortable and Jimi just seemed to be oblivious to anything in his way. He just marched through it like a gentleman."

Even so, Emerson recounts one night – December 2, to be precise – when there was a problem. "We were playing at the Dome in Brighton and my mother and father, who lived not far away, came to the show. My mother thought Jimi was too loud."

Eire Apparent's Henry McCullough reckons that the tour had "the air of the music hall about it". As part of the band cutting their teeth in the world of rock, he says, "It was pretty new to us having so many people on tour and it was odd to be on the road for beer money with the likes of the great Jimi Hendrix."

Being on a bus with players from Floyd, The Nice and Amen Corner was "like a boy's outing", according to McCullough who, less than two years later, would be on the bill with Hendrix at Woodstock as a member of Joe Cocker's band. "There was a bit of smoking and a few pints and all the velvet jackets. And there were no riders in those days, so you all went out to eat and then went back to do the show."

As one of the youngest and least experienced players on the tour, McCullough never expected to get close to Hendrix. "I never spent any real time with Jimi, although we'd all have a smoke together backstage. I didn't know what to say to him and he never really started a conversation. In fact, to be honest, I was a bit afraid of him. He was taller than me but he sort of hunched over you and was a bit scary.

"It was how he played the guitar that really frightened the life out of me. It was overwhelming. I watched him almost every night and that was the beauty of being there. It was impossible not to stand in awe of what was going on."

McCullough enjoyed a close-up view of what Hendrix did on stage, including his tricks of playing the guitar with his teeth and behind his neck. "I suppose if you practise they weren't too difficult, but I had never seen anybody else do it," he explains, before analyzing another aspect of Hendrix's act. "Of course his show was sexually orientated, which was a big plus. At the end of the day he was the real deal."

If sex was a major part of Hendrix's stage show, his appeal to his female fans – and his never-ending appetite for them – was something show host Drummond experienced wherever they went. "Girls just threw themselves at Hendrix throughout the tour. At the stage door it would be packed with girls and he did have to rebuff some of them because he just couldn't take them all on, although he would have given it a good go."

Drummond had a close encounter one evening when, after a few post-show drinks, he left his bag in Hendrix's room. "I went back to get my bag, knocked on the door and heard a lot of giggling. Jimi asked who it was and when I said it was me and I had come to collect my bag he said, 'You can come in, but you gotta get into bed.'"

Unaware of what exactly lay in waiting for him behind the hotel-room door, the presenter repeated that all he wanted was his bag. "Jimi shouted through the door, 'You ain't comin' in

COME IN, BUT YOU GOTTA GET INTO BED

unless you get into bed.' So I said 'OK' just to get into the room, and when I walked in there were two girls in the bed and Jimi standing there smiling," recalls Drummond. "I just grabbed my bag and ran out."

Confirming that it was his understanding that Hendrix did get a cut of the gate – "Chas had done a good deal for him" – Drummond also remembers how a roadie would stand behind the stack of speakers during Hendrix's set. "With his fag still going, he would put his hand up against the speakers ready for Hendrix to bang his guitar into them. His job was to stop them falling over.

"I watched his show every night and it was great – like watching the Jerry Lee Lewis of the guitar with all the playing behind the neck and with his teeth," says Drummond. "But off stage he was very polite and a very pleasant man."

David Arden recollects that this tour signalled a change in the way package shows were presented. "Radio 1 had just begun and you now had DJs rather than comedians like Jimmy Tarbuck, Johnny Ball and Norman Vaughan as the host." But radio presenter Drummond's skill was in presenting and playing records, not being on stage in front of thousands of screaming pop fans. "I was totally lost. I wasn't a stand-up comic and I got booed off most of the time," he recalls, before explaining that the one person who used to help out on occasions came from Pink Floyd. "Roger Waters was funny and he used to occasionally give me a joke to tell the audience."

Drummond still found it tough being on stage, although, as he explained to Hendrix one night, it had its benefits for the other acts on the bill. "I used to say to him that no matter how badly you played, by the time I introduce you the audience are so pissed off with me that you can come and play anything and they'll love it. He used to say, 'I know it, I understand that.'"

It seems Hendrix also had his own particular way of tormenting the broadcaster when he was doing his 'bit' on stage, joining in with the fans when they abused the show's host. "Jimi asked me quite a few times if I saw him during the evening's show. I'd say, 'No. Why? What were you doing?', and then he'd tell me, 'I was at the back of the stage shouting 'fuck off' at you, along with the rest of the audience.'"

When the tour made a stop in Coventry on November 19, Trevor Burton took time out to visit his family in the Erdington district of Birmingham – and took a special guest with him. "Jimi did come round to my house to meet my mum during the tour. He had a cup of tea and some cake, I think, and she loved him. He was absolutely charming to her, but then he was always very polite."

JIMI HENDRIX MADE IN ENGLAND

8

Declaring that Hendrix was "the loudest guitarist anyone had ever heard at that time", Burton has only vague memories of the time spent in the car with Hendrix as they motored around the UK. "He was very funny, I remember that. He had a great sense of humour but he never talked much about music – but then he never talked about very much at all," he says. One of the reasons for that, according to Burton, was because "he was very stoned most of the time. We were both pretty smashed and we just mumbled to each other a lot."

While Burton the guitarist admits to being "absolutely" influenced by Hendrix's playing, he recalls The Experience's bass player being less impressed. "Noel used to say about Hendrix's playing, 'It's all volume, he gets away with murder. I can do that.'"

After 31 shows spread over 22 days (there was only one on opening night at the Albert Hall), the tour came to an end in Glasgow at the famous Green's Theatre. Pete Drummond has special memories of the last night .

"They told me not to tell any jokes about Protestants or Catholics or Rangers or Celtic in order to avoid any trouble," he says, before admitting to his mistake. "I started to tell a joke about a Protestant and a Catholic walking down the street, and before I could finish this guy came running down the aisle towards the stage and I swear he had a knife."

Thanks to the notoriously high stage at Green's, Drummond was confident that the man couldn't actually get to him, but security stepped in anyway. "I was taken off stage by one of the crew and bundled out of the back door. Hendrix couldn't go on for a long time after that because the audience was so incensed about what had gone on with me. I don't think they were on my side."

The two shows in Belfast on November 27, 1967 marked Jimi's 25th birthday and brought a spontaneous round of 'Happy Birthday' from the crowd. There were concerns that the performances – part of the Belfast Arts Festival – were in danger of damaging the historic Whitla Hall in Queen's College.

With the balcony vibrating and the support columns visibly shaking, Hendrix added to the excitement by destroying Mitchell's drum kit. Then, as Trevor Burton recalls, "Jimi finished by throwing his guitar – it was a Flying V – through a window at the back of the stage that was about 20 foot high. You could see it hanging outside into the alley at the back of the theatre and it was still feeding back."

After that, the band returned to London for a three-day break, during which time Hendrix received his belated birthday present from Kathy Etchingham – a Basset hound puppy which he named Ethel Floon. "Jimi thought the world of that dog. It would bound around the room banging head first into the furniture, which used to have Jimi in fits of

8

laughter," she recalls. She also remembers that the problems came as the dog grew bigger and louder. "Because of the constant barking and complaints from the neighbours, we felt she would be better off in the country, so Jeff Beck took her."

Four days after his birthday, as Hendrix made his way to Kent to play two shows at the Town Hall in Chatham, the Experience's second album hit the shops. Jimi, who simply said of his new release, "I wanted to be listened to", was not altogether happy with either the release date or the album cover.

"The album was made over a period of 16 days, which I am very sad about", he said, "but we had to get it out to put in all the kiddies' stockings for Christmas. It could have been much better." It came out on December 1 with a cover reflecting the mid-Sixties enthusiasm for all things mystical and Eastern following The Beatles' dalliance with the Maharishi Mahesh Yogi.

Designed by David King and painted by Roger Law, it featured the heads of Hendrix, Mitchell and Redding on a multi-armed Indian God. "When I first saw that [cover] design, I thought, 'It's great, but maybe we should have an American Indian,' explained Hendrix. "Three of us have nothing to do with what's on the Axis cover."

He added further insight into how much he was actually involved in the design of his second album cover – at a time when The Beatles had personally overseen the creation of their Sgt Pepper sleeve – by admitting, "I liked the inside of the cover best, really. Like, they have an Indian painting about us. Well it's alright, you know." Hendrix's preferred inside cover shot was a gatefold black and white photograph of all three members of the group taken by Donald Silverstein.

Despite his reservations, the cover was picked out for special mention by Record Retailer in their review, which told dealers, "Superb cover design that will help boost sales of this album, which is surprisingly subdued music-wise for Hendrix. He is now in that privileged league of poppers who are assured of sales regardless of the album."

Hendrix nevertheless saw the end product as a major step forward, both in terms of writing and recording. "It's made with stereo in mind ... we've tried to get the most freaky tracks right into another dimension" was his explanation, while he described the album as, "The story of a guy who's been on Earth before but on a different turn of the axis – and now he's come back to find this scene happening."

The album was well received by the critics, with Nick Jones, in his London Notes column for Rolling Stone magazine, suggesting that while the album cost £10,000 to record, "It's very freaky – and at times shatteringly beautiful." In Melody Maker, the same writer added,

JIMI HENDRIX MADE IN ENGLAND

8

"It's too much. Amaze your ears, boggle your mind, flip your lid, do what you want to do, but please get into Hendrix like you never have before."

The NME's Keith Altham waxed lyrical, telling his readers, "Next time you spot an unidentified flying object crashing across the night sky with electric blue flames streaming out behind, look closely for it might just be that traveller in time, space and sound – Jimi Hendrix." He went on to confirm Jones' assertion that the album cost £10,000 and added "the most impressive sleeve for an LP I have seen" cost a further £3,000.

Within a week of release, Axis: Bold As Love had raced into the UK chart at Number 8 before peaking at 5. It would have to wait until 1968 before getting a shot at the US chart.

For Brian May, the second album from The Experience represented a defining moment in the history of recording. "We became great disciples of his studio technique, and on Axis it's part of the great bible of how to behave in the studio." The album also reinforced May's belief that the line-up of The Experience was nigh-on perfect. "A three-piece was absolutely right for Jimi – a rhythm guitar would have made things too stiff," says the Queen guitarist who worked in exactly the same format.

"Jimi's relationship with Mitch was just phenomenal and they could feel out every little variation in tempo and you can hear them working off each other on the live takes," explains May. "I was a huge fan of Mitch and his jazz-based drumming, but it's sad that Noel didn't seem to enjoy his time with Jimi."

Eire Apparent's McCullough had crossed paths with Redding many times as they gigged around the London club scene. "He had the urge to go out and play anywhere and I think all along he had a plan where he could go back and play lead guitar," he suggests. "But playing bass for Hendrix wasn't such a bad gig – and it paid the wages. To get to play bass with Jimi Hendrix you've got to be doing the right thing."

The release of Axis threw The Jimi Hendrix Experience into direct competition with Cream, their chief rivals for the title of top progressive/underground/psychedelic/freaky band of the day. The trio of Eric Clapton, Jack Bruce and Ginger Baker released their second album, Disraeli Gears, in November '67, just a few weeks before Hendrix's follow-up, and both peaked four places off the top behind The Sound of Music and Sgt Pepper, which, by the end of 1967, had notched up 68 weeks and 26 weeks respectively at Number 1.

Although Cream's second album came out just as Axis was being issued, it seems that it was Hendrix's debut LP that had caused Clapton most discomfort. They had finished recording Disraeli Gears in New York's Atlantic Studios just as Are You Experienced hit the shops and the charts in May 1967. "I was angry because he'd come here to England and

COME IN, BUT YOU GOTTA GET INTO BED

we'd gone to America and we'd made Disraeli Gears there and came back to deliver and nobody wanted to know. That was because everybody had Are You Experienced. That was all they wanted to talk about – I was furious." The situation probably wasn't helped by the fact that both acts' albums were released in the UK by Polydor.

"Everywhere you went it was wall-to-wall Jimi and I felt really down," says Clapton. "I thought we had made the definitive album, only to come home to find that nobody was interested. It was the beginning of a disenchantment with England where it seemed there wasn't really room for more than one person to be popular at a time."

Ironically, both Disraeli Gears and Axis: Bold As Love peaked at the identical UK Number 5 chart position. And while there was rivalry between the two three-piece outfits, Hendrix was rarely heard to pronounce on Clapton's band; most recorded comments were flattering ones about his personal musical prowess.

Axis: Bold As Love toned down the pyrotechnics of their debut release to focus more on Jimi's melodic side and his Dylan-esque lyrics. Whereas most of 'Are You Experienced' had been road tested, It featured many songs not previously performed live, and indeed most were destined never to be. Only 'Spanish Castle Magic' was to become a concert regular.

Of the remaining tracks, 'Little Wing' was granted an occasional live outing. It's a short track which would have been shorter had it not been slowed from its rehearsal tempo by producer Chandler – in live performance it was only extended by a minute or so. 'EXP' and 'Up From The Skies' were attempted live just a handful of times. However, 'Wait Until Tomorrow' and 'Little Miss Lover' were included on an October 1967 BBC Radio 1 session recording.

One of the album's earliest tracks, 'If Six Was Nine', was recorded as an instrumental jam, lyrics/overdubs being added later. The song was later featured in the movie Easy Rider. Effects were prominent in tracks like the funky 'Little Miss Lover', Jimi playing the percussive riff through a wah-wah pedal and using Roger Mayer's Octavia effect in the solo. This hard-edged funk track was at one time considered for release as the next single after 'The Wind Cries Mary'.

The Noel Redding composition 'She's So Fine' was the first track to be recorded for the album in early April 1967. It saw its writer take lead vocals and was very much from the British psychedelic school of pop, Noel penning the lyrics after seeing a hippie walking around with an alarm clock hanging round his neck on a piece of string. Jimi attempted to beef things up as best he could with some Who-style power chords.

Sci-fi reared its head in album opener 'EXP', with Mitch Mitchell, as radio announcer, and

8

can seen as a precursor to the more fully realised 'sound paintings' on the 'Electric Ladyland' album. The second half of the track was originally known as 'Symphony Of Ideas' and was recorded at the initial sessions for the album in May 1967. It segued into 'Up From The Skies' which, lyrically, was a sequel to 'Third Stone From The Sun'. The Experience played this live only a handful of times, an attempt at San Francisco's Winterland in February 1968 ending prematurely when Mitch's brushes disintegrated on-stage, much to the amusement of Jimi and Noel.

The use of panning for the vocals and guitar on the R&B-flavoured 'One Rainy Wish' presaged the far more complex production work on Electric Ladyland. Jimi played three guitar parts, obtaining an almost semi-acoustic tone from his Strat, while the song itself was also multi-layered, a dream-like verse in 3/4 time contrasting with a heavier middle section and the chorus in regular rock 4/4. The lyrics used colour metaphors – Jimi would often tell engineer Eddie Kramer how he visualised certain sounds in terms of colours and he would attempt to realise these by use, or misuse, of the available studio machinery and effects.

Inspired lyrically by the Spanish Castle club in Jimi's home town of Seattle, 'Spanish Castle Magic' brought another change of mood and saw him, unusually, play piano. He is said to have re-recorded sections of the bass in Noel Redding's absence. The lead guitar licks on the short, sub-two-minute 'Ain't No Telling' were panned hard to the right channel and followed the melody line of a soul-styled call and response vocal. There was no guitar solo as such, although the song ended with a flurry of notes.

As if in deliberate contrast, 'Wait Until Tomorrow' was a simple one-guitar song that was originally envisaged as a 'joke' song. The lyrics about Jimi trying to get his girlfriend to run off with him were on the corny side, and the extremely high-pitched backing vocals by Mitch and Noel sounded like parody; Jimi can be heard laughing at their efforts. However, by the time of the final take the song had become a fully-fledged composition.

On first hearing, 'You Got Me Floatin'' appears to have a straightforward production, but on closer inspection many details reveal themselves. A backwards guitar lick opens proceedings and reappears at various points. The funky main guitar is choppy and infectious; the solo guitar pans wildly, while an almost hidden speeded-up backwards guitar lurks behind it. Noel used an eight-string bass on this track, while Trevor Burton and Roy Wood of The Move contributed harmony vocals. 'Castles Made Of Sand' contains some of Jimi's finest lyrics. They deal with a failed marriage, a theme which features in some of Jimi's other songs – his parents' divorce obviously had a great impact.

Title track 'Bold As Love' was the crowning glory of the album it closed. The influence

COME IN, BUT YOU GOTTA GET INTO BED

of Bob Dylan is strongly felt in the lyrics, with Jimi's own colour imagery once more coming to the fore. The guitar-playing, too, could be described as lyrical. Again Jimi replaced certain portions of Noel's bass. The song was split by a short drum solo treated with a phasing effect. 'Bold As Love' is claimed to be the first example of stereo phasing (the Small Faces single 'Itchycoo Park' used the same effect – more correctly a mixture of both phasing and flanging – but was in mono). The second half of the song, an instrumental tour de force in which Jimi's lead guitar soars and heads for the heavens, provided a glorious and majestic finale to the album.

While Axis was not issued in America in 1967 – the US version featured the same tracks as the UK issue but with a slightly different running order – another album featuring Jimi Hendrix did come out in December of that year and it was highlighted as part of Capitol Records' special Christmas full-page advert in the December 9 issue of Billboard. Get That Feeling was announced as including both Jimi Hendrix (in larger type) and Curtis Knight (in smaller type) and featured the tracks Hendrix had recorded in New York during the summer under the direction of Ed Chalpin.

As the year came to an end, Get That Feeling entered the US albums chart at Number 194 – eventually rising to 75 – while in the UK it crept into the Top 40 following its delayed release in February 1968. According to Rolling Stone reviewer Michael Lydon, the album "is not what it appears, Hendrix's latest release. The record is barely representative of what Hendrix is now doing and is an embarrassment to him as a musician," continued Lydon. "It is so badly recorded to be of little historical value."

The Los Angeles Times were no more impressed with what they heard and saw as they warned fans, "Beware when an album shrinks the featured vocalist's name [Knight] in small type beneath the twice as large name of a back-up musician [Hendrix] … for what sounds suspiciously like no more than a demonstration record with some after-the-fact engineering tricks."

If anyone was in any doubt about the circumstances and quality of the album, Hendrix made his feelings clear about the collection that bore his name as soon as he heard of the album's release. "The Curtis Knight album was from bits and pieces of tape they used from a jam session … tiny little confetti bits of tape," he stressed. "Capitol never told us they were going to release that crap. That's the real drag about it … that cat and I used to be friends."

The response from those representing Hendrix in America was a follow-up full-page advert in the next issue of Billboard announcing the release of his new American single 'Foxey Lady' (sic). Once again, the photo was just Hendrix without Mitchell or Redding, with

8

a cover shot of the Are You Experienced album.

To make a point about the way they felt about the Get That Feeling album, along the bottom of the ad was a strap line which read:"Notice! All Current & Future Recordings by The Jimi Hendrix Experience Appear Exclusively on Reprise Records!"

Whether the advert was bought and placed by Track Records, ANIM or Reprise Records is unclear, although Reprise's chief creative force Stan Cornyn is adamant that it wasn't the US record label."I can't imagine we – me, actually – putting such a clumsy ad in Billboard. Utterly not our style," he says.

Less than three weeks after the release of his new album and after they had completed their round of recordings for the Jonathan King television show, Radio 1's Top Gear and a Top Of The Pops special, Hendrix and his band found their way back at Olympic Studios for four days in December to begin work on tracks intended for the next album.

Working on 'Crosstown Traffic','Dance' (which eventually saw the light of day as the track 'Ezy Ryder') and Redding's unfinished and unreleased 'Dream', Hendrix, who was joined in the studio by Traffic star Dave Mason, played piano, bass and kazoo.

With the year coming to an end, there was the usual business of music polls and chart performances to consider and the UK music trade paper Record Retailer's analysis of the year showed The Experience as the fifth most successful group in the Top Singles section and at Number 13 in the Top LP listing behind – yet again – The Sound Of Music (1) and Sgt Pepper (6).

The annual New Musical Express Readers' Poll wasn't as generous to Hendrix as the fans from their rival Melody Maker had been a few months earlier. This time Hendrix, Mitchell and Redding won nothing at all, although they were listed in four categories. The Experience came in at Number 12 in the Best World Vocal Group section (The Beatles were at 1 and The Beach Boys at 2) and were voted fifth Best New Group behind the likes of the Bee Gees and Traffic.

Meanwhile, Hendrix came in at a lowly Number 18, behind winner Elvis Presley, as the Best World Male Singer, and at a much more respectable fourth place as Top World Musical Personality behind both Elvis and John Lennon.

The band's sessions at Olympic were interrupted by the extraordinary Christmas On Earth Continued concert in the Grand and National Halls at London's Olympia featuring Hendrix, The Animals, The Move, Pink Floyd, the Graham Bond Organisation and Soft Machine. There was also a funfair and a paddling pool on offer for those who paid 25/- on the door or £1 in advance for their tickets.

COME IN, BUT YOU GOTTA GET INTO BED

Organized by the publishers of Image magazine, the concert ran from 8pm on December 22 through to 6am the next day, but Christmas On Earth Continued turned out to be a financial flop when the attendance failed to reach anywhere near the anticipated 10,000. Hendrix, Mitchell and Redding finally got to go on stage at 2am, with the frontman urging the crowd, "Plug your ears, watch out for your ears, watch out for your ears, okay?", before opening with 'Sgt Pepper' and finishing with 'Wild Thing' after also running through 'Foxy Lady' and 'Red House'.

During the afternoon's rehearsals Hendrix managed to upset the shop steward of the in-house electricians, who asked him to turn down the volume as there had been a complaint. Hendrix's response was to turn it up and he only relented when the union man threatened to call out his workers and cancel the whole show.

Redding's recollection of the night was being on stage with the latest development in concert lighting. "It was the first time I'd been exposed to strobes. I could not handle strobes in those days," he recounted. "These things started going off and it was insane. Jimi loved them, he'd just go mad."

The 1967 Christmas extravaganza was another chance for Brian May to get to see his guitar idol, as his band 1984 were booked – although not listed in the adverts – on the same show. It turned out to be one of the last gigs May played with the band, who were specially groomed for the occasion with guardsman's jackets and a dab or two of make-up.

After watching The Move and Pink Floyd perform from their artist-only spot in the gallery, and even spotting Hendrix in the canteen, 1984 had to get through their own set. This began even later than Hendrix's performance which, for May, was "stimulating and baffling … I was just completely entranced. It was wonderful when he played – like the heavens opening."

It wasn't just Hendrix's playing ability that touched Queen's guitarist. "Even though he was being a guitar God on stage, his humanity was still there," explains May, looking back over 45 years. "He would turn to the side of the stage, smiling and slightly dismissing himself. He had a wonderful persona, very warm and modest. I really wish I had known him."

Over the years, there have been endless theories about Hendrix's 'upside-down' style of playing and having his instruments re-strung so he could play them left-handed. "The reason he played like that was because you couldn't buy left-handed guitars when he started out," explains Roger Mayer. "They might have made a few in the early Sixties but they were pretty rare, so he had no choice but to turn them over and have them re-strung."

Les Fleur de Lys player Haworth agrees. "I would have thought that when he was growing

8

up, left-handed guitars might not have been readily available to him so he would have learned to play on a right-handed guitar. For him it just became first nature. It was only later that left-handed models started coming out, but by then Jimi had perfected his own way of playing."

Whatever the reason, May was suitably impressed and a little baffled at what he saw on stage. "His back-to-front, upside-down way of playing is completely foreign to me and it makes it very difficult to figure out what he was doing. There are a lot of people who spend their lives trying to figure out what Jimi did and how he did it, but I'm not one of them. I just like to absorb it and enjoy it. And I haven't tried to reproduce any of it."

May also has no doubt that the band he came to fame with would not have progressed as they did without Hendrix. "He was one of our biggest influences in starting Queen, and all the stuff that influenced him was the sort of music that also influenced us."

The year of 1967 ended for The Experience with a New Year's Eve Party at the guitarist's favourite watering hole, the Speakeasy, where Jimi saw in 1968 alongside Eric Clapton, Eric Burdon, Steve Winwood, Ginger Baker and Georgie Fame. In traditional style, the assorted characters swung into a unique rock'n'roll rendition of 'Auld Lang Syne' which lasted half-an-hour.

On piano that night was Phil Ryan from Welsh band Eyes Of Blue, who refused to give up his seat in order to be part of the revelry. He recalls how the year went out for Hendrix. "Most of them were playing it ['Auld Lang Syne'] pretty straight but Hendrix, in his inimitable way, mutated it into something else completely. What a brilliant way to bring the New Year in."

The year which undoubtedly made Hendrix into a global superstar had come to end. He had won awards, hit the charts in places as far apart as New Zealand and Norway, played to packed concert halls across America, throughout the UK and around Europe and been feted by the great and good of the music business as being the best rock guitarist on the planet.

As Chas Chandler, the man who brought him to the UK as a complete unknown and steered him on the path to glory, proudly announced, "From September 1967 he was enormous." Sadly, the success story was never going to last forever.

THE GROUP WILL ALWAYS BE TOGETHER

9

RECORDS IN NEW YORK – SPLITS FROM CHANDLER – DISBANDS
EXPERIENCE – APPEARS AT WOODSTOCK – TOURS AMERICA –
APPEARS AT ISLE OF WIGHT – LAST PERFORMANCE

In the 15 months which had passed since his arrival in Britain, Jimi Hendrix achieved every aspiring musician's dream. He was now a global rock superstar and it was thanks to what he delivered as a songwriter, singer and performer during 1967 that he was able to start a new year with new ambitions.

But not everybody was on his side. Indeed, one of his harshest critics turned out to be a British singer who was actually signed to the same US record label.

Former child star Petula Clark made her feelings about Hendrix known to Melody Maker. "Jimi Hendrix is a great big hoax, but if he can get away with it good luck to him," she said in the first issue of the music paper in 1968. "I saw him in Los Angeles. I think he's unexciting and he doesn't move me. The fact that he isn't a big success with the general public proves something." Before the month was out, readers of Melody Maker had written in with their views on songstress Pet.

"No Petula, it isn't for you, but for teenagers he is the most exciting act in the country," wrote one presumably young fan, while another fair-minded Hendrix supporter added, "She is entitled to her opinions, however misguided they may be." On the other hand, the 35-year-old singer with an impressive string of 24 hits to her name had her supporters.

"Viva Petula Clark," wrote one. "At last someone has the audacity to express their true feelings about Jimi Hendrix, king of this new weird 'music'." Another added, "If more people like Pet would speak up I'm sure the untalented people would be deterred from inflicting themselves on the pop scene."

While it's unlikely that Hendrix was stung by Clark's comments – or those of the readers of Melody Maker – he had decided before January was over that his future, and

9

that of his band, lay in his homeland. Mitch Mitchell, for one, was not surprised. "[There] was Jimi's realization that he'd made it in America and wanted to live permanently in New York."

Reflecting on the prospect of a move away from the UK, the drummer added, "This, of course, was completely alien to Chas and Noel, and even to me at that stage. It took me about a year to realize how important New York had become."

Fellow American Joe Boyd was not surprised that Hendrix had decided to return to the States at the end of 1967, and to New York in particular. "He had been scuttling around New York for years and I think to return to New York in triumph was pretty irresistible to him."

Before they left the UK, Hendrix, Mitchell and Redding gathered in Olympic Studios to continue recording tracks for their third album, which at that time was still nine months away from release. One of the tracks was a cover of a song by one of Hendrix's greatest influences – Bob Dylan.

Hendrix arrived in the States to see 'Foxey Lady' (with 'Hey Joe' as the B-side) reach a disappointing Number 67, two places lower than 'Purple Haze' had achieved three months earlier. However, within just a couple of weeks he saw Reprise swing into action with a campaign that included a major, full-colour, full-page advert on the prized back page of Billboard.

The text – no doubt written by the label's chief copywriter Stan Cornyn – announced the company's plans for the new Axis: Bold As Love album. "A typically thunderous Reprise promotion begins to invoke, extol, incite The Jimi Hendrix Experience!" The ad went on to detail how the label was going to flood the country with posters, radio spots, banners, window displays and newspaper and magazine inserts, signing off by proclaiming: "America is not likely to escape The Jimi Hendrix Experience."

The album was equally well-received by Billboard's music reviewer, who reckoned, "The Jimi Hendrix Experience has another album winner in the second Reprise LP, although this one has more jazz-orientated numbers than their first." The net result was a new high for Hendrix as Axis: Bold As Love swept up to Number 3 – two places higher than where Are You Experienced peaked.

Its rise up the US chart began with an undistinguished entry at Number 140, but within two weeks it had jumped to 24 and then on to 3, taking with it the group's first album, which swept back into the upper reaches of the chart to give Hendrix two albums in the American Top Ten at the same time.

THE GROUP WILL ALWAYS BE TOGETHER

While he failed to get past French bandleader Paul Mauriat, who, together with his orchestra, headed the chart for five weeks with his Blooming Hits collection, and both Bob Dylan and Aretha Franklin, who took the Number 2 spot, Hendrix's achievements were well received by his record company. "Having two Top 5 albums felt very good," confirms Cornyn. "In that time – '67 to '68 – we had embraced Hendrix, which is easy to do when you have an outrageous success in your tribe, and many other 'underground' artists."

Hendrix set about consolidating his Stateside success with a mammoth three-month tour before embarking on six months of recording in New York's Record Plant. But as he swept across the US, Hendrix was exposed to his country's growing unrest about the war in Vietnam.

The year of 1968 kicked off with a short Scandinavian tour, warming up the Experience for a second ever tour of the United States. Dissatisfaction was growing in the ranks, most notably in the shape of Noel Redding. The bass player resented his lack of creative input – and, while he'd been allowed to contribute a track to Axis: Bold As Love (and would do likewise on Electric Ladyland)this was unlikely to satisfy him for long. One disagreement in Gothenburg led to Jimi destroying a hotel room in a fit of rage, for which he spent a night in the cells.

Redding wasn't the only unhappy Experience member. Jimi was beginning to feel trapped by his audience's expectations, having to engage in destruction and acts of showmanship every night. A three-piece format left little room for disguising an off night, so Hendrix's insistence that the music spoke for itself was a high-risk strategy, especially when there was dissention behind the scenes.

Protest marches were kicking off in cities all around the world with American students and peace protesters at the forefront, something Hendrix could not have missed even if he'd tried. Early on during his time in London, he had spoken about the Vietnam War and, perhaps because of his time in the military, he did not appear to be against the conflict.

"The Americans are fighting in Vietnam for the complete free world," he explained, before going on to warn, "as soon as they move out, they'll be at the mercy of the communists. For that matter the yellow danger [China] should not be underestimated. Of course, war is horrible, but at present it's still the only guarantee to maintain peace."

Eric Burdon recalls watching anti-war riots on the TV with Hendrix and asking the ex-paratrooper, "What do you think of that?" Hendrix's reply was to say, "Oh, if you

9

really understood the situation you'd understand why the American Government is trying so hard in Vietnam because of the 'domino effect' and it would eventually fall into the hands of the Chinese." His views may not have been hip or along appropriate lines for a leading figure in the 'underground', but it seems they were heartfelt and worn on his sleeve for all to see.

It wasn't just America's involvement in a war in south-east Asia that was brought closer to home for Hendrix when he returned to the US. Noted author and commentator Charles Shaar Murray reckons that, by returning to New York City in 1968, Hendrix became the focus of attention for a host of people who sought to gain from his fame. "It wasn't until he relocated to New York and found himself in a social scene with white radicals and radical brothers from the black political scene that he started to take on board some information that he hadn't had before."

Whether he was moved or persuaded by either America's continuing anti-war protests or the growing Black Power movements is unclear, although he did donate $5,000 to a memorial fund for Martin Luther King.

Hendrix chose to return to the UK for just a few days in the summer of 1968 when he played a date at the Woburn Music Festival in the grounds of the Duke of Bedford's estate. After earlier gigs in Italy and Switzerland, his show on July 6 – sharing the bill with Geno Washington, Tyrannosaurus Rex and Family – lasted a mammoth 48 minutes and included ten-minute versions of 'Red House' and the then-unreleased 'Tax Free', plus an eight-minute rendition of 'Purple Haze'. He would not play Britain again for a further five months.

On the record front, Hendrix broke new-ish ground with the release of Smash Hits, a collection of the group's four British hit singles – including B-sides – plus four tracks from the Are You Experienced album. Hits compilations from the major British groups were still fairly few and far between in early 1968, although both The Beatles and The Rolling Stones had issued their first collections in late 1966.

In the UK Track Records also considered it vital to get another LP on the shelves as there would be a 10-month gap between the release of Axis: Bold As Love and Electric Ladyland – a lengthy pause in the fast-moving Sixties' music scene. The album was released in the UK in April 1968 and peaked at Number 4 in Britain in April. It would eventually hit Number 6 in America, but not until July 1969 after Electric Ladyland and was considered to be a stopgap until a new studio album could be completed. Reprise reasoned that The Experience did not have enough US hits by early 1968 to justify

9

its release. When it did come out – with an uncredited cover photograph featuring a single image of Hendrix repeated three times – it would feature his much-vaunted version of 'All Along The Watchtower'.

In Britain, the cover version of the Dylan song reached Number 5 to become the band's fourth Top 10 hit single, while in America it became their first and only Top 20 hit when it eventually peaked at Number 20 in September 1968. Hendrix had apparently first heard the song at a party he went to with Dave Mason and recorded it on the same night, playing Redding's right-handed bass while Mason supported him on acoustic guitar.

Mitchell, whose drumming was included on the track, recalled that his bandmate was not entirely happy with the way things panned out. "I think Noel got pissed off and was in the pub, but the track didn't suffer," he said. Jimi had explained, "I felt like 'Watchtower' was something I had written but could never get together", while the composer wrote about Hendrix's version in his own 1985 Biograph set. "It's not a wonder to me that he recorded my songs, but rather that he recorded so few …"

The resulting version earned Hendrix the accolade of producing the Best Cover Version, in the opinion of the music critics on Britain's Daily Telegraph newspaper. Their verdict, published in 2004, was that "Hendrix's version of a so-so track from Dylan's John Wesley Harding album completely outgunned the original. A light, scampering ballad re-emerged as a mini-epic of foreboding with Hendrix's heavy three-chord intro hanging like a thunderstorm and Dylan's lyrics sounding an ominous epitaph for the Sixties."

Writing in America's Spin magazine a year earlier, respected US rock writer Greil Marcus was equally gushing in his praise for the record. "Jimi Hendrix's version of the windstorm has been riding the airwaves for 25 years; it's probably the strongest cover of a Dylan song anyone has ever produced."

Kathy Etchingham opts for the Dylan cover as her favourite Hendrix record. "It gets me every time. I love it. When I first heard him play it, it was 'Wow, did I really hear that?'," she explained in 2011. "I was in the studio when he played it. It was so fluid and just came out in one go. It was completely spontaneous. That's probably why it's so good."

The year of 1968 would prove eventful indeed. By the time the tour reached California in February, crowds at the Anaheim Stadium saw him refusing to live up to their expectations. Unfortunately just playing the music was mistaken for apathy. Back

9

in Britain, he was being criticised for spending too much time in the States, where he was signed to Frank Sinatra's Reprise label. His schedule represented 54 concerts in 47 days, so it was little wonder performance levels dropped dramatically.

In April Hendrix cancelled a show at Virginia Beach on learning of Martin Luther King's assassination. Then in Zurich in May one of two 'Monster Konzerts' at the Hallenstadion was temporarily suspended when a most un-Swiss riot broke out during 'Stone Free'. More happily, that same month saw Hendrix and Mike Jeffery purchase the lease on the recently closed Generation Club in New York. Jimi would later turn it into Electric Lady studios.

September saw him follow in the footsteps of the Beatles when he played the Hollywood Bowl supported by Soft Machine, Eire Apparent and Vanilla Fudge. But the mood had changed by the end of November and he deliberately missed a plane to Detroit on the last day of the month as he did not want to play. He was eventually persuaded to travel to the Cobo Hall in a private Lear Jet and fulfil the gig.

On October 25, just a month after the release of the single 'All Along The Watchtower' (and a similar period after Reprise's US issue), the album Electric Ladyland – which had been started in London in December 1967 and finished off during a mammoth session in New York during the summer of 1968 – finally came out in the UK. It was issued with a controversial double gatefold cover featuring Hendrix surrounded by a bevy of 19 naked ladies. The country's record retailers promptly refused to display it but were happy to carry on selling it – as long as it was in a brown paper cover!

It seems Hendrix's request for a photograph of the group with some small children on the statue of Alice In Wonderland in New York's Central Park, which had been taken by Linda Eastman (later to become Mrs Paul McCartney), was either ignored by his record company or arrived too late for their production deadlines.

In a note hand-written on stationery from New York's Cosmopolitan Hotel, Hendrix apologized for the delay in sending along his detailed instructions for the album artwork, explaining, "We have been working very hard indeed doing shows AND recording." The note is included in the 2008 double CD re-release which, 40 years on, finally featured the 1968 Eastman shot on the cover.

The album rose to become a Number 6 hit in the UK, while in America it took Hendrix, Mitchell and Redding (plus assorted guest musicians such as Al Kooper, Steve Winwood and Buddy Miles) to the coveted Number 1 spot for the first and only occasion in the lifetime of The Experience – albeit with another cover design. It chimed

9

in with the title of the album which was Hendrix's homage to groupies, "some (of whom) know more about music than the guys."

The original nude cover shot – taken by award-winning photographer David Montgomery and reputedly disliked by Hendrix, who never actually approved it – was changed in America to a more acceptable psychedelic fuzzy orange and yellow close-up portrait of Hendrix taken by Karl Ferris. The change of design undoubtedly helped American sales of the album and it held on to the top spot for two weeks in November 1968, ahead of Big Brother & The Holding Company, featuring Hendrix's former friend Janis Joplin.

The album had been predominantly recorded in the States at New York's newly opened Record Plant. The studio boasted state-of-the-art 12-track recording machines, and one of the engineers at the new facility was none other than Eddie Kramer, whose growing reputation had seen him lured away from Olympic Studios in London. Sessions had started in April and included the transfer of recordings made in England during late 1967 and early 1968 to the new tape format.

In contrast to the recordings for the first two Experience albums, the sessions had no fixed time frame. Unsurprisingly Jimi felt he had earned the chance to spread out, and a double album would be necessary to contain everything he wanted to achieve. 'Electric Ladyland' was the first Experience album to be mixed solely in stereo, mono versions of the album being merely the stereo mix 'folded' into mono.

Kicking off proceedings, '…And the Gods Made Love' used varispeed backwards vocals and psychedelic panning to take the listener on a mindbending journey into Electric Ladyland. Originally known as 'At Last The Beginning' built on the same musical foundations as (but was a far more successful attempt than) the experimentation of 'EXP'.

Track two, '(Have You Ever Been To) Electric Ladyland', inspired one of Jimi's finest vocal performances; he was so pleased that, on hearing the playback, he shouted "I can sing, I can sing!" 'Crosstown Traffic', one of the first tracks to be recorded for the album back at Olympic in December 1967 was tweaked in the States. Jimi's piano emphasised the chord changes, while Dave Mason of Traffic contributed backing vocals on the chorus which contained the name of his then band – was this deliberate or just coincidence?

The 15-minute 'Voodoo Chile' recreated the many nights Jimi had spent jamming in New York clubs during this period. Mitch Mitchell was on drums, but bass came

9

from not Noel Redding but Jefferson Airplane's Jack Casady, with organ by Traffic's Steve Winwood. In total contrast 'Little Miss Strange' was a slice of psychedelic whimsy written by Redding, who supplies lead vocals and rhythm guitar. While Jimi's weaving lead guitar patterns attempted to lift the track, it is apparent that, in this exalted company, 'Little Miss Strange' was second-rate.

'Long Hot Summer Night' was a chunk of urban soul with Dylan sideman and Blood, Sweat and Tears pianist Al Kooper guesting. Jimi again doubled on bass and also provided intricate gospel-style backing vocals. Next, the Earl King blues standard 'Come On (Pt. 1)' featured the basic Experience line-up; this was the last song to be recorded and sounded like it.

The riffy, syncopated 'Gypsy Eyes', its blues format similar to Muddy Waters' 'Rollin' And Tumblin'', required a stamina-testing 40-plus takes to complete, its earthiness contrasting with the electronic sound collage/sci-fi jam '1983 (A Merman I Should Turn To Be)' This in turn segued into 'Moon, Turn the Tides...Gently, Gently Away' and was one of the earliest recordings ever made on a 16-track tape machine which the Record Plant had now upgraded to.

Jimi felt 'Burning Of The Midnight Lamp' had been unfairly criticized when released as a single, so was adamant that it should appear on his next studio release in an expansive stereo mix A further reason for its inclusion was that the song had not been issued as a single in the States. Current 45 'All Along The Watchtower' was also included, in further contravention of the early 'no singles on albums' edict.

'Rainy Day, Dream Away' featured jazzy jamming in the vein of organ maestro Jimmy Smith's early-Sixties quintet whose line-up of organ, guitar, drums, sax and congas Jimi sought to replicate. To this end Buddy Miles on drums, Mike Finnegan on organ, Freddie Smith on sax and Larry Faucette on congas were assembled. Jimi played the Kenny Burrell (Smith's guitarist) role. The bass parts were either overdubbed by Jimi later or Finnegan provided them, Jimmy Smith-style, using bass pedals.

'1983 (A Merman I Should Turn To Be)' and 'Moon, Turn the Tides...Gently, Gently Away' evoked an underworld world, the seagull effects being produced by capturing the feedback from a set of headphones as they were moved towards a microphone. Although titled and sequenced as two tracks, the join between them is indistinguishable. In these pre-automated days, mixing became a performance in itself as Jimi and Eddie jumped around the board, creating the final piece in one session without edits.

'Still Raining, Still Dreaming' continued where 'Rainy Day, Dream Away' left off. The

9

two tracks were recorded as one and it was only during mixing sessions that the idea of splitting them into separate songs came up. Jimi's wah-wah guitar took over the song while the rest of the band continued to pin down the rhythm, Jimi duelling with himself at one point. By the end of the track he has taken the Jimmy Smith sound on by several light years. 'House Burning Down' featured a wealth of superbly executed and complementary guitar overdubs, improbably welding together a full-tilt chorus and a strict tempo funk march verse.

The closing 'Voodoo Child (Slight Return)' was taped with the Experience the day after the blues jam version, it has often been reported that a film crew had arrived at the studio to film Jimi and company and this was what they launched into. Crossing a 'Foxy Lady'-type riff with 'Catfish Blues' (an old blues tune the band had often jammed on), the peaks reached by the song were exhilarating. It would become a posthumous Number 1 single in the UK and was an obvious choice, condensing as it does the very best of Jimi Hendrix into just five minutes.

If this album marked a new level of success for the band in America, it also heralded some significant changes in the life and times of Jimi Hendrix. As he pushed forward with his own ambitions to be both a performer and a producer, so he seemingly alienated his mentor, manager and producer Chas Chandler.

His insistence on being in control of all aspects of The Experience's musical output was noted by the critics, Melody Maker pointing out that Electric Ladyland was "mixed up, muddled, mutinous and menacing". This, they felt, raised a huge question mark over his new role. "Jimi produced and directed, and whether his work in the control booth is a success is a matter of opinion."

Somewhere in the midst of the 1968 sessions in New York's Record Plant studio Chandler walked out, leaving the musician he had found in Greenwich Village and taken to stardom to fend for himself. Despite the album's cover claim ('Produced and directed by Jimi Hendrix'), Chas had produced 'Crosstown Traffic', 'Burning Of The Midnight Lamp' and 'All Along The Watchtower' before his departure.

The studio had been ruled by Hendrix's sometime friend Devon Wilson, who organised his social life and, to Chandler's chagrin, decided who was and was not allowed to attend sessions. An increasing number of hangers-on crowded the control room who Jimi proceeded to try to entertain rather than play for the tape machines. Strained relations with Noel Redding resulted in Jimi playing bass on the majority of the tracks; a number of guest musicians also featured.

9

It didn't end there, as Chandler was also in disagreement with his partner Mike Jeffery over the exploitation and commercialization of Hendrix. David Arden recalls that "Chas told me that part of the reason that he wanted nothing to do with Hendrix any more was because he couldn't stand what Jeffery was trying to do with Jimi."

Kathy Etchingham was also on the receiving end of Chandler's outrage as he told her, "My relationship with Jimi is finished. I'm no longer his manager." This meant that he was no longer prepared to let her and Hendrix share his family home in Upper Berkeley Street. While she searched for a new home for the two of them – eventually settling on Brook Street – she also tried to find out what was behind the split. While Hendrix refused to say anything at all, Etchingham discovered through third parties that it was drugs plus differences over production and musical control that drove a wedge between them.

After Chandler had formally dissolved his partnership with Jeffery in December 1968 by selling his share in The Experience to his former business partner for $300,000, Etchingham reflected on their time together. "Chas was one of the only people who told Jimi a straight story. When Jimi lost him he was then only surrounded by 'yes' men." However, she wasn't prepared to totally dismiss Jeffery as the bad guy.

"Some biographers have painted Mike [Jeffery] as the monster who ruined Jimi's life, but that wasn't quite the case," she says. "He may have taken all the money and hidden it off-shore somewhere but that didn't worry Jimi as long as he had enough for his immediate needs." Those needs seemed to focus on clothes and jewellery and food and drink bills in clubs on both sides of the Atlantic, plus recording time. Then there were drugs, which seemingly increased Hendrix's paranoia about interference in his beloved music. "Jimi was impossible for anyone to manage," says Etchingham.

If Jimi was impossible to manage, it seems he was also difficult to play with. In the midst of the furore surrounding Chandler's departure, Mitchell and Redding also decided to split. Both flew back to Britain at the end of the band's US tour, a decision that brought a reaction from Billboard's Ed Ochs when he saw Hendrix in New York in December 1968: "Arrogant as a bar-room bully and erotic to the point of outright invitation."

Another New Year brought another change of heart, however, and both sidemen were beside Hendrix when he appeared on the BBC's Happening For Lulu TV show on January 4, 1969. This was when Jimi caused chaos by bursting into an unrehearsed and unscheduled version of Cream's 'Sunshine Of Your Love'.

The reason fir this was the recent (November) disbandement of Cream, the

9

supergroup having run its tempestuous 30-month course. Rather than rejoicing at the departure of his band's greatest rivals from the scene, Jimi was clearly genuinely upset.

At the same time, he was telling the world, "My Jimi Hendrix Experience will not be disbanded. What rubbish. We cannot have it better than today." He also proclaimed, somewhat melodramatically, "The group itself will always be together as long as we are still breathing." However, it still wasn't all sunshine within the camp, and on February 24 The Experience played their last UK show to a sell-out audience at London's prestigious Albert Hall. It was a high note to go out on for the group that had been created in Britain just 28 months earlier.

Even though there was to be another US tour, the days were well and truly numbered for the Experience and, on June 29, 1969, the established line-up played their last ever show together at the Denver Pop Festival in the Mile High Stadium.

Redding, whose new band Fat Mattress were on the same bill as support, was first to go when, after hearing rumours that he was about to be replaced, he caught a plane to Britain and never returned to the fold. Reflecting on his departure he observed, "I was 20 when I joined Jimi Hendrix, but I feel fulfilled and I'm still here." He added that he also had another ambition to achieve. "I'd like to write the truth about Hendrix and get into the legalities. I've been told I lost about $2 million, which is pretty cool!"

While rumours about Mitchell's future flew around the business, the story was that Hendrix was considering dropping 'Experience' from the act's name in order to include other writers and musicians in the developing of a 'creative commune'. Within a week, Mitchell had joined Redding in confirming his permanent departure from the group, although he did team up with his old boss for a July appearance at the Newport Jazz Festival. The golden age of The Jimi Hendrix Experience had come to an end.

In the middle of August 1969, Hendrix and his new band Gypsies, Sun & Rainbows stole the headlines at the first Woodstock Music & Arts Fair in Bethel, New York, both as the highest-paid act – the fee was reported to be $125,000 – and for their rousing closing version of the US national anthem. "I don't know, man, all I did was play it" was Hendrix's simple explanation of his August 18 late-night rendition of 'The Star-Spangled Banner'. "I'm American so I played it. I used to have to sing it in school. They made me sing it in school, so it's a flashback."

For Greil Marcus, in his Rolling Stone review of Woodstock, the performance took on a different and far more eloquent meaning. "As he [Hendrix] told it, 'The Star-Spangled Banner' was the story of a nation ripping itself to pieces then stitching up

9

the flag as a crazy quilt. His face is still on it."

By the end of 1969, the Woodstock band had been downsized into a new three-piece with drummer Buddy Miles and bassist Billy Cox. This time they operated solely under the name Jimi Hendrix, although they were quickly dubbed the Band of Gypsys.

Despite setting up his new 'creative commune' of musicians, Hendrix was also hatching a plan which would involve his former bandmates. In a new project which he dubbed as "a farewell tour" of the US, UK and Europe, he wanted Mitchell and Redding to re-join him on the six-week journey. He told the music press in early 1970, "Right now, I'm just concentrating on … for us to get back together again. We're gonna take some time off and go out somewhere … to get some new songs and new arrangements … so we'd have something to offer, you know something new."

Neither Mitchell nor Redding responded publicly to the offer and the tour never took place, which meant that Hendrix and his new band remained in the US for the first half of 1970, touring and recording at Electric Ladyland Studios in New York which he had bought and refurbished.

The new trio's debut live recording Band Of Gypsys, cut at the turn of the year at the Fillmore East, was handed over to Capitol Records for release in America as part of a settlement to compensate sometime producer Ed Chalpin, who also received a percentage of previous albums. The LP peaked at Number 5 in the US and 6 in Britain, where it was released on the Track label.

With no Experience reunion in sight, Hendrix played more and more dates across America, including a return to his home town of Seattle in July; he was honoured by Garfield High School, the school he attended but never graduated from. However, the next month saw Hendrix make a surprise return to perform in Britain for the first time in 18 months – and only the second time in three years.

The third Isle of Wight Festival took place at East Afton Farm in Godshill and attracted over 600,000 fans to see the likes of Procol Harum, Emerson, Lake & Palmer, The Doors, Joni Mitchell, The Who, Sly & The Family Stone, Joan Baez and Jethro Tull. Hendrix, who closed the proceedings at 3am on August 30, with Mitch Mitchell once again behind the drum kit.

He chose to open with a rendition of 'God Save The Queen' and his performance moved the NME to write, "Dressed in a multi-coloured outfit that must have been designed by a hallucinating tailor, he opened with, of all things, the National Anthem. Needless to say it has never sounded like that before", later declaring that Hendrix was

THE GROUP WILL ALWAYS BE TOGETHER

9

"without doubt one of the biggest hits of the festival".

After the success of his August Bank Holiday appearance on the Isle of Wight, Hendrix moved on to tour Denmark and Germany, where he played his last ever concert at the "Love And Peace" Festival on the Isle of Fehmarn on September 6, 1970.

I'D HAVE LOVED TO DO THAT GIG AGAIN

I'D HAVE LOVED TO DO THAT GIG AGAIN

JAMS AT RONNIE SCOTT'S – DIES OF OVERDOSE –
POSTHUMOUS NUMBER 1 'VOODOO CHILE' – FINAL OFFICIAL
ALBUM THE CRY OF LOVE – HIS MUSIC IS HIS LEGACY

On his return to the UK, Jimi Hendrix had made a call to Tony Bramwell, the man who ran the Saville Theatre who had booked him to play there four times during 1967.

"He phoned me up after the Isle of Wight Festival and asked if he could play the Saville again," recalls Bramwell. "He was heartbroken when I told him it had closed down and was now an ABC cinema," he says. "Jimi just said, 'I would have loved to do that gig again, it was my favourite.' They were the last words he ever said to me."

Bramwell also remembers that, when the Saville Theatre was being knocked down, he walked past the site and spotted a load of tapes in a skip. When he asked about them, the workers told him that they had found lots of artists' tapes and had sent on the ones they could identify and thrown the rest out. "There were The Beatles, Led Zeppelin, The Stones and Hendrix and I passed them on to the guys I knew," he explains.

He gave the Hendrix tapes to Chas Chandler, "but as he died soon after I don't know what happened to them. There were some tracks I didn't recognize, so there may be some tapes of unreleased Hendrix material from the Saville out there somewhere."

Back in England and anxious to catch up with old friends, Hendrix spent the evening of September 16 on stage at Ronnie Scott's club in London, jamming with his buddy Eric Burdon. He spent the night with a girlfriend, Monika Dannemann, in the Samarkand Hotel in Bayswater – a stone's throw from Blaises nightclub, where, in December 1966, he had been tipped by Melody Maker to become "one of the big club names of '67".

On the morning of September 18, Hendrix was found unconscious and rushed to St. Mary Abbot's Hospital in Kensington, where he was pronounced dead on arrival.

JIMI HENDRIX MADE IN ENGLAND

Tragically, he had left a message on former manager Chas Chandler's answering machine in the early hours of the morning, in which he said, "I need help bad, man."

At an inquest ten days later, the coroner reported that Hendrix died as a result of inhalation of vomit caused by barbiturate intoxication and recorded an open verdict. The man from Seattle was duly flown home for a funeral service and buried in the Greenwood Cemetery in Renton, Washington.

Looking back on Hendrix's premature death at just 27 – the same age as Brian Jones, Janis Joplin, Jim Morrison, Kurt Cobain and Amy Winehouse – Roger Mayer says, "I was in a studio in New York with Stevie Wonder and we just pulled the session immediately. It was a total surprise to me, and people who were close to him said he was going back to London to meet up with Chas again and put things back together."

Queen guitarist Brian May recalls, "I was at home when he died and I think Freddie phoned me up and told me. Then he and Roger [Taylor] came round to the flat. We were all very despondent and very sad."

For Keith Emerson, Hendrix's death didn't come as too much of a shock, but to this day it has very personal poignancy. "My son Aaron was born just a month later on October 9, 1970, in the same ward of St. Mary Abbot's Hospital in Kensington where Jimi died," he explains, before reflecting on Hendrix's death. "At that time it wasn't that much of a shock. Janis [Joplin's] and Jim Morrison's departures seemed inevitable. Everyone was looking at each other and going, 'Who's next, Elvis?'"

ELP dedicated 'Barbarian' to him, Emerson confirms. "We went on stage the night he died and announced to the audience, 'This song's for Jimi', because it started with 'Purple Haze' chords."

Daevid Allen looked on what happened to his one-time friend as a cautionary tale, and much affected his own attitude to success. 'When fame took hold of him he disappeared into a cloud and that was that. It's the way the system works: you get sucked dry and then you die, in one form or another … I know very, very few people who've survived the fame trip.'

For Pete Townshend, Hendrix 'lived his whole life squashed into 26 years, and got more out of life than most people get in. And as far as I'm concerned he had done it … how could he ever have surpassed what he'd done?'

Oddly, none of the major British music papers carried any sort of tribute to Hendrix from either record or management companies, and it was left to his American label and friends to make public declarations of their loss.

I'D HAVE LOVED TO DO THAT GIG AGAIN

10

Reprise Records took a full-page in Billboard and the lengthy text – undoubtedly written by Stan Cornyn – included these lines: "We never really knew Jimi well, though we did know him some. Jimi was the stuff heroes were made of. He had it all going: black, just back from England, a super head, a lightning guitarist, an electronics wizard, the archetypal lust dream of every father's daughter. He was a cinch to be a hero."

In the same issue, the Monterey International Pop Festival added their sympathy with a full-page advert which read simply, "To A Black Gypsy Cat Who Rocked The World When It Needed To Be Rocked. Sleep Well."

Before the year was out, the single 'Voodoo Chile' would bring the deceased rock star his first and only British Number 1, although Hendrix's death had little or no immediate impact on album sales. The Band Of Gypsys album re-entered the US Top 30 for just one week, while Smash Hits also made a brief, one-week appearance. In the UK, Band Of Gypsys crawled back into the chart at Number 28.

The final 'official' Jimi Hendrix album, The Cry Of Love, came out in March 1971 and featured much of the music he had been working on for a planned concept release, The First Rays Of The New Rising Sun. Released by Track in the UK and Reprise in the US, it made the Top 3 in both territories and meant that all the approved Hendrix albums – Are You Experienced, Axis: Bold As Love, Smash Hits, Electric Ladyland and The Cry Of Love – had been Top 10 hits, a total of five in four years.

The first 20 years after his death, a total of over 300 different recordings were issued by various record companies, plus a host of illegal bootlegs. Over 20 'new' albums entered the UK chart between 1971 and 2002, but 2010 saw the release of the significant Valleys Of Neptune, featuring unreleased tracks from London and New York sessions spanning 1967 to 1970.

Hendrix's BBC recordings appeared as a single disc in 1989 (entitled Radio One) and as a 2CD set (BBC Sessions) nine years later. Highlights included the instrumental 'Driving South', Howlin' Wolf's 'Killing Floor' tackled at a punishing tempo and Muddy Waters' '(I'm Your) Hoochie Coochie Man', with Alexis Korner on slide guitar. Particularly historically valuable were a stripped-down version of 'Burning Of The Midnight Lamp' with a new ending and 'Wait Until Tomorrow', a track rarely played live.

'Love And Confusion', recorded in February 1967, was radically different from the studio-overdubbed original, while alongside the hits were covers ('Hound Dog') and album tracks ('Little Miss Lover'). Rolling Stone concluded that Radio One 'is probably the closest the tape machines came to recording the private, searching Hendrix during

JIMI HENDRIX MADE IN ENGLAND

that roller-coaster year … This is the sound of Hendrix reinventing rock'n'roll.'

Despite selling millions of records around the world and commanding huge fees for his live appearances, Hendrix left only $20,000 in his estate, which was inherited by his father Al. However, during the two years after he died, Hendrix's business affairs were still controlled by Mike Jeffery until he died in a plane crash over France in March 1973.

Even then, rumours of shady dealings persisted, some suggesting that the manager had in some way faked his own death and disappeared with Hendrix's cash. This story is disputed by Kathy Etchingham, who says that few if any bodies from the crash were ever identified and adds, "All I know is that he is buried in Croydon cemetery. I found that out around 15 years ago."

In 2009, an even more bizarre claim was made by former roadie James 'Tappy' Wright, while publicizing a Hendrix biography, when he alleged Jeffery had admitted to him that he had murdered Hendrix.

In the same year as Jeffery died, both Mitchell and Redding negotiated deals with the Hendrix estate and his record companies that saw them give up all future royalties from the Hendrix catalogue. Mitchell agreed a sum of $300,000, while Redding oddly settled for $100,000, although some years later he would claim that he had been defrauded of '£8 million in royalties'.

In 2010, a British national newspaper looked at the earnings of musicians, film stars and writers in the years following their deaths. Under the heading "The Dead Rich List", the Daily Mail concluded that Elvis had earned his estate a cool £1 billion since his death in 1977. Behind 'The King' came John Lennon with posthumous earnings of £200 million, and Michael Jackson with an impressive £168 million, earned in just one year.

Further down the list – between 13th-placed reggae star Bob Marley (£38 million) and scientist Albert Einstein, with £30 million thanks to licensing deals with Disney, McDonald's and Nestlé, was Jimi Hendrix. They calculated that his £35 million in earnings since 1970 came from back-catalogue sales and a licensing deal with Sony, plus £2.5 million from a successful lawsuit brought against his half-brother Leon Hendrix by Experience Hendrix, the company run by the star's stepsister Janie, over an unlicensed product called Hendrix Electric Vodka.

Hendrix's extraordinary influence as a performer and guitarist was well established during his lifetime, but in death, as is so often the case, it was elevated to a new level as he took on legendary status in the rock world. He was cited as the "most influential electric guitarist to date … the first black rock star, setting a visual style that would

I'D HAVE LOVED TO DO THAT GIG AGAIN

influence such artists as Michael Jackson and Prince".

Bruce Springsteen admitted that hearing Hendrix "showed us there was a deep ecstasy to be had", while Neil Young, who was signed to the same American label as Hendrix, observed, "For my money he was the greatest electric guitar player who ever lived." The one-time member of Crosby, Stills, Nash & Young took to wearing a Jimi Hendrix badge on his guitar strap during his 1978 Rust Never Sleeps Tour.

In the years after his death, Hendrix was lauded, applauded and honoured by America's music and entertainment institutions and organizations. He was given a Star on the Hollywood Walk Of Fame in 1991, inducted into the Rock And Roll Hall Of Fame in 1992 (by Neil Young) and, in the same year, was awarded NARAS' (National Academy of Recording Arts & Sciences) Lifetime Achievement Award at the 34th Grammy Awards.

Four years after these last two awards – and two years after he himself was inducted into America's Rock And Roll Hall Of Fame as a member of The Animals – Chas Chandler, the man who found his future through Hendrix's guitar-playing, died in his home town of Newcastle Upon Tyne. He was 58 years old.

In 2003, the same year Hendrix topped Rolling Stone's poll of all-time great guitarists, Noel Redding, the guitarist who became a reluctant bass player, died at his home in Ireland, aged 57. Five years later, the final link with the original Experience line-up disappeared when 61-year-old Mitch Mitchell was found dead in his hotel room in Portland, Oregon, just days after finishing a string of dates on the 2008 Experience Hendrix Tour, a tribute featuring Buddy Guy and Jonny Lang among others.

The memory of Jimi Hendrix lives on for many people, and not just through his music. He left a collection of pictures which were gathered up over the years by some of those who had travelled and worked with the musician. It seems that Hendrix's schoolboy interest in drawing turned into a relaxing pastime during the hours and days on the road. According to former roadie Wright, "Jimi would do two things when he was travelling around. He would either write songs or draw and paint. Most of the drawings he would just crumple up and throw away."

In 2010, to commemorate the 40th anniversary of Hendrix's death, the Handel House Museum, based at 25 Brook Street where both Handel and Hendrix lived, brought together a collection of photographs, letters and clothing plus the Flying V guitar he played at the Isle of Wight Festival weeks before he died.

At the same time, the hotel listed on Hendrix's death certificate as his 'place of residence' – the flat he died in was officially Monika Dannemann's home – decided to mark the anniversary by creating a special 'Jimi Hendrix Suite' on the fifth floor.

The market for Hendrix memorabilia has continued to soar. Top money is reserved for items of clothing and his guitars. The coat he wore the night before he died – a plain grey jacket – went to auction in 2011 carrying an expected sale price of £25,000.

Over 20 years after he took his old, battered guitars into the Selmer shop to part-exchange them for new ones, the sale of guitars 'owned' or 'used ' by Hendrix had become big business. In 1990, Mitch Mitchell put up for sale the white Strat used by Hendrix at Woodstock and raised £198,000, only for Microsoft founder Paul Allen to buy it some years later for a massive $1.3 million.

Roger Mayer reflects on the number of 'Hendrix guitars' that have turned up over the years. "There seems to be 300 to 400 out there. We did have guitars stolen on the road and in the studio but Kathy [Etchingham] and I once worked out that Hendrix had 'lost' more guitars than he ever owned – and we couldn't remember him being that careless!"

Kathy Etchingham adds that "There are a load of fake Hendrix guitars out there. If you believed all these people who claim to have one then he must have spent all his time giving away guitars, but he never actually had that many guitars."

The two albums The Experience recorded and released during the first full year Hendrix spent in Britain are, 45 years on, established among the top echelon of rock titles. Are You Experienced, considered by many one of the finest debut albums in rock history, has now sold over four million copies in America, where it racked up over 100 weeks on the chart. Both Mojo and Guitarist magazines placed it at Number 1 in their list of all-time Best Guitar Albums, while TV channel VH1 ranked it at 5 on their list of the all-time Greatest Albums and Rolling Stone placed it at 15 in their poll of the 500 Greatest Albums.

The Encyclopedia Of Albums described it as the "cornerstone of a legend", while the popular collection entitled 1001 Albums You Must Hear Before You Die classed Are You Experienced as "one of the greatest debuts ever" which "stunned the Sixties rock aristocracy".

The same publication commented on the follow-up, Axis: Bold As Love, and said, "There is no arguing ... with the brash, scintillating songs, the grasp that Jimi and his cohorts had on the studio technology at their disposal and the lyrical beauty of Hendrix's guitar playing." It was also ranked at Number 7 on Guitarist's collection of

I'D HAVE LOVED TO DO THAT GIG AGAIN

Most Influential Guitar Albums, while Rolling Stone ranked it at 82 among their list of the 500 Greatest Albums.

These two albums – plus four hit singles – marked an exceptional period in Hendrix's life when he came to England and found his true calling as a musician of the highest calibre. Those first 15 months saw his record sales increase, his live appearances reach new heights in terms of excitement and controversy, laying the foundations of a career that would ultimately see him crowned as a genuine icon of rock music.

Jimi Hendrix may have been born in the USA, but he was made in England during the swingin' Sixties. No wonder he once said, "Nineteen-sixty-seven was the best year of my life."

INDEX

INDEX

INDEX

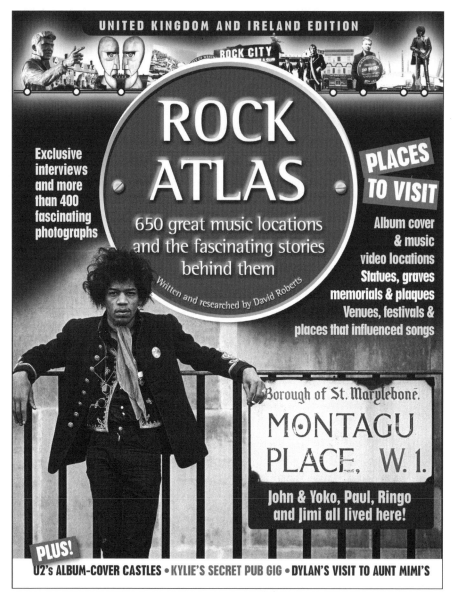

UNITED KINGDOM AND IRELAND EDITION

ROCK ATLAS

650 great music locations and the fascinating stories behind them

Written and researched by David Roberts

Exclusive interviews and more than 400 fascinating photographs

PLACES TO VISIT

Album cover & music video locations
Statues, graves memorials & plaques
Venues, festivals & places that influenced songs

Borough of St. Marylebone.

MONTAGU PLACE, W. 1.

John & Yoko, Paul, Ringo and Jimi all lived here!

PLUS!
U2's ALBUM-COVER CASTLES • KYLIE'S SECRET PUB GIG • DYLAN'S VISIT TO AUNT MIMI'S

ROCK ATLAS

The ultimate rock guide
304 pages in full colour

CLARKSDALE